SOUTHERN ENCLOSURE

SOUTHERN ENCLOSURE

SETTLER COLONIALISM AND THE POSTWAR TRANSFORMATION OF MISSISSIPPI

JOHN H. CABLE

UNIVERSITY PRESS OF KANSAS

© 2024 by the University Press of Kansas
All rights reserved

Published by the University Press of Kansas (Lawrence, Kansas 66045), which was organized by the Kansas Board of Regents and is operated and funded by Emporia State University, Fort Hays State University, Kansas State University, Pittsburg State University, the University of Kansas, and Wichita State University.

Library of Congress Cataloging-in-Publication Data

Names: Cable, John H. (History professor), author.
Title: Southern enclosure : settler colonialism and the postwar transformation of Mississippi / John H. Cable.
Description: Lawrence : University Press of Kansas, 2024. | Includes bibliographical references and index.
Identifiers: LCCN 2023004227 (print) | LCCN 2023004228 (ebook)
  ISBN 9780700635832 (cloth)
  ISBN 9780700635849 (ebook)
Subjects: LCSH: Choctaw Indian—Land tenure—Mississippi. | Land tenure—Mississippi History—20th century. | African American farmers—Mississippi—History—20th century. | Agriculture—Social aspects—Mississippi. | Settler colonialism—Mississippi—History—20th century. | Mississippi—Race relations—History—20th century. | BISAC: HISTORY / United States / State & Local / South (AL, AR, FL, GA, KY, LA, MS, NC, SC, TN, VA, WV) | HISTORY / African American & Black
Classification: LCC HD211.M7 C33 2024 (print) | LCC HD211.M7 (ebook) | DDC 333.709762—dc23/eng/20230628
LC record available at https://lccn.loc.gov/2023004227.
LC ebook record available at https://lccn.loc.gov/2023004228.

British Library Cataloguing-in-Publication Data is available.

Printed in the United States of America

10 9 8 7 6 5 4 3 2 1

The paper used in this publication is acid free and meets the minimum requirements of the American National Standard for Permanence of Paper for Printed Library Materials Z39.48–1992.

*Woe to those who add house to house
and join field to field
until everywhere belongs to them
and they are the sole inhabitants of the land.*

—Isaiah 5:8

CONTENTS

Acknowledgments ix

Introduction 1

  1. Land, Labor, and Race in the Prewar Years 10

  2. Sea Change: Settler Agriculture after World War II 30

  3. Frantic Resistance: Mississippi and the Decolonial Zeitgeist 50

  4. Enclosure: Settler Agriculture in the 1950s 81

  5. Mississippi's 1960 108

Conclusion 125

Notes 133

Bibliography 179

Index 203

ACKNOWLEDGMENTS

Thanks to my editor, David Congdon, as well as to Andrea Laws and the rest of the staff at the University Press of Kansas for believing and investing in this project. I feel fortunate to have worked with such a wonderful, caring team.

This book would not have been possible without the early support of the history faculty at Florida State University, especially Maxine Jones. Andrew Frank talked me out of a very different project and helped steer this one in the right direction. Many thanks to Katherine Mooney, Will Hanley, Maxine Montgomery, and Paul Renfro for their tireless support and for reading these chapters in their earliest form, which cannot have been fun. Additionally, conversations with Peter Garretson, Rafe Blaufarb, Ron Doel, Claudia Liebeskind, Suzanne Sinke, Meghan Martinez, Jenna Pope, James McCallister, Josh Butler, Kyle Harris, Lauren Thompson, Chris Crenshaw, and John Whitehurst were always stimulating.

Beyond Tallahassee, many others gave generously of their time and expertise in ways that made this a better book. Pete Daniel and Adrienne Petty read early versions of the chapters. Their comments and criticisms were invaluable. Paul Rosier and Daniel Cobb graciously fielded my frantic questions via email. Conversations with Tore Olsson, Justin Randolph, Dina Gilio-Whitaker, Marilyn Lake, Kevin Bruyneel, and Michael Witgen helped me think about the project in new ways. J. D. Sears provided legal advice. My friends and mentors Mark Huddle, Aran MacKinnon, and Rob Sumowski always made time to talk. My new colleagues at Abraham Baldwin Agricultural College, especially Russell Pryor, lent moral support through the final stages of revision and publication. Thanks to readers Katherine Osburn and Emma Folwell, as well as to the anonymous readers whose sharp critiques of the manuscript forced me back to the drawing board a time or two.

While researching this book, I had the pleasure of working with many great archivists and librarians. Thanks especially to Amanda Bell at the Chahta Immi Cultural Center, Jennifer McGillan at Mississippi State University, Leigh McWhite at the University of Mississippi, and the reference assistants at the Mississippi Department of Archives and History, the University of Southern Mississippi, the Philadelphia-Neshoba County Public Library, the National Museum of the American Indian, the National Archives (College Park, Washington, DC, and Kansas City), and the Library of Congress. Very special thanks to Adam Beauchamp, Mohamed Berray, and the rest of the social sciences librarians at FSU's Strozier Library; they bent over backward to assist with this project.

My family—Jim and Kathy Cable, Mark and Betty Jo Wallace, and Paul, Ashley, Graeme, Eleanor, and Silas Cable—has been supportive from the start. My dad was my traveling companion on several trips to Mississippi, and my mom and mother-in-law helped with childcare.

Janet and Wallace Cable are the two loves of my life. Their sacrifices above all others made this book possible. I dedicate it to them and to the labor, delivery, and NICU nurses at Phoebe Putney Memorial Hospital in Albany. Life is so precious.

SOUTHERN ENCLOSURE

INTRODUCTION

> Alex Bell of southwest Winston grieved himself to death because Indians left the country.
> —a Winston County, Mississippi, settler, 1937

In the late 1930s, as the Works Progress Administration (WPA) was compiling a guide to the state of Mississippi, residents of Kemper County recalled how the place had looked to their parents and grandparents. "Dotted about over this section were spaces of open land, an acre or less in extent," one report read, "on each of which was to be found what appeared to be the remains of a burnt cabin." The cabins belonged to Choctaws, most of whom the United States government had deported after the 1830 Treaty of Dancing Rabbit Creek. Enslaved people, trafficked to Mississippi by white settlers, encountered the burned-out cabins as they were clearing land for cotton cultivation. Aware of the recent mass expulsion, the slaves reported hearing "distressing sounds . . . proceeding from those places either in the field or near by." They took them to be the sounds of "Indians mourning for their homes." The white narrator, a century removed from the events she described, mocked the slaves' "superstitious nature," musing that "if labor had been free then, those fields would never have been cultivated by negroes."[1]

Stories like this one reveal a society deeply rooted in dispossession. After Dancing Rabbit Creek, vastly fewer Choctaws inhabited the wide, diagonal swath of central Mississippi ceded to the United States. Remaining native people faced the predation of settlers who ruthlessly purloined the rest of their land, occupied their homes, and left them destitute. For the better part of a century, Choctaw removal remained an ongoing process, never truly finished. Against the backdrop of that orgy of land grabbing, the subject of this book appears tragically unexceptional. In the years after the WPA published its *Guide to the Magnolia State*, deserted homes again dotted the landscape. Empty tenant houses marked the involuntary exodus of entire classes of farmers after World War II. Local white elites expelled sharecroppers and tenant farmers—disproportionately, though not entirely, Black and native people—and forced many small, landowning farmers off the land. They redeployed the basic tools of settler-colonial dispossession against non-elites, both native and non-native. The result was an upward redistribution of land and wealth, the effects of which, like the Choctaw expulsion of the nineteenth and early twentieth centuries, continue to bedevil the state.[2]

This latest dispossession, which spanned the American South and had parallels abroad, occurred in a milieu of racial panic. The civil rights movement had begun to threaten the social relations that had evolved in Mississippi since the Treaty of Dancing Rabbit Creek. White opponents of civil rights, many of whom still occupied the same confiscated land as their settler parents or grandparents, observed post–World War II political trends with trepidation. One man, who claimed that his "grandparents were among Mississippi's first pioneers," warned Senator James O. Eastland in 1949 that civil rights legislation would "bring about the greatest upheaval our State has ever seen." There would be "wanton blood-shed, murder and very many perfectly innocent people will suffer the worst kind of outrages." At such a politically fraught time, landowners moved to consolidate, mechanize, and escape their dependence on labor. Once a mechanical cotton picker became available, the Delta planter on whose land it was to be demonstrated stressed the machine's potential to "make our racial problem easier to handle" by displacing Black people. Just as Jim Crow collapsed, then, so, too, did the labor-intensive farm structure that had been the very basis of Mississippi's settlement.[3]

Historians have long been interested in the concomitant unsettling of Southern political and agrarian regimes. It is a commonplace to say that the "Southern enclosure movement"—mechanization and land consolidation—placed limits on Black Southerners' enjoyment of civil rights victories by pulling the economic rug out from under them. This book takes issue not with that argument's basic thrust but, rather, with the narrow framework in which it is typically advanced. Much of the excellent work on the intersection of US Southern agriculture and civil rights altogether ignores native people and native land, past and present. That elision naturally marginalizes not only historical actors but also critical interpretive tools. Colonial invasion, clearly a constitutive element of Mississippi society, should play a far greater role in shaping histories of the modern South (much as it has come to shape the histories of places like Canada and

Australia). That Mississippi settler towns like Philadelphia and De Kalb sit atop the ruins of Choctaw towns—Halunlawi asha and Holihta asha, respectively—must inform our notions of land and racial justice. Quite simply, as Margaret D. Jacobs argues, "We will need to reckon with the history of settler colonialism." This book seeks to do exactly that.[4]

In its most basic form, settler colonialism is a process that involves the dispossession of native people and resettlement of their land by outsiders. The term itself has been around for a long time, but as a conceptual framework, settler colonialism took shape in the work of the late Australian anthropologist Patrick Wolfe. Wolfe pointed out that settler colonialism fundamentally differs from ordinary "franchise" colonialism. While colonizers in the latter form are content to rule native people, settlers want to replace them. He commonly juxtaposed the franchise colonialisms of British India and Dutch Indonesia with the settler colonialisms of Australia, Israel/Palestine, and the United States. Yet as some scholars have suggested, his enormously important insights could also be reductive. For instance, he famously insisted that settler colonialism's primary agenda was the "elimination of the native," and, thus, that settlers desired only *land* from native people—*labor* they could find elsewhere. A cursory look at the plight of twentieth-century Choctaw sharecroppers complicates those claims. Hence, even as this book relies on the work of Wolfe and others in the burgeoning field of settler-colonial studies, it questions some of their tidy formulations.[5]

Nevertheless, reframing modern Southern history as settler-colonial history reshapes our understanding of the region in important ways. In making territoriality—the "fusion of people and land"—its analytical center, the settler-colonial framework necessarily concerns itself with indigeneity. Scholars of Native American history have long called for a paradigm shift that moves Indians out of the margins of Southern history. The work of Jacobs, Theda Perdue, Malinda Maynor Lowery, Angela Pulley Hudson, Andrew Frank, and Kristofer Ray (to name just a few) points the way. But as recently as 2017, Frank and Ray observed that "to study southern history is [still] to explore a biracial story." Bringing Indians back into the story does not simply graft a new group onto the standard black-and-white narrative but rather challenges and enriches that narrative, as Perdue has argued. For instance, the experiences of Mississippi Choctaws with the federal government's mid-twentieth-century relocation program—which sought to mainstream Indians by enticing them off reservations and into cities—cast the Southern enclosure movement in a new light. Not only did enclosure displace vulnerable farmers, as is well known, but it also served the aims of federal Indian policy by making the Choctaws' ancestral homeland inhospitable to the many members of the tribe who made a living sharecropping.[6]

The settler-colonial reframing of the modern South, and of Mississippi in particular, also prompts comparisons with other settler societies. Here, I deal mostly with southern and eastern Africa, where similar timelines, racial regimes, agrarian transitions, and cultures of reaction and resistance to decolonization linked the societies across what Gerald Horne calls the "white Atlantic." If James C. Cobb could claim in 1999 that "southernologists" were largely blind to the wider world, that is no longer the case. This study draws from a rich body of scholarship (some of it quite old, notwithstanding Cobb) that sees the South not as isolated or exceptional, but as part of larger worlds of connection like the African diaspora, global capitalism, and white supremacist politics. Much of the work dealing with the twentieth century, however, has focused on transnational networks of activism. While this book is attentive to what I call the decolonial zeitgeist of the 1940s–1960s, its primary concern is not political activism. Rather, in its engagement with the transnational, it looks at the ways colonial land-grabbing and agricultural modernization placed limits on decolonization. After three-quarters of a century, contemporary calls for land reform as "a precondition for true freedom" in places like South Africa, Zimbabwe, Kenya, and, indeed, Mississippi bespeak the urgency of such an approach.[7]

If a comparative and transnational perspective affords a more sophisticated understanding of the issues of land, labor, and race under scrutiny here, those issues still call for the sort of nuanced treatment that only a local study can render. *Southern Enclosure* focuses on east-central Mississippi, most of whose nine counties (Attala, Kemper, Lauderdale, Leake, Neshoba, Newton, Noxubee, Scott, and Winston) are located at the base of the north-central hills, a region characterized by rich bottomlands and moderately fertile hills. Parts of Noxubee, Winston, and Kemper Counties also lie in the black prairie and flatwoods regions, the former of which (mainly in Noxubee) is more fertile and conducive to large-scale agriculture. As a whole, east-central Mississippi has more in common with the hill country to the north than with the much-studied Delta region to the west. In most of the nine counties, whites came to outnumber Black and Choctaw residents, if only slightly, and compared to the Delta, farms tended to be smaller. "One-mule farms" were more common than sprawling estates. Like many others in the Southern upcountry, between the late-nineteenth and mid-twentieth centuries, farmers in east-central Mississippi grew cotton as their primary "money crop," a fact that did much to shape how land and people were used and, often, abused.[8]

East-central Mississippi might seem an odd focus for a book like this. Studies of the Southern enclosure movement have often looked to the Delta, a region that contained enormous plantations where mechanization and land consolidation had a more sweeping impact. That section, with its Black-majority counties and planter aristocracy, has also been where scholars have turned to draw comparisons to places like sub-Saharan Africa. The "startling juxtaposition of white affluence and black poverty" in the Delta *seems* colonial. However, the sustained presence of Choctaws in east-central Mississippi provides an important reminder that colonization is no metaphor and that the involuntary exodus of farmers that followed World War II—while different in important ways from Choctaw removal—was part of a much longer, multilayered history of dispossession. Moreover, shifting the focus away from the Delta gives a clearer picture of the poor and vulnerable of all races that faced displacement as elite whites profited. White sharecroppers, tenants, and small farmers also left the land without much choice, even if local industries softened the blow with preferential hiring.[9]

Focusing on east-central Mississippi also affords an interesting view of the different experiences of Choctaws and Black Mississippians under Jim Crow—differences that I argue are most legible through the lens of settler colonialism. In general, Blackness and Indianness as racial signifiers derived from a key difference in the roles white settlers initially expected those groups to play. "One drop" of African blood was said to make a person Black—a "mystic hyperpotency" that Patrick Wolfe attributes to whites' desire to maximize the number of unfree or exploitable laborers. The opposite logic held true for Indians—because whites generally wanted Indians' land, not their labor, they attempted to define Indians out of existence through blood quantum discourse. But the selective mutability of the latter formulation becomes clear in Mississippi. By the late nineteenth century, whites had, for the most part, already acquired most of the Choctaws' land, whether through treaty making or outright theft. Hence, there was little incentive to write Indianness explicitly into the state's infamous Jim Crow–era constitution. Choctaws attempted to preserve their own identity in a biracial system, yet whites often subjected them to the same abuses as they did Black Mississippians, as both nonwhite groups now faced exploitation specifically as laborers. That is not to say that there was no splitting of hairs on the race issue when circumstances dictated, as they sometimes did. Rather, it reminds us of the very social construction and, thus, inherent instability of race itself.[10]

Moreover, in the post–World War II period, Choctaws and Black Mississippians had their own discrete political goals that were deeply rooted in their respective historical experiences. Choctaws desired land, sovereignty, and, otherwise, to be left alone. But "land is the main thing," tribal chairman Emmett York declared in 1951. "I'd rather have my own land." While not unconcerned with the question of land, Black Mississippians generally pushed for political equality; civil and voting rights were their primary focus through the mid-1960s. (Yet issues of territoriality were never far off, as Black activists often risked eviction, the denial of credit, or some other economic reprisal that ended in their removal from the land.) Distinct ambitions, to say nothing of the complex politics of race, kept these two groups from forming any sort of lasting solidarity during the Jim Crow era. In fact, by most accounts, Choctaws intentionally avoided contact with Black Mississippians, both to preserve their own identity and to avoid the oppression that Blacks faced.[11]

If the region's social relations are best understood through the interpretive lens of settler colonialism, the question of vocabulary is trickier. Most people are not used to thinking about *colonizers* and *colonized* in Mississippi (at least not after the eighteenth century). Moreover, for most Americans, *decolonization* is something that happened elsewhere. Therefore, I use the

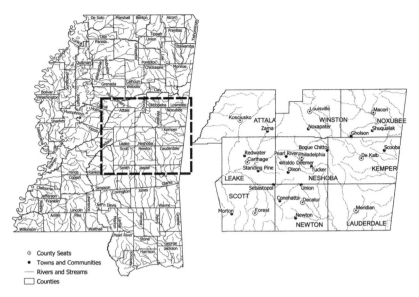

East-Central Mississippi. Map by C. B. Crenshaw.

conventional vocabulary of empire only sparingly. But I do make reference to *decolonization* because, while it is a relative neologism (and a loaded one at that), it is still the word that best describes the global process that most white settlers, including those in the American South, resisted tooth-and-nail in the mid-twentieth-century. In nonsettler colonies, decolonization signified imperial retreat or divestment, as in places like India and Ghana. In settler states like Rhodesia (Zimbabwe), South Africa, and, I argue, Mississippi, it meant the demise of undemocratic, white supremacist regimes. Particularly in settler states, decolonization strictly in the political realm left much to be desired in the realm of the economic, especially with regard to land distribution. One of my objectives in *Southern Enclosure* is to situate Mississippi within that global history using language that, while precise, does not alienate readers.[12]

This account relies on the records of agricultural leaders whose work in the post–World War II period delivered much of the Choctaws' ancestral land to a handful of large operators. The ways in which those leaders promoted enclosure dovetailed with the aims of segregationist groups like the White

Citizens' Council and the Mississippi State Sovereignty Commission (indeed, some agricultural leaders also organized Citizens' Councils), as well as with the efforts of the federal government to snuff out Indian tribal sovereignty. While other scholars have assembled compelling narratives of agrarian transition using these annual extension reports, demonstration records, meeting minutes, and correspondence, I view them as a record of ongoing colonization. As the Mississippi Choctaws looked for ways to recover their land or get fair compensation, the agencies of the United States Department of Agriculture (USDA) actively pursued an opposing, consolidationist agenda that involved ridding the land of "inefficient" small farmers, tenants, and sharecroppers (some of them Choctaws). The agricultural leaders who served these agencies at the state and county levels were, often wittingly, instruments of dispossession, and their paper trail merits close scrutiny.[13]

I have also relied on the oral accounts compiled by the Center for Oral History and Cultural Heritage at the University of Southern Mississippi and the Native American History Project of the Samuel Proctor Oral History Program at the University of Florida. They, along with the constituent files of long-serving US senators James O. Eastland and John C. Stennis, give a sense of how ordinary Mississippians felt about the forces transforming their society in the 1940s and 1950s. The records of the Mississippi Band of Choctaw Indians, particularly the Tribal Council minutes, as well as the Choctaw files of the Association on American Indian Affairs and the National Congress of American Indians, are indispensable to telling the story of tribal rebirth and struggle during this period. And the records of numerous government agencies outside the USDA, especially those of the US Commission on Civil Rights, are also essential.

Southern Enclosure tells the story of an embattled settler society confronting big historical changes. It begins with an overview of land, labor, and race before World War II, with emphasis on the centrality of labor control as a concomitant to land seizure. The political shifts of the wartime and postwar periods posed serious problems for white landowners dependent on a disproportionately nonwhite labor force, and mechanization emerged as both an economic and political solution. In east-central Mississippi, mechanization and diversification promoted land consolidation, which was, by turns, cause and consequence of the displacement of large numbers of small farmers and almost all of the region's tenants and sharecroppers. As this study emphasizes, there can be no separating the Southern enclosure movement from its political context. Elite whites weaponized enclosure to resist the civil rights movement. At the same time, and no less importantly, enclosure was the culmination of more than a century of settler-colonial land grabbing. By 1960, when this study ends, the old farm structure was practically dead, much of the region's land was in the hands of a few large operators, and Mississippians of all backgrounds struggled to adjust to the new economic reality. As the conclusion suggests, enclosure and its effects were the rocks on which the ship of political reform ran aground in the 1960s and 1970s.

LAND, LABOR, AND RACE IN THE PREWAR YEARS

I

> *The Chairman: Do you own any land, Mr. Tubbie?*
> *Mr. Tubbie: No; they won't let me have any.*
> —Congressional Hearing on the Condition of the Mississippi Choctaws, 1917

In 1909 a Mississippi planter declared that cotton was "the greatest money crop in the world." But, he lamented, "we cannot farm without labor." The "labor question," which especially bedeviled cotton planters but was not theirs alone, had an unsubtle racial connotation in the state, as it did in other societies dominated by white settlers. The explosive growth of settler colonies in the nineteenth century had left whites in possession of vast amounts of indigenous land but dependent (in part or in whole) upon people of color to make the land productive. Aside from land acquisition itself, perhaps no single factor was more instrumental in shaping settler societies than the manner in which they resolved the labor question.[1]

The most direct way to make the reliable labor force that settlers required was to put to work the very people whose land had been taken. A version of this happened in British southern and eastern Africa. In the late nineteenth and early twentieth centuries, white South African farmers, along with mine owners, insisted that the African peasantry there be crushed and forced to work for wages. Colonial authorities pushed a slew of measures toward that end, culminating in land laws that effectively proletarianized the peasants. A similar process occurred in Southern Rhodesia, where prosperous African peasants were systematically driven "off the land and into the workplace." In Kenya, British colonization alienated the best land in the Rift Valley to a tiny handful of white settlers, although African "squatters" there retained more autonomy than their southern African counterparts. In each instance, the basic aim of settler-colonizers was to take land and mobilize labor in one motion.[2]

Mississippi's white settlers also recruited indigenous labor, although not primarily so, as in the African examples. While the purpose of the Treaty of Dancing Rabbit Creek (1830) was unequivocally to expel the Choctaws, Article 14 of the treaty reserved land for anyone who chose to stay in the state and live under its laws. But that provision fell apart in short order, as the federal agent charged with enrolling allottees became too drunk and belligerent to perform his job. Avaricious settlers and speculators took advantage of the situation. In many early cases, whites simply invaded the homes of Choctaws who had chosen not to leave. Hiram Walker drove an elderly Choctaw man named Oakalarcheehubbee from his home with a whip. Choctaws Elitubbe and Abotaya each returned from hunting to find white families living in their homes. A sympathetic settler named Grant Lincecum confirmed the harrowing accounts of white intrusion, reporting in 1836 that "those [Choctaws] who occupied good land have generally met with this fate." James Oxberry, a Choctaw man who had unsuccessfully attempted to register for an allotment with the federal agent, lamented that the dispossessed families were "completely destitute, and depend upon game and charity for their support." The Choctaws' land base in Mississippi evaporated, and toiling on settler farms emerged as one of very few options for those electing to stay. As one Choctaw leader later recounted, "Landlord use 'em almost like a slave, but not quite."[3]

Far more numerous by the mid-nineteenth century, though, were enslaved Africans, about a million of whom settlers ultimately trafficked from the Atlantic seaboard to the Southern interior to grow cotton. While there were only a few thousand Choctaws left in Mississippi, by 1860 the nine counties of the east-central portion of the state contained 47,169 slaves. As settlers in places like Australia, Hawaii, and Israel/Palestine would also learn, there were advantages in driving indigenous people out in favor of an exogenous labor force. Unlike Choctaws, after all, enslaved Africans had no prior claim to the land in question and, thus, posed no serious problem to settlers in terms of a competing sovereignty. But the effort to rid Mississippi of indigenous people was not entirely successful, as plenty still lingered in hopes of recovering their land. Unable or unwilling to clear marginal lands of every remaining Choctaw, settler planters had few qualms about using them to augment their labor force.[4]

The end of chattel slavery in the 1860s transformed labor relations. In the immediate aftermath of the Civil War, most white landowners hoped that the new free-labor system would resemble the old slave system, although some worried about sharing social space with Black freed people they had so recently treated as property. "We are encumbered with a dependent race of people," the *Meridian Daily Clarion* editorialized in the fall of 1865, "who must dwell among us till provision is made for their colonization elsewhere." Settlers in Noxubee County feared that freed people would "fight & kill off the white population." But rumors of a general uprising never materialized. Nor did the prospect of redistribution, which would have confiscated land wrested from native people just a generation before and parceled it out more equitably among settlers and ex-slaves. President Andrew Johnson ensured that all such moves were blocked or reversed. The primary post-emancipation task of white Southern landowners, then, as they saw it, was to find new ways to solve their labor problem. During Reconstruction, they did so on terms not of their own choosing. Black political power and the presence of the Freedmen's Bureau often stood in the way of the most repressive measures. But the overthrow of Reconstruction by the mid-1870s cleared the way for tighter labor control.[5]

Crucially, the fact that ruling white settlers could, by then, devote their attention almost exclusively to labor control owed to their having eliminated or subdued native claimants to the land. Indeed, the growth of capitalist agriculture in east-central Mississippi was predicated on the availability of land, conditioned on the dispossession of Choctaws formally through treaty making and informally through outright theft. Yet the imperialist truism that whites *belonged* on the land—that their belonging was intrinsic, self-evident, even commonsensical—elided the foundational role of indigenous dispossession. Even the failed push for land reform immediately following the Civil War—which had advanced the then radical idea that Black Americans, too, belonged on land of their own—was premised on a notion of economic justice that effaced native people. The land question was, of course, far from settled in the minds of Mississippi Choctaws, but for white landowners, it took a back seat to the labor question. The settler-colonial violence and racial chauvinism that had, in just a few short decades, transformed the Choctaws' homeland into a "white man's country" now underwrote a relentless drive to secure a rural proletariat and make the land pay. For their part, Choctaws recognized land theft and labor exploitation as two sides of the same coin.[6]

I

Ruling whites reasserted control during and after Reconstruction in part by using the law to forge a new system of land tenure that favored landowning planters. Two basic, distinct tenure arrangements (with seemingly endless permutations) had by then emerged: tenant farming and sharecropping. An existing body of law governed the landlord-tenant relationship, in which the tenant paid rent to the landlord, sometimes in a share of the crop. The sharecropping system, while outwardly similar, was, in fact, new and different. "Croppers" were, in essence, wage workers paid with a share of the crop. As Harold Woodman explains the distinction, "The cropper . . . was a wage laborer, his wages being a portion of what he produced paid to him by the landlord," while "the tenant was a renter who paid rent to the landlord for use of the land." Moreover, between the end of the Civil War and the 1880s, Mississippi's state legislature joined other Southern states in passing lien prioritization laws rendering the landlord's lien for rent and advances superior to all other claims on the crop. This way, landowning farmers could raise and market a crop without worrying about the claims of tenants, croppers, or merchants eating into their profits. Clearly, the system to which these changes gave rise was ripe for abuse, and Mississippi landowners seem to have lost few opportunities to use their legally superior position to reduce labor's bargaining power.[7]

Additionally, post-Reconstruction changes in land-use rights made it harder for poor and landless people to survive without renting land or working for wages. During the antebellum and Reconstruction eras, all classes of Southerners had enjoyed common access to any unenclosed land (the "open range") for livestock grazing, hunting, and fishing. Once landowning planters regained control of Southern state legislatures in the 1870s, they introduced stock laws, which shifted the burden of fence-building (and the liability for crops damaged by livestock) away from planters. Stock laws negatively impacted poor whites, freed people, and Indians still residing on marginal lands by cutting off access to customary, noncapitalist means of subsistence. In Mississippi, not surprisingly, stock laws arrived earliest in counties with larger planters and more freed people. Noxubee, Attala, and Kemper Counties had each passed stock laws by 1880, while for the time being, the rest of east-central Mississippi remained open range. A statewide game law, which similarly curtailed subsistence outside of the cotton economy and contained strong incentives for local enforcement, was passed in 1876. Anti-enticement (1890) and vagrancy (1904) laws were the final coffin nails for labor mobility, a fact that nonwhite Mississippians, largely disfranchised by the 1890s, had little power to change.[8]

These sorts of legislation reflected the power of landowning planters to shape a system that suited their interests above all others, codifying forms of labor control that would survive well into the twentieth century. The system was dynamic and continued (albeit in new forms) the work of dispossession begun with the taking of land. If the plundering of Article 14 claimants had affirmed that Mississippi was a "white man's country," the land-use and labor control measures passed after Reconstruction augured a constrained existence for the already disinherited. Moreover, the elite bias of such laws and the increasingly multiracial character of east-central Mississippi's rural proletariat suggested that the emerging system of land tenure would impoverish white as well as Black and native people.

Augmenting the new legal basis for postbellum labor control were the informal forms of intimidation and coercion that many whites adopted. Just as the forced-labor system of *chibaro* (and its Portuguese counterpart, *chibalo*) plagued southern Africa in the early twentieth century, de facto slavery thrived in the red clay hills, piney woods, and cotton fields of east-central Mississippi after Reconstruction. As Douglas Blackmon has shown, there existed in the United States a "constitutional limbo in which slavery as a legal concept was prohibited . . . but no statute made an act of enslavement explicitly illegal." The late nineteenth and early twentieth centuries found the South's most vulnerable workers ensnared in forced-labor arrangements for which there were few if any legal proscriptions. Sometimes, enslavers used debts or broken contracts as pretext, while other times, they simply kidnapped their victims. East-central Mississippi's Black, Choctaw, and even some poor white workers supplied the region's farms, sawmills, and turpentine camps with plenty of unpaid labor during those years, and there was considerable public support for the system.[9]

As early as the turn of the century, the federal government was aware of slavery's persistence in the Deep South. In 1903 an unprecedented wave of peonage cases shook the Alabama Black belt, and a year later, the wave reached Mississippi. The Justice Department learned that Kemper County planters J. E. Henderson and a pair known as the Leggett brothers were holding a Black man named Shep Griffin against his will. Griffin allegedly owed the planters ten dollars, a debt that several white citizens had offered to help him pay. But the planters declined the payment because, as the *Jackson Daily News* reported, "it was work and not money they wanted." Individuals identified as "reputable white citizens" reported that Henderson and the Leggetts had on one occasion "stripped and severely whipped" Griffin for attempting to escape the farm. For nearly a week, Griffin's clothes stuck to the gashes on his tattered flesh. A second escape attempt—this time to neighboring Neshoba County—ended when armed whites captured him, tied him to a horse, and dragged him back to the Kemper County farm.[10]

On the evening of March 7, 1904, deputy US marshals arrived in Kemper County to seize Griffin on a bench warrant. R. C. Lee, US attorney for the Southern District of Mississippi, wanted his testimony in the government's case against Henderson and the Leggetts, and the bench warrant seemed the only way to extricate him. Authorities detained Griffin in a Meridian jail so that he would not have to return to Kemper County, where he would have faced retaliation for cooperating with the government. But local resistance made it exceedingly difficult for crusading district attorneys like Lee to prosecute peonage cases, and United States v. Leggett—like United States v. Pickett, a similar peonage case originating in the same county around the same time—remained stalled for two years. Special agent A. J. Hoyt, whom the government had charged with collecting evidence in the Mississippi peonage cases, lamented that "the white Planters stand to-gether and will not give a Negro a verdict over a white man, no matter what the evidence may be." Such planters, he informed Attorney General William H. Moody, were "as much in the Negro Traffic in my opinion as they were before the [Civil] War," and would close ranks to protect their own. By 1906 Lee had decided to drop both cases. As he explained to the attorney general, "The trial would end in a verdict of not guilty—indeed, we have no sort of doubts about this."[11]

Not surprisingly, the relatively few peonage indictments in the first decade of the twentieth century failed to snuff out the region's slave rings, and the practice continued. At the end of 1917, a Choctaw man named Tom Stephens dictated a letter to Interior Secretary Franklin K. Lane, describing how a white man named Vance Posey had "robbed me of everything I had and beaten me nearly to death." Posey, who lived in Deemer, a small community in Neshoba County, had hired Stephens and his two sons in December 1915 to clear land—a job for which Posey paid them five dollars per acre. But afterward, Posey detained Stephens and his sons, forcing them to perform more than a year's work without adequate provisions or pay. On June 28, 1917, sensing that Posey was in a violent mood and not wanting to work for him in that day's driving rain, Stephens stayed away. That night, Posey and three other men awakened Stephens and beat and flogged him at gunpoint. Stephens played dead, then limped five miles to a friend's house. In the days that followed, his mother and sons escaped and joined him. Posey retaliated by keeping all of the family's possessions, including clothing, beds, and quilts. Stephens contacted Secretary Lane as cold weather was approaching, fearing that he and his family "may all freeze to death" if no one intervened on their behalf. "The white men (some of them) have treated the Choctaws this way all the time since the Dancing Rabbit Creek Treaty," he lamented. "Everything the Choctaws get the white men take away from them. *This is the way they drove our grandfathers from their homes, and now they take everything from us.*"[12]

Stephens viewed white landowners' ruthless labor control measures as a direct extension of colonial invasion. His parting observation makes clear that settler-colonial dispossession was not a discrete event but, rather, a structure and a process unfolding over time. Landless and politically powerless—and having endured an excruciating "second removal" just a decade prior to Stephens's letter—Choctaws fell prey to the same sorts of forced-labor tactics that ensnared black Mississippians and some poor whites. For Stephens, such practices were all the more degrading for their occurrence on stolen Choctaw land, the taking of which was, of course, the condition of possibility for the whole rotten system.[13]

The end of World War I brought hard times for farmers across the country, as overproduction pushed farm prices down. A wave of outmigration to the urban North made cheap, tractable labor seem scarce. In Mississippi, the onset of the agricultural depression coincided with the last gasp of the old timber industry—soon to collapse from decades of reckless clear-cutting that left most forest lands denuded. As hard times set in, whites longed for cheap labor in the form of enslaved workers secured through bogus vagrancy charges. "Look on the streets of any town," a Newton County newspaperman urged readers, "and you will discover one cause of the scarcity of farm labor." He castigated "loafing idlers," suggesting that anyone not actively engaged in farm work should be compelled to do so. "If we only had marshals and officers to enforce the vagrancy laws in the towns," the journalist opined, "and a Ku Klux Klan in the country to see that those 'who toil not, neither shall they eat,' labor conditions would improve."[14]

To be sure, plenty of whites still solved their labor needs by simply enslaving fellow Mississippians. On May 13, 1925, the Federal Bureau of Investigation (FBI) received a typewritten letter from Sebastopol, on the border of Leake and Scott Counties. Its author, a white man named Robert McLendon, reported the kidnapping and enslavement of "a 16 year old half white negro boy, an orphan." The young man had apparently been passing through the area in search of work when a prominent white landowner named Nick Lang enslaved him on his farm. "I cannot recall the name of the boy," McLendon wrote to the FBI, "but an early trip to Mr. Nick Langs home . . . will find the boy in slavery all right." On three separate occasions, the young man had attempted to escape the farm, whereupon Lang had recaptured and beaten him. East-central Mississippians would undoubtedly close ranks to protect such enslavers; as McLendon related, "Hell is an icehouse when you seek to investigate slavery and moonshining and bootlegging." McLendon assured the FBI that there were "many other slaves over Mississippi, Alabama and Ga., being smuggled."[15]

Two years later, National Association for the Advancement of Colored People (NAACP) secretary James Weldon Johnson forwarded a similar letter to the FBI that he had received from Kosciusko, in Attala County. A man calling himself Frank Jones alleged that the local justice of the peace and his constable, Jeff Therrell, were "in a conspiracy to arrest colored as well as white people on trumped up charges and find them guilty." Someone from the sawmill and logging camp at Zama, a small settlement southeast of Kosciusko, would show up to pay the imposed fines and take the prisoners back to the camp, where they remained "indefinitely." W. P. Brown & Sons, a Louisville, Kentucky, lumber operation, had purchased Zama, forty miles of railroad, and 30,000 acres of virgin timber in 1924. Jones wrote that Therrell had once been a whipping boss there and was appointed constable at the county seat "in order to furnish negroes for the Zama camp." He explained that Therrell and the justice of the peace had the routine "down to a science." If they needed more workers than the usual array of trumped-up charges would yield, the pair enslaved those who could not pay the local road tax, and there was "no appeal if it's a negro." Such local officials, Jones added, had "absolute authority over the negro," and, lest the NAACP think it was an isolated problem, he assured Johnson that this sort of thing "prevails throughout the state."[16]

More than half a century after emancipation, whites still felt a sense of ownership over "their" labor force, much as they did over "their" land. That much is evident from a 1929 incident that occurred in Noxubee County. Around the time of the cotton harvest, a man named J. T. Wilson of Wirewood Plantation, near Greenwood in LeFlore County, attempted to hire twenty-three Black families from Noxubee County to pick cotton in the Delta. When businessmen and planters in the Noxubee County seat of Macon caught wind of Wilson's plan, which probably ran afoul of the anti-enticement statute, they formed a posse to deter him. After taking one of Wilson's Black associates to the outskirts of town to beat him, the posse forced the Greenwood men to leave without the families. George Padmore, then a globetrotting union organizer for the Communist Party, wrote of the incident in *The Life and Struggles of Negro Toilers*, a 1931 pamphlet that likened Southern "Jim Crowism" to colonialism in sub-Saharan Africa. Padmore's account had the posse publicly stripping and flogging the Black families "as a warning to other blacks never to attempt to migrate."[17]

According to R. J. Enochs, a white doctor and federal agent serving the Mississippi Choctaws, it was "custom" for landlords to keep indebted sharecroppers "in captivity" until they had paid in full. Race apparently mattered less than social class or tenure status. "All the people who move from place to place—the poorer white people, the Indians, and the negroes in this country," were vulnerable to such abuse. "It amounts to an unfortunate state," Enochs told members of a Senate subcommittee of the Committee on Indian Affairs in 1930. "But that is the custom which [the landlords] have among themselves."[18]

Similar reports of coercion and intimidation emanated from east-central Mississippi until the early 1940s, but, as at the turn of the century, there remained little hope of bringing the perpetrators to justice. That was in part due to the active involvement of local law enforcement officials. It also stemmed from elite Mississippians' broad approval of forced labor. The persistence of slave rings and gentleman's agreements among white landowners contributed to a climate of fear among the region's most vulnerable workers. Tenants and sharecroppers who might have otherwise challenged their landlords, contested the terms of their employment, or demanded a fairer shake at settlement time must have recognized the futility in doing so when whites could enslave them with impunity. Moreover, for Blacks and Choctaws in the late nineteenth and early twentieth centuries, there was yet another powerful incentive to toe the line.

II

Extralegal killing was not uncommon in settler societies before World War II. Just as the founding of such societies had been predicated on violence, so, too, was their preservation. Certainly, the fear of revenge, however unfounded, played some role in whites' brutality. In Neshoba County, for instance, whites asked Lillie Jones, a Black woman born in 1892, "If it ever gets to where you all will be over us, like we are you, would you turn us a favor?" As Jones recalled, "They have been so bad, harsh, on the Negroes, till they figured that the Negro, if they ever got the chance to do anything to them, they'll sure do it." Blacks accused of murdering or attempting to murder whites could be tortured and killed before ever facing the formal judicial system. Sexual fear also incited whites to violence, paralleling the "Black peril" scares in Kenya, Southern Rhodesia, and South Africa. Indeed, as in other settler states, proximity to Black people in and of itself could constitute a crisis for whites. K. Stephen Prince points out that lynching was one among several "desperate responses of a people whose very survival was at stake," or so they seemed to believe. To be sure, whites enjoyed a numerical majority in the counties of east-central Mississippi (unlike in some Delta counties or in the African examples, where they constituted only a small percentage of the overall population). But fear could sometimes obscure that fact or render it irrelevant.[19]

Like involuntary servitude and slavery, lynching fostered a psychic terror that served white landowners' desire for labor control. Memory of a spate of lynchings in the late nineteenth and early twentieth centuries hung like a dark cloud over Black and Choctaw communities in east-central Mississippi. Obie Clark, a Black man born in Kemper County at the start of the Great Depression, grew up hearing stories of family friends who had challenged the region's strict social order. "They showed us oak trees where black men were hung and shot until the rope broke," Clark remembered. "They knew what would happen to a black person who attempted to live as a first-class citizen." Clint Collier, of Neshoba County, remembered stories of a first cousin shot and killed for speaking to a white woman, and of a great-uncle killed by white vigilantes at the turn of the century. The lynching of family friend Willie Tingle traumatized Newton County residents Medgar and Charles Evers when they were young. Whites dragged Tingle behind a wagon, then hung him from a tree, and finally "shot him full of holes." They left his clothes "lyin' in that field, all bloodstained," Charles Evers recalled decades later, "and Medgar and I would see 'em every day. I can close my eyes and still see 'em, real as life. . . . It shocked the daylights out of us." Such stories reminded Blacks and Choctaws of the consequences of defying white supremacy.[20]

Lynchings in east-central Mississippi tended to be swift and brutal. The most common triggers were accusations of murder or attempted murder and sexual transgression. On February 16, 1891, friends and neighbors of a prosperous white farmer named Ben Pierce hanged John Bull, a Choctaw man, in Neshoba County. The *Jackson Clarion-Ledger* reported that Bull was the prime suspect in Pierce's murder, and that the whites had moved as one to capture him and send "his poluted [sic] soul to meet his God from the limb of a convenient tree." Six years later, whites in the same county captured a Black man named Jim Cooper who they alleged had attempted to kill a white man named Mulholland. After hanging Cooper, they slit his throat from ear to ear. Four years after that, Neshoba whites hanged a Black man named Sam Hinson for allegedly assaulting a white woman. The next year, a posse shot and killed Dick Hill for allegedly killing a white man. Before World War I, accusations of murder or attempted murder were also behind lynchings in the counties of Kemper (1905 and 1909), Lauderdale (1883, 1889, 1910, and 1911), Newton (1908 and 1911), Leake (1899), Winston (1891 and 1894), and Noxubee (1882, 1899, and 1912). Although whites periodically revived the Ku Klux Klan and similar vigilante groups, most lynchings seem to have been the work of spontaneously organized groups of ordinary citizens.[21]

The frequency and persistence of lynching, in addition to being characteristic of the Jim Crow South, betokened a deep well of settler-colonial anxiety decades after the disappearance of a "frontier." That the dispossession of indigenous people was a formative experience for whites in east-central Mississippi is undeniable. Most locals in the early twentieth century could trace their family lineage to the initial settlement period, and everyone knew what it had taken to wrest complete control of the region from its native inhabitants. "Instead of a land sale, it was more of a land steal," admitted Mary Lillian Whitten, a white woman raised in Noxubee County on what had once been the land of Choctaw leader Mashulatubbee. "I think the white people have been ashamed."[22]

Violence—including the quiet violence of occupying stolen land—had become a way of life, and something about that fact haunted whites. In the early twentieth century, a Noxubee County woman named McGraw told of how, at night, her mother was "frightened by howls of wolves and by the Indians, who were numerous in these parts." And even as he watched Choctaws pick his cotton, Kemper County planter T. B. George recovered abandoned tools, weapons, and jewelry from an idle pasture on his property, the site of a former Choctaw town. Such ruins were an unsubtle reminder of founding violence—that the place George called home was also a site of destruction. Moreover, the farm economy of the late nineteenth and early twentieth centuries forced whites to share social space with those they had dispossessed or enslaved. When they felt their control threatened, they sometimes fell back on old patterns of violence that recalled the anxieties of the frontier and early settlement periods.[23]

Turn-of-the-century lynchings, only a generation or two removed from the mass dispossession of the Choctaws and within living memory of slavery, prefigured the violence of the interwar years. Sometimes, these were quite similar events in which mobs of white men captured and killed a single Black or Choctaw man suspected of murder or inappropriate behavior toward white women. On July 18, 1924, lumbermen in the Kemper County town of Scooba (site of a 1906 riot) broke into the local jail and lynched a Black man named Harry Shelton for "insulting proposals to a white woman." Whites "severely whipped" an eighteen-year-old Black man in Neshoba County on March 20, 1927, for the same reason. Three months later, whites in the Winston County town of Noxapater burned two Black men that they had stolen from police custody. The men stood accused of murdering a local sawmill superintendent. Two white men faced a grand jury indictment in the 1940 murder of Choctaw farmers Lampkin Amis and Tommie Thompson, but probably only because the victims were tenants on the farm of Gene DeWeese, a prosperous farmer from a very prominent Neshoba County lumber family.[24]

Racial violence in the interwar years could also reflect more purely economic resentment. In June 1921, the New Deemer Manufacturing Plant in Neshoba County closed after a white mob terrorized the Black section of the small company town two nights in a row. There had long been a lumber operation at Deemer, and before 1921, all the employees had been white. A short time before the terror attacks, the company had begun hiring Black workers. On the night of June 20, angry whites fired into the houses of the sixty or so Black families in the town. The next night, a few sticks of dynamite exploded in the same section, signaling the start of a second round of gunfire from whites encircling the neighborhood. Afterward, the company offered to hire protection for the Black families, but they fled the town instead.[25]

III

The system of labor control that ruling whites arranged after Reconstruction looked much the same until economic catastrophe in the 1920s and 1930s prompted federal intervention and the beginning of a new order. The end of World War I had brought curtailed foreign demand for American farm goods, which, combined with farmers' growing productive capacity, meant that prices slumped. The situation for Southern cotton farmers, who had recently had to deal with the arrival of the boll weevil, was particularly difficult. Although cotton prices fluctuated in the late 1910s and 1920s, the nagging problem of overproduction meant that they did not reach parity with the more stable prewar period of 1909–1914. To make matters worse, farmers habitually tried to make up for falling cotton prices with increased plantings, which left less acreage for other crops and caused cotton prices to fall still further. Federal and state governments expended an enormous amount of energy trying to devise a solution for overproduction, but none worked particularly well for cotton farmers, and by the time President Franklin Delano Roosevelt took office in 1933, the problem demanded a new approach.[26]

The Agricultural Adjustment Act, signed into law in May 1933, revolutionized Southern agriculture. For cotton farmers, its cornerstone was a domestic allotment program. Since previous attempts to reduce cotton acreage (and, thus, induce higher prices) had necessarily been on a voluntary basis, noncooperators—farmers electing to capitalize on others' acreage reduction—had been a perennial concern. The plan of the Agricultural Adjustment Administration (AAA) was to pay farmers to reduce cotton acreage. If enough farmers signed a formal contract to comply, the program would go into effect. In July 1933, with about a million cotton farmers (or about ten million acres) committed to the reduction effort, the program commenced. In exchange for planting only their allotted acreage in cotton, farmers received benefit payments from the federal government. AAA payments came in the form of rental payments and parity payments, a portion of which the landowner was supposed to share with tenants. The first year, east-central Mississippi's farmers committed tens of thousands of acres for a total of $876,879.12 in benefits; the state as a whole received $9,924,837. Cully Cobb, onetime Mississippian and head of the AAA cotton section, called the acreage reduction campaign a "battle for economic existence" that "saved the South from the disaster of four cent cotton."[27]

As the AAA began to prop up landowning cotton farmers with rental and parity payments, tenants lost a significant amount of bargaining power. With smaller acreage allotments came the possibility that tenants and sharecroppers might be evicted, despite lackluster government efforts to prevent such an outcome. Heads rolled in the AAA cotton section, as a handful of employees who stood up for the landless farmers lost their jobs. The Supreme Court's January 1936 ruling in *United States v. Butler* that the AAA's processing tax was unconstitutional did little to stem the slow but certain erosion of tenants' and sharecroppers' overall economic security, as the domestic allotment program proceeded through other legislative means. Moreover, the federal government had never attempted to directly facilitate the fair division of parity payments between landlord and tenant for fear of disturbing the Southern social order. While some landlords claimed to have credited tenants' share of the payments "to their accounts," the accounts in question had long been instruments of the landlords' own subterfuge. Plenty of landlords simply changed the status of tenants and sharecroppers to that of day laborer and used the payments to buy labor-saving machinery. Disputes between landlord and tenant now landed before county committees consisting of local landowners rather than in state courts; the committees' (unpublished) decisions generally favored the landlord. As one team of social scientists observed, the "AAA as finally administered . . . proved to be merely a subsidy to planters."[28]

While planters prospered under the AAA, tenants and sharecroppers languished. In February 1937, US Secretary of Agriculture Henry A. Wallace transmitted a report on farm tenancy to the president, citing a multitude of factors contributing to tenants' plight. The *Report of the Special Committee on Farm Tenancy* especially highlighted the ill effects of a land policy of fee simple absolute, in which owners were entitled to unrestricted use (and abuse) of "their" land. "Erosion of the soil has its counterpart in erosion of our society," the report stated. "Instability and insecurity of farm families leach the binding elements of rural community life." That tenants and sharecroppers tended to move from farm to farm with great frequency, cultivating a money crop with little regard for the long-term health of the soil, only worsened the situation. In July of the following year, the *Report on the Economic Conditions of the South* further highlighted the sorry state of Southern land tenure, similarly linking concerns of labor to those of land use and the environment. "No other similar area in the world gambles its welfare and the destinies of so many people on a single crop market year after year."[29]

IV

Like in most of the cotton South, the number of tenants and sharecroppers in east-central Mississippi had risen since Reconstruction as small landowners fell into debt and lost their land. Many tenants and sharecroppers in this part of the state were white, although the rate of tenancy (including sharecroppers) was higher for Black and Choctaw farmers, who had less hope of escaping their debts. Clint Collier, mentioned earlier, remembered that whites "found all kinds of techniques to exploit [Black sharecroppers]" and inhibit their advancement to landownership. Collier's father "farmed on halvers" in the first half of the twentieth century and paid usurious rates for basic supplies like clothing and fertilizer at the Mars Brothers store in Philadelphia. He reckoned that while white tenants and sharecroppers were not necessarily getting a fairer shake, they were freer to challenge the landlord or merchant: "If he wanted to, [the white tenant] could demand his rights more than we could." In other cases, sharecroppers had to go through their landlords to obtain supplies from local merchants—an arrangement that could double the interest and result in the cropper forfeiting all or most of their share of the cotton at settlement time. Again, Black farmers were in no position to haggle. "Sharecropping, this plantation system . . . it has used the black man quite a bit," Collier lamented.[30]

Most Choctaws in the early twentieth century were sharecroppers on white farms, and peonage was common. In 1918, Commissioner of Indian Affairs Cato Sells made a pass through the area and described "pitiable poverty," noting that the Choctaws "were almost entirely farm laborers or share croppers." A miniscule number owned any land outright, and sharecropping seemed the surest way to secure shelter and enough cornmeal to live on. Most avoided sawmilling because they had had little training in that sort of work and rightly considered it dangerous, while some traveled as far as the Delta for steady work picking cotton (a trend that would continue for decades). Some Choctaw sharecroppers, like Olmon Cumby, attempted to purchase their own capital goods but were cheated by settlers. When Cumby paid a settler thirty-five dollars for a cow, the settler took the money and kept the cow. Cumby did not pursue the matter because he "didn't want to have any trouble with him." Others gave up on any but a hand-to-mouth existence under the thumb of a white landlord. Phillip Dixon, a Choctaw sharecropper working for a Leake County man named Ed Freeny, reckoned that "I just never will be able" to purchase land or tools. "I just have been in bad luck all the time, you see." The year of the commissioner's visit, following testimony from a number of other Choctaw farmers, several of whom seemed on the verge of starvation, Congress appropriated $75,000 in relief, and an Indian agency set up shop in Philadelphia.[31]

The federal government's assumption of some responsibility for the well-being of the Mississippi Choctaws meant material improvement on a few fronts. The Office of Indian Affairs (OIA) opened schools for Choctaw children at Pearl River, Tucker, and Bogue Chitto (Neshoba County); Standing Pine and Redwater (Leake County); Bogue Homo (Jones County); and Conehatta (Newton County). "We are colonizing [grouping] them as much as possible," a government agent reported in the 1920s, "more to give them school advantages than for any other reason." To be sure, the school curriculum reflected the government's preoccupation with assimilation—federal policy since the Dawes Act of 1887. But Choctaw families made the most of the schools, often using them as community centers. In 1926 the agency added a thirty-five-bed hospital.

Still, the question of land loomed largest for most Choctaws. In 1920, Frank McKinley, the agent appointed by the OIA, reported on the land situation as he perceived it. Of the roughly half a million acres allotted to the Mississippi Choctaws over the years, most were "being occupied by white settlers" who, "as a matter of true record . . . have no more title to same than a man in China." While many of the current occupants might be "innocent as to [their] occupancy," McKinley was sure that "the original entry to most of this Indian land has been with deliberate and conspired fraud." He concluded in no uncertain terms that the Choctaws had "been practically driven off of [their] own land." McKinley soon attempted to acquire farms for them on treaty land that settlers had stolen. Yet the process of reappropriating the land was exceedingly complex and angered many settlers. McKinley "[ran] into guns and ammunitions," as one Choctaw leader later reflected. "[White] people didn't want to lose what they got on the land there, which . . . belonged to the Indians, but they were using it." Although a few Choctaw families obtained reimbursable loans for farms on agency land, the interwar years still found most Choctaws working as sharecroppers under the thumb of whites. McKinley's successor noted in 1927 that "under the present landlord and tenant system the Mississippi Choctaw has no chance at all to be anything except a slave."[32]

Choctaws thus experienced not only land dispossession on a grand scale but also subjugation as laborers on that land. Article 14 claimants and their descendants had been robbed not only of their land but also of their means of subsistence outside the cotton economy, which elite white settlers had rigged in their favor. This seemingly unalterable situation found a majority of Choctaws no closer to recovering a land base (and, thus, a shot at prosperity) in the 1930s than at almost any time since the Treaty of Dancing Rabbit Creek a century earlier.

As it developed in the late nineteenth and early twentieth centuries, land tenure in settler societies was nakedly exploitative, privileging white farmers at all others' expense. In that regard, Mississippi differed little from southern and eastern Africa. As settlers there consolidated their hold on the land, they forced African peasants into relationships of dependency. After World War I and as they became more confident as farmers, settlers in the White Highlands of Kenya attempted to reduce the independence of the Kikuyu squatters that were their principal labor force. Progressively more draconian Resident Native Labor Ordinances (RNLO)—culminating in the 1937 RNLO—gave settlers a freer hand in dealing with squatters as they saw fit, which generally meant reducing their independently cultivated acreage and their livestock holdings. Squatters unable or unwilling to adapt faced an unenviable choice between the city and the crowded, over-farmed reserves. Even before the extensive mechanization of settler agriculture in Kenya, the assault on the squatters' autonomy fostered much of the resentment that would reach its apogee in the Mau Mau emergency of the 1950s.[33]

Southern Africa looked similar in the sense that settlers were increasingly able to restrict African peasants' access to the means of subsistence and force them to work as tenants or for wages. Aided by successive Land Apportionment Acts, Southern Rhodesia's white settlers occupied the best farmland, while inferior lands were held in reserve. Uprooted Shona and Ndebele had little choice but to work for whites. As one settler remarked in the 1930s, the "relative abundance of labour in Rhodesia is not the least of its charms." In South Africa, sharecroppers like Kas Maine could own certain capital goods like farm implements and work animals, but (mainly undercapitalized) settlers owned the land. As Maine remarked near the end of his life, "The seed was mine, the ploughs were mine, the oxen were mine. All was mine, only the land was his." In the early twentieth century, before tractors arrived in great numbers, Highveld sharecroppers like Maine had some bargaining power in their oxen. This worried some settlers, and the South African Parliament, through the Natives' Land Act of 1913, attempted to eliminate sharecropping altogether in favor of wage labor or some other form of tenancy. By the 1930s, settlers had embarked on what would be a decades-long drive, first for "influx control," then to abolish tenancy altogether in favor of low-paid wage labor.[34]

Whatever autonomy poor and nonwhite farmers maintained as World War II approached, landowning settlers everywhere had the backing of the state, and their power was difficult to resist. In Mississippi, big landowners emboldened by the overthrow of Reconstruction set up a legal framework for controlling labor and benefited from an informal regime of de facto slavery and racial terror. But labor control there was contingent on several factors. Poor, rural Mississippians had to remain moored to the cotton economy; peonage needed to continue unhindered; Black and Choctaw Mississippians had to remain politically disenfranchised; the labor movement needed to be kept weak; and, in general, outside interests could not be allowed to interfere. Even if most of those conditions held, the status quo could stand. But almost none of them did. By 1945 a new day had dawned in the South. Fortunately for white landowners, a revolution in science and technology—led by USDA agencies that favored large operators—would soon render the labor question irrelevant and foster a consolidation of settler-colonial landholding.

SEA CHANGE SETTLER AGRICULTURE AFTER
WORLD WAR II

2

Machinery everywhere.
—Homer Croy, Harper's, 1946

"When these picking machines begin to move into the cotton fields," inventors John and Mack Rust wrote of their mechanical cotton picker in 1936, "they will of necessity steadily crowd the sharecroppers and other hand pickers off the cotton land." The Rust brothers hoped that some provision might be made for workers displaced by their machine, lest they "be added to the ranks of the unemployed." Almost a decade later, a prototype was slated for demonstration in the Mississippi Delta, where planters and agricultural leaders were not worried about labor displacement—in fact, they were counting on it. "I am confident that you are aware of the serious racial problem which confronts us at this time and which may become more serious as time passes," Clarksdale plantation manager Richard Hopson wrote local planters in advance of the demonstration. "Mechanized farming will require only a fraction of the amount of labor which is required by the sharecrop system," he assured them, "thereby tending to equalize the white and Negro population which would automatically make our racial problem easier to handle." Rarely were the social and political implications of mechanization so clearly spelled out, as everyone in the cotton South knew what was at stake.[1]

Since emancipation, landowning farmers had had to

contend with the labor question—specifically, how to mobilize and control workers in a nominally free-labor system. The labor question was inextricable from what Hopson referred to as "our racial problem," as nonwhite tenants and sharecroppers were a disproportionate share of the farm labor force. After World War II, the growth of the civil rights movement at home and decolonization abroad filled many whites with apprehension—planters perhaps most of all. For if Jim Crow collapsed while white planters still depended on Black and indigenous labor, labor control as whites knew it would end. In part to avoid such a calamity, the Southern agricultural establishment pushed to completely mechanize cotton production and diversify farms that were too small or hilly for mechanical pickers, as was the case in much of east-central Mississippi. The result was a farm structure that was less labor-intensive and more capital-intensive than ever. By design, the transition virtually eliminated tenant farming and sharecropping, and it led to the consolidation of land in fewer, whiter hands.[2]

In the late 1940s, that process was still beginning. But from the start, agricultural leaders imagined that Mississippi and the rest of the cotton South would soon be free of "inefficient" small farmers and that large, white landowners (the "real farmer," as one member of the elite Delta Council put it) would predominate. The labor question would mostly be a thing of the past. Settlers elsewhere imagined similar possibilities as machinery became available. In fact, wherever white settlers farmed, they realized distinct advantages over indigenous and other nonwhite farmers thanks to their almost exclusive access to modern equipment and expertise. Not only in southern and eastern Africa, but in French Algeria and Tunisia, whites enjoyed a near-monopoly on imported tractors, combines, and other heavy equipment. Mechanization rewarded big farmers who could take advantage of economies of scale and freed up the land of less competitive farmers, leading to consolidation.[3]

In Mississippi, this meant that the most prosperous descendants of the pioneering settlers enjoyed an ever-larger share of the ill-gotten gains of colonization. This chapter describes a shift in the dynamic of settler colonialism that commenced when technology emerged as a solution to problems of economy, land use, and, importantly, labor control. Its consolidationist logic was upwardly redistributive and poverty-inducing over the long term. While the century following the Treaty of Dancing Rabbit Creek had witnessed the exploitation of Black and native people as laborers on taken land, the post–World War II period gave rise to an entirely new set of social relations wherein laborers were rendered disposable. If the labor question had once presented unique problems for landowners in the settler South, increasingly after World War II, labor *was* the problem. A granular look at this shift, as promoted by state and local agricultural leaders and set against postwar political trends, gives a sense of why and how the mode of settler colonialism changed in Mississippi.

I

A combination of factors made the post–World War II period a watershed for the cotton South. In 1945 growers were unsure of what the future held economically, and memories of the aftermath of World War I made them pessimistic. As one Southern farmer put it, "It'll be like the last war— a real slump. That's what I'm planning on." Small farmers and tenants were particularly worried, although few farmers of any status felt totally secure. Many expected oversupply and low prices, especially as veterans and defense industry workers returned to the farm after the cessation of hostilities. Some feared recession would accompany peace, and USDA agricultural economists acknowledged as much in a bulletin titled *What Peace Can Mean to American Farmers*, arguing that the fate of American agriculture "depends more on the level of business activity and nonfarm employment that can be maintained after the war than upon anything else." As economist Stuart Chase put it in the *Nation*, "When workers have jobs, farmers have prosperity." Their assessment was in line with the growing consensus that peacetime prosperity meant full employment, generous wages, and, thus, mass purchasing power. If nonfarm employment was not available, not only would the domestic market for cotton-based products (and other farm products) shrink, but still more workers might choose to return to the land, making the overall situation worse. Adding to the uncertainty were shifting foreign consumption patterns and the growing market share enjoyed by manufacturers of cheaper synthetic fabrics like rayon. Many observers concluded that Southern cotton had to become competitive to survive.⁴

In a set of congressional hearings between 1944 and 1947, lobbyists, experts, and big cotton growers responded with calls for "economy and efficiency in production." Clarence Dorman, director of the Mississippi Agricultural Experiment Station, told members of the House Cotton Subcommittee of the Committee on Agriculture in December 1944 that branch stations were perfecting full mechanization. They had found "that the cost of mechanizing 500 acres is less than the tenant houses on the farm before you go into feed, mules, or anything else on a regular system." In July 1947, Frank J. Welch, dean of the Mississippi State College School of Agriculture, further stressed the link between efficiency and modernization. Efficient cotton growing, Welch argued, would require increasing the size of farms and supplying enough capital to employ the latest methods on the larger units. Neither testimony completely ignored the obvious human cost. But, as Welch rather callously stated, "There are at present too many people on the land for efficient combination of labor and other productive factors under the proposed better balanced and more efficient system." Welch's idea of "efficiency," in other words, required that all but the biggest operators would have to go.⁵

In east-central Mississippi, the shift from labor-intensive to capital-intensive cotton farming began in earnest in the late 1940s. Partial mechanization had occurred before World War II only on a small percentage of farms. A few Farmall tractors were in use in Neshoba County in May 1937, and eighty-three local farmers reported owning a tractor in 1940. But that number represented only about 2 percent of the county's farmers. During the war, the process quickened somewhat as landowners bemoaned their loosening grip on labor. County agents helped landowners overcome the decline in cheap, tractable labor—which agents and landowners tended to misleadingly characterize as a labor *shortage*—by securing tractors, fuel, tires, and other equipment. "Stress has been placed on using as much farm machinery as available so as to save labor," one county agent reported. In the absence of mechanical solutions for two of the more labor-intensive steps in the cotton-growing process—weeding and picking—many more clung to animal traction and family labor until after the war. "Although it has been possible to dispense with negro labor to some extent in planting and cultivating," explained a Leake County agricultural leader before the war, "it has not as yet become possible to do without the negro when the time comes to harvest the cotton." But by the end of the war, Mississippians were reading about the development of mechanical pickers and flame throwers that could burn weeds and grass growing close to the cotton stalk. Although it would be a few more years before preemergent and post-emergent herbicides would replace the flame thrower, by 1945 full mechanization was no longer a distant dream.[6]

County agents made sure that local people knew about the farmers in their midst who were already employing the new methods. As early as 1943, local newspapers featured a profile of a white Kemper County farmer, Evie Skipper, who was coping with wartime changes by mechanizing. That year, Skipper had thirty-four acres in cotton, twenty-one in oats, fifteen in corn, thirteen in wheat, and six in soybeans; he also raised hogs. Not long before, Skipper had employed four sharecroppers and two wage hands. Soon, he was able do without all but the two hired workers—a Black farmer and his wife. By the summer of 1943, the total workforce amounted to Skipper; his wife, Florrie; and daughters, Fetha, Joyce, and Evie Jo. The farmer could pare down to such a degree because he had invested in a combine, a tractor, and "other modern farm equipment." This, of course, meant that Florrie, Fetha, and Joyce (credited almost as an afterthought in the article) had to chop thirty-four acres of cotton. Without a mechanical alternative to hand-thinning, and in the years before flame throwers and herbicides were widely available, female members of partially mechanized farm families were sometimes expected to perform extra hand labor—a "second shift" of sorts—in addition to their normal work around the house. The agent made no mention of what became of the sharecroppers and other wage hands.[7]

Norveil Johnson, who ran a farm near Philadelphia, also touted the benefits of mechanization. "There are two principal ways to operate a farm," he explained in 1946, "with tenants, mules, and a share-crop system or by machinery. I prefer the machinery method." Like Skipper, Johnson had acquired some of his equipment during the war, but he planned to purchase more, including a corn binder, before 1947. Not only did he save on labor costs, but Johnson also joined the ranks of well-capitalized farmers using their new machines to do custom work for those who did not want to employ croppers or day laborers but did not yet own their own equipment. Such custom work meant that tractors and other machines paid for themselves in short order. In drawing attention to farmers who were mechanizing their row-cropping operations, county agents made a virtue of abandoning labor-intensive methods. Moreover, they did so in ways that decentered social costs like unemployment and an unequally gendered restructuring of the division of labor. That the local newspaper was the site of that important obfuscation meant that the community learned to view mechanization as unproblematic, even progressive. But portions of east-central Mississippi faced topographical obstacles to mechanization that other cotton regions (such as the Delta) did not, and the profiles of Skipper, Johnson, and others also demonstrated the importance that hill-country extension agents were beginning to attach to another labor-saving, capital-intensive turn: diversification.[8]

II

For decades, dairy had been a valuable (if minor) non-cotton-related enterprise in east-central Mississippi. The poor postwar outlook for cotton led the region's agricultural leaders to place greater emphasis on dairy as a means of diversification. "Since cotton is in a rather discouraging position," Neshoba County agent C. I. Smith announced in January 1945, "we think it would be wise for more farmers to begin to make plans for a well rounded dairy program [to] supplement the income from cotton." Agent Smith and J. C. Brister, manager of the local Pet Milk plant, attempted to sell dairying as a way for landowners to "finally . . . make their farms pay" by converting surplus feed and grass into profit (in the form of milk), selling calves, and saving manure for fertilizer. Additionally, whereas the new machines that were replacing animal traction and hand labor in cotton farming worked well in the flat Delta region, the sloping terrain of the hill country presented safety problems. Cattle grazing allowed farmers to make productive use of such land without worrying about erosion or tractor accidents. For a variety of reasons, enough east-central Mississippi farmers began raising livestock that, as agricultural economist Clayton Ellis put it in 1946, the "milk pail and churn are replacing the picking sack and the cotton gin." The shift was so immediate in Neshoba County that between 1945 and 1949, local farmers more than doubled their earnings in dairy products sold. In a sign of the times, C. I. Smith resigned as county agent to work for Pet.[9]

A boon to landowners, the transition to dairy meant more output with less manpower. One farmer near Union, in Newton County, boasted that dairying made him less dependent on tenants and hired labor. "I will not plant a seed of cotton another year," the man said. "With a few days hired help and the help of my wife and daughter, I will work my entire farm through my dairy program." Clearly dairying, like the transition to full mechanization in cotton, found women performing essential work as their husbands realized handsome returns that they no longer had to divide among workers. "The profit on my farm will not have to be shared with anyone," bragged the same farmer. "Hereafter I expect to farm in such a way that I will never be dependent on much labor again." Norveil Johnson, the Philadelphia man who had quit employing tenants and hired labor in favor of mechanized cotton farming, also experimented with dairying. "For the amount of labor and capital involved," he crowed, "my milk cows pay me many times as much as my cash crops do in proportion." Farmers able to afford the initial investment could run a highly efficient dairy operation with a milking parlor and the latest labor-saving equipment.[10]

Perhaps no area farmer was more celebrated for successful dairying than Irby W. Majure of Union. C. S. Norton, a former AAA district agent who replaced C. I. Smith as Neshoba County's extension agent, wrote glowingly of Majure in the *Neshoba Democrat* and the *Jackson Clarion-Ledger*. Before the war, Majure and his tenants had grown cotton and corn on 327 acres, but neither his land nor his finances seemed to be improving from year to year. The turning point, wrote Norton, was when Majure "let all his tenants go except two men." Along with Mrs. Majure, these two helped him transition from almost exclusively row-cropping to a sophisticated dairy operation. Majure pared down to 140 acres—still well above the local average at that time—and used the money to fertilize and seed grazing crops, purchase new equipment, and add twenty cows to his herd. Keeping only seven acres of row crops (mainly corn for feed), he followed the advice of Norton and the State College soils lab religiously, arranging nine different pastures that consisted of various oats and grasses. As their operation expanded, the Majure family enjoyed "city conveniences amid the quiet life of the country," including a freezer full of vegetables and a pantry stocked with canned goods. Norton made no mention of the fate of the evicted tenants.[11]

While it was less common than dairying, some east-central Mississippi farmers turned to raising beef cattle in the early postwar years. The Extension Service's Test Demonstration program kept records on Lauderdale County farmer Robert E. Payne between 1946 and 1950. During that time, Payne followed a prescribed plan that called for increasing acreage devoted to pasture and decreasing that given to row crops like cotton and corn. He acquired fifty-seven head of cattle (bringing the total to eighty, up from twenty-three in 1946) and purchased an array of new planters, cultivators, seeders, and fertilizer distributors for use on a tractor. There were five sharecropper families on Payne's farm when the program selected it. Five years later, there were only two. The agent reporting on Payne suggested that the "improvements made on this farm from 1946 to 1950 could and should be made on nearly all farms in the county." Yet again, the fate of the displaced sharecroppers garnered no mention.[12]

Cotton gave way to other types of farming at the same time that Mississippians began to think more seriously about forestry. In the nineteenth and early twentieth centuries, before the advent of responsible silviculture, overcutting for short-term gain had rid the state of most of its virgin timber. Wartime demand and the postwar building boom afforded Mississippi timber companies an incentive to adopt more farsighted practices. In 1945 a young extension forester named Dick Allen moved to Neshoba County and, in short order, accepted a position as the first forester for Philadelphia's long-established A. DeWeese Lumber Company. Working across Neshoba, Leake, Kemper, and Winston Counties, Allen helped DeWeese introduce a regional program of tree farming, the likes of which the company's owners had first witnessed while visiting the Crossett Experimental Forest in Arkansas. The program involved sustained-yield harvesting of mature timber that would leave a "capital stock" of trees for use in the future. Since the DeWeese company could not afford to purchase the amount of acreage it needed, it offered private landowners forest management services in return for right of first refusal on their timber, for which the company promised competitive prices.[13]

County agents cooperated closely with Allen, as did east-central Mississippi's newly hired extension foresters. They helped make tree farming—and forestry in general—an important feature of the region's agricultural landscape in the years after World War II. In Kemper County, agent B. H. Dixon noted that farmers were "beginning to consider their woodlands as a crop just as with cotton and corn." Extension personnel marked private timber for selective cutting, organized communities for fire prevention, supplied farmers with creosoted fence posts so that they would not have to dip into their valuable timber for that purpose, and distributed pine seedlings for replanting. They also made forestry a staple of 4-H work, knowing that club members were the farmers of the future. "Forestry is beginning to receive the attention it deserves in the county," agent C. S. Norton observed in his 1947 report on the Neshoba County 4-H program. But tree farming, like dairying, required far less labor than the old method of cotton farming around which the local economy had developed since the region's settlement. And, like dairying and mechanized row-cropping, tree farming would simultaneously be a boon to large landowners and a drag on local employment.[14]

III

In championing mechanized and diversified farmers, agricultural leaders rarely said much about the social consequences of following their advice. As *Fortune* magazine's farm columnist suggested in 1945, it might not have mattered if they had: "Farmers seem bent on sharing the savings that mechanization brought to industry whether it creates farm unemployment or not." Certainly, some landowning farmers were counting on the labor displacement that modern farming would bring. But no one—especially not the experts whose job it was to dispense advice to farmers—could claim that layoffs and evictions came as a surprise or were largely unintended. Well before displacement began to soar in Mississippi in the 1950s, observers had thought through the implications of new, labor-saving technology—particularly the mechanical picker—and its attendant capital and acreage requirements. The restructuring of Southern agriculture would almost certainly produce an army of displaced farmers whose only salvation would be industry's capacity to absorb them as wage workers.[15]

Ironically, one of the early warnings about mechanization came from none other than John and Mack Rust, inventors of an improved spindle cotton picker. They had spent their childhood years picking cotton by hand and wanted farmers to benefit from their machine. But they did not want to be the authors of what they estimated would be 75 percent unemployment among sharecroppers. "We are not willing that this should happen," John Rust stated in 1936. "How can we prevent it?" Indeed, when the Delta Experiment Station field-tested the early Rust machines in the mid-1930s, few could ignore the obvious social implications. "Song of Dixie Darkies Will Fade Away If New Cotton Picker Success," ran one front-page headline. Oscar Johnston, an AAA official and Mississippi native, witnessed one of the tests on August 31, 1936, and remarked that the machine would likely "spell the end of the small farmer." Memphis political boss Ed Crump went so far as to declare that the mechanical picker should be outlawed. Despite their misgivings, the Rust brothers eventually reached agreements with Allis-Chalmers, Pearson, J. I. Case, and Massey-Harris-Ferguson to use Rust designs in their respective spindle pickers.[16]

In the late 1930s, journals like *Rural Sociology* brimmed with warnings of the probable consequences of mechanization. The consensus view was that mechanization would bring disaster for small operators. By the 1940s, though, some observers began to emphasize pull factors and voluntary outmigration, rather than displacement per se. In this view, many who left the land either deployed or worked in wartime defense industries and did not return. When economic recovery led to greater civilian consumption, former tenants, sharecroppers, and small farmers found off-farm employment and never looked back. This supposedly led to a labor shortage for which landowners had to compensate by mechanizing. Oscar Johnston, who had earlier warned that mechanization would mean the end of small farmers, changed his tune in May 1947. "Mechanization is not the cause, but the result, of economic change in the area," he wrote in the *Saturday Evening Post*. "Mechanization is progress, and progress is inevitable." Mississippi home economist Dorothy Dickins flatly stated that "there is no problem of a displaced labor supply; in fact, there is a scarcity of labor on some plantations."[17]

Some scholars have stressed the difficulty or futility in establishing cause and effect regarding mechanization. What is certain is that there was a concerted drive—clearly expressed in the deterministic language of cotton lobbyists in congressional hearings and agricultural leaders everywhere—to mechanize every stage of cotton production in the interest of large landowners. Wartime migration supplied a temporary defense against charges, such as those from the nation's Black press, that the "transition in the South from cotton to beef and mechanized farming . . . will throw millions in the bread lines." But the truth was that farm labor was not in short supply in postwar Mississippi. Laborers simply were not as controllable as they had once been. So, even as they worked to suppress wages and cut costs in the short term, big planters and their allies made labor-displacing mechanization a key component of the postwar push for consolidation and efficiency in cotton farming.[18]

As Mississippi extension economist H. J. Putnam outlined in an unpublished 1946 report, displacement was built into the new farming model in the state. Putnam explained that there were two primary reasons for the declining farm population: World War II and mechanization. Military service and war industries had pulled farmers off the land while the war lasted, but in the postwar decade, mechanization would "probably play a much greater part in bringing about change on Mississippi farms." Both factors would lead to fewer and larger farms, which he considered a positive development that meant more profits for large landowners. "It seems unquestionably true," Putnam averred, "that those farmers who remain on the land will enjoy a higher income and a better level of living if some of the farm population is lost to other occupations." The Extension Service's Test Demonstration program in the state (for whom Putnam wrote the report) thereafter deemed farms with tenants and sharecroppers to be inefficient "'problem' farms." For large landowners to prosper, most other farmers would have to disappear.[19]

A fundamental contradiction attended the purposeful abandonment of whole tenure groups by the Extension Service—the government agency charged with assisting *all* farmers. At times, county agents seemed as though they were trying to both support and displace. Reporting on the progress of extension work in Neshoba County at the end of 1946, agent C. S. Norton revealed the cognitive dissonance that now suffused his work. In his discussion of the farm labor situation, Norton first affirmed that the alleged shortage was over: "Quite a few of the labor problems have been relieved this year, since the veterans are back on the farms." Yet the drive to adopt more and more labor-saving technology accelerated. Tractor-use was making terracing less labor-intensive, he declared. Ditching with dynamite "has saved much labor to the farmer." With more farmers turning to timber as a crop, Norton was arranging demonstrations of the pulpwood saw and power saw, which, "as soon as they are available . . . will mean a labor saving device to farmers in harvesting their forest products." Norton cited "some" voluntary out-migrants, even as he institutionalized the use of equipment whose purpose it was to further thin the ranks of farm labor.[20]

However Southerners resolved the chicken-and-egg questions around mechanization and outmigration, few disputed that one somehow accompanied the other. East-central Mississippi, like the rest of the cotton South, would suffer in the wake of those transformations. To be sure, some Black, Choctaw, and poor white farmers found richer, more stable lives elsewhere. US industrial might—resuscitated during the war—temporarily rendered cities havens for *some* lucky rural migrants. Yet for many others, displacement was but the latest in a continuum of injustices, generating new problems for both the rural South and the urban North in the decades to come.

IV

Aside from the plans and interventions of experts, what made elite whites in east-central Mississippi and elsewhere abandon labor-intensive farming in full view of the likely social consequences? It would be wrong to completely ignore the role of wartime migration. Moreover, many cotton growers did feel the squeeze of economic pressures whose immense scale and complexity prompted them to exert greater control where they could. But the political context of the 1940s suggests other incentives for white landowners to make the shift. Though often more symbolic than substantive, threats to white supremacy and labor control appeared more frequently during this period, placing the region's already paranoiac white supremacists on the defensive.

First, there were signs that the federal government was taking a stronger line on involuntary servitude and slavery in the South. Attorney General Francis Biddle's Circular No. 3591 (1941) had signaled as much in directing US attorneys to consider prosecuting cases not strictly limited to debt peonage. And a 1948 revision of the federal criminal code further clarified the government's position. Such changes coincided with the Supreme Court's anti-peonage rulings in *Taylor v. Georgia* (1942) and *Pollock v. Williams* (1944), which, by themselves, were unlikely to have had much effect on the persistent problem of slavery. In east-central Mississippi, new investigations into slavery allegations meant that it would be tougher for landowners so inclined to force individuals to work for free. While investigations still outnumbered convictions, the implications for landowners' authority—and not merely their balance sheets—were lost on no one.[21]

To be sure, dead-end cases in the early 1940s involving east-central Mississippi landowners Roy Smith and Ethyl Kilgore still suggested that neither the FBI nor district attorneys wanted to risk time and resources on unlikely prosecutions. Smith had allegedly held a white sharecropper named Milton Lee Bulman, his wife, and six of their nine children on his Newton County farm, forcing Bulman and three of the children to work out a $200 debt. In a letter to her brother in Memphis, Mrs. Bulman claimed that Smith had threatened to kill her husband if the family left his farm. The allegation highlighted the exposure of poor whites to forms of abuse typically associated with Black and native people. But the case went nowhere. Nor did that of Kilgore, a Winston County landowner who had allegedly held Black tenants Bob and Delma Thomas against their will. District Attorney Toxey Hall informed the Justice Department that he was "of the opinion that we could not get a conviction." Responding for Attorney General Biddle, Assistant Attorney General Tom C. Clark agreed.[22]

But the case of Donald Castle demonstrated the bureau's willingness to pursue justice in accordance with Biddle's recent turnabout on civil rights when a conviction seemed likely. On March 17, 1943, a grand jury returned an indictment charging Castle with peonage. The indictment alleged that Castle had taken a Black man named Rossy Wyse "with the intent that he ... be held as a slave" at Castle's Lauderdale County sawmill. It detailed how Castle had shackled Wyse to a bed with a log chain that attached to his neck and used "threats, intimidation, whipping and beating" to force him to work in payment of a debt. In September, Castle pleaded guilty and received a $500 fine, a suspended sentence of two two-year jail terms, and two years' probation. The successful prosecution of the Castle case served notice on white landowners and other employers of low-skill workers that a long-established tool in their arsenal—slavery—faced new obstacles.[23]

Meanwhile, as the Supreme Court's decision in *Smith v. Allwright* (1944) outlawed the white primary and launched what one scholar called a "revolution in black political participation," Southern Democrats in Congress mobilized for war. As Ira Katznelson has noted, "Every potential law, including the vast bulk of proposals not overtly concerned with race, was assessed for how it might affect the region's autonomy." Using their considerable leverage, Southern legislators routinely defeated anti–poll tax bills and manipulated soldier-voting bills to suit their own preferences. Sectional concerns trumped party loyalty, and the long-strained New Deal coalition—built on cooperation between Southern and non-Southern Democrats—began to crack. For instance, Southern Democrats joined Republicans in forcing the return of the US Employment Service (USES) to state operation, worrying that federal government control of labor policy could seriously threaten white Southerners' supply of cheap, tractable labor.[24]

Given the rising labor militancy after World War II, Southern Democrats had reason to be concerned. Of particular significance for Mississippians was the intersection of race and class fears that manifested from a short-lived postwar Southern labor drive. In 1946 the Congress of Industrial Organizations (CIO) announced "Operation Dixie" to organize Black and white workers on an equal basis. Operating out of Jones County, in the southeastern part of the state, Mississippi CIO organizers had some success with workers at the Masonite plant in the county seat of Laurel. There, the CIO union beat out the American Federation of Labor (AFL) affiliate with the help of Black workers. But white supremacists used familiar race-baiting tactics to thwart interracial unionism in the state. *Jackson Daily News* editor Fred Sullens warned readers that CIO organizers were "more dangerous than rattlesnakes." Despite a few other notable election victories, Operation Dixie left Mississippi in 1949, citing diminishing returns. But its effect on white supremacists was to further telescope labor and race.[25]

Black agricultural workers also organized in the postwar period, alarming Mississippi's agricultural elite. "I have discovered I have a problem on my hands in regard to labor joining unions," Sunflower County planter Joe Dockery told the influential Delta Council's Labor Committee in May 1946. Dockery likened unionization drives on his plantation to the CIO's organizational efforts in the urban North. Labor leaders, he asserted, were anti-planter and anti-mechanization. They were "out to hurt the farmer or land-owners, to slow down or cripple him, and to break up machinery." Moreover, "they publish a newspaper that attacks the planter," and "there is a picture of the mechanical cotton picker with the comment that it will bring hardships, displacing the man with the hoe." Unsettled by this news, Washington County planter Dudley Miller linked the threat of union activity on the Dockery plantation with the growth of civil rights activity more broadly, citing rumors that the "NAPC" [sic] was organizing in the Black town of Mound Bayou. An important nerve center of Mississippi agriculture, the Delta Council helped determine the structure of farming not only in the rest of the state, including the hill country, but also across the cotton South. With close allies in Congress, the Farm Bureau, and equipment manufacturers and dealers, the group had significant sway. If the Delta Council determined that labor control was in jeopardy, their concern reverberated widely.[26]

Under such circumstances, fair employment legislation provoked considerable acrimony. Between 1944 and 1950, several bills were introduced in the US House and Senate to permanently extend President Roosevelt's wartime Fair Employment Practice Committee (FEPC), which banned discriminatory employment practices in government, defense industries, and unions. The debates over such legislation reveal the depth of white Southern anxiety. Testifying in a 1947 Senate hearing, Mississippi governor Fielding L. Wright predicted "strife, turmoil, confusion, and even bloodshed," should the current FEPC bill pass; it was, he declared, "the most dangerous legislation ever presented to an American legislative body." Whites in east-central Mississippi agreed. A year earlier, L. L. McAllister of Lauderdale County had thanked Senator James Eastland for "the splendid fight you have put up in the defeat of one of the most vicious pieces of legislation ever before Congress, namely, the 'FEPC.'" Henry J. Dorsey of Attala County wrote Senator John Stennis on "a subject near and dear to [Dorsey's] heart (white supremacy)," urging Stennis to "fight like hell the negro bills before Congress." Stennis assured him that he would "keep on using every means at my command to defeat each and every one of the Bills aimed at the Southland."[27]

As FEPC proposals foundered, labor legislation that did pass bore the mark of anxious southern racists. The Taft-Hartley Act of 1947, a set of amendments to the mostly labor-friendly 1935 Wagner Act, widened the latter's agricultural exclusions. At the behest of Southerners like the late Senator Pat Harrison, the Wagner Act had not protected "any individual employed as an agricultural laborer, or in the domestic service of any family or person at his home." Taft-Hartley expanded the exclusion to encompass workers involved in "handling, planting, drying, packing, packaging, processing, freezing, grading, storing, or delivering . . . any agricultural or horticultural commodity." The exclusions disproportionately affected nonwhite workers, who remained vulnerable to the sorts of abuses and unfair labor practices that the National Labor Relations Board purported to police.[28]

Whites in east-central Mississippi tended to be of one mind with their elected leaders on such issues. When Representative Arthur Winstead of Mississippi's fifth district announced his reelection bid in May 1946, he courted white supremacist constituents with direct references to the intersection of labor and civil rights. "I have supported all legislation to curb radical CIO leadership during the war and reconstruction period," he reminded voters. "I have opposed such legislation as Anti-Poll Tax, FEPC and other measures directed at the South." Adding to the urgency of the political moment, Winstead's reassurances came as local Black veterans like Medgar and Charles Evers of Newton County were defying local custom by attempting (unsuccessfully) to exercise their right to vote. In the July primary—the only election that mattered in the absence of a viable second party—Winstead trounced his opponent, the more moderate J. O. Hollis of Leake County, by nearly 2 to 1. He would go on to serve until 1964, when further cracks in the once-solidly Democratic South found the eleven-term congressman defeated from the right by a Republican.[29]

In the 1940s, then, white Southerners scrambled to shore up Jim Crow along the axes of labor and civil rights. Fissures in the New Deal coalition—including the rise and fall of the States Rights Democratic Party (or Dixiecrats), who opposed measures like President Harry Truman's establishment of a Committee on Civil Rights—suggested the seriousness of perceived threats to white supremacy. There can be little doubt that existential fears loomed large as well-to-do white landowners reevaluated their reliance on a disproportionately nonwhite labor force. When Evie Skipper, Norveil Johnson, and Irby Majure dismissed all their tenants, and when the Union dairy farmer boasted that he would "never be dependent on much labor again," they did so in a political climate beset by racial anxiety. It was a context in which issues of class—particularly for well-to-do whites—were nearly inseparable from race. To consider the needs of poor and landless farmers in the region, as Gilbert Fite has pointed out, "meant assisting black producers, whose spokesmen and leaders were supporting school integration and other changes which threatened racial segregation."[30]

To be sure, the anxieties that surfaced in the 1940s and metastasized in the 1950s were not new. As Dane Kennedy has suggested, in settler-colonial contexts, whites' nervousness had always rivaled their brazen sense of supremacy: "Power was matched by fear, arrogance by anxiety, disdain by suspicion." By ending landowners' dependence on labor, mechanization afforded a way to hedge against the social upheaval they so feared. Moreover, some hoped not only to lessen their dependence on labor but also to force Black people off the land and out of the South for good. "The [mechanical cotton] picker is going to put people out of work. Nothing gets around that," as Oscar Johnston quoted columnist John Temple

Graves at the 1947 Beltwide Mechanization Conference. But "if it lessens our Southern percentage of colored population and increases it in other places, the race problem will be easier for us to handle and for other places to understand." Such logic accompanied a fundamental pivot in how settler colonialism operated in the region. If Mississippi Choctaws had long since been lumped into the category of exploitable laborer in which Black farmers were overrepresented, Black farmers would increasingly find themselves forcibly displaced as Choctaws had once been.[31]

V

The agricultural shifts that transformed Mississippi and the rest of the cotton South had close parallels in the settler states of Africa. White farmers there enjoyed generous state assistance, and during and after World War II they parlayed their advantage into capital-intensive operations that reduced their need for African labor. Credits and tax breaks subsidized mechanization. Tractor purchases soared, while work oxen died and were not replaced. African farmers, from smallholders to tenants, faced displacement. Much of this change coincided with developmentalist rhetoric—outwardly concerned with soil conservation and often informed by American agricultural experts—that painted Africans as careless farmers. Displacement forced many of them onto even smaller, more crowded plots of worn-out reserve land or into urban areas.[32]

Mechanization in Kenya was an extension of decades of direct state intervention in the interests of settler farmers. While the state had not always functioned *solely* as an instrument of settler power—some African "collaboration," after all, kept the colonial state viable—it supported settler farmers in classically uneconomic ways. It early insulated them from African competition, for instance, and lowered freight rates on settlers' exports while raising them on Africans' imported consumer goods. A Land Bank further propped up settler farmers, who were notoriously poor credit risks. It took the outbreak of World War II—with its heightened demand for maize, sisal, and pyrethrum, and Britain's willingness to carry the risk for farmers—to place settler agriculture on firm footing. The wartime boom afforded settlers access to the capital they needed to invest in labor-saving machinery, much of it imported from the United States. Production committees dominated by settlers made sure that whites were the ones that benefited. As a staffer on the central Production Board characterized its racist logic, when it came to "the skilled control that is needed by so many modern agricultural processes . . . [Africans] just cannot begin to make the grade." Given the pressure that measures such as the Resident Native Labor Ordinance already placed on squatters, mechanization in the White Highlands was a final, devastating blow to their livelihood, displacing thousands.[33]

Settlers in South Africa began to mechanize around the same time and under similar circumstances. State supports had long propped up uncompetitive white farmers, the goal having been to keep as many whites viable as possible. By the late 1930s, settlers were using Control Boards to push for subsidies, tariffs, and export quotas for the same reason, and the Land Bank was an important crutch. But in the 1940s, when farmers' tight control over labor came into question, some began pushing to replace workers with machinery. Stefan Schirmer has demonstrated that their motives were often quite political; they wanted to reduce or end their dependence on "troublesome" labor. In the Transvaal alone, tractor ownership increased from 5,782 in 1945 to 42,867 in 1960. As one white farmer declared in 1948, "the time has passed for us to be dependent on native labour and to plough with spans of oxen." Transvaal sharecropper Kas Maine heard such talk and worried about the consequences, but, without state largesse or much property of his own, he knew that his best bet was to "remain on good terms with the landlord" as long as possible.[34]

Before World War II, settler landowners had little choice but to farm in ways that required a steady supply of labor. Their dependence on labor—enmeshed with their steadfast commitment to racial hierarchy—shaped the status quo. The war and its aftermath changed everything. In the cotton South, agricultural leaders took steps to ensure that large landowners remained viable at the expense of smaller farmers. In Mississippi, farm agencies set out to rid "problem farms" of tenants and sharecroppers. They encouraged some hill-country farmers to switch from row-cropping to cattle raising or tree farming, and they helped well-capitalized farmers acquire the machines and chemicals that would make them successful in the new era of large-scale, highly mechanized agriculture. The social effects of those changes were easy to predict, as scholars and farmers alike had long discussed the likelihood of human displacement. Indeed, plenty of the displacement that accompanied mechanization was cultivated, viewed as a way to make farms more efficient and rid landowners of labor problems in an unpredictable social climate. Parallel shifts in southern and eastern Africa suggest that a similar set of concerns shaped the ways that settler societies around the globe confronted the postwar period.

There can be no denying the pervasiveness of white racism in the changes that were unfolding. But as Patrick Wolfe has argued, race is a "site-specific" trace of colonial history, "instantiating a particular colonial relationship." Considering how prominently territoriality figured in Mississippi's postwar transformation, that colonial relationship remained rooted in the land. As the next two chapters demonstrate, while escalating movements for civil rights and self-determination posed unprecedented threats to the racial status quo, elite whites responded not merely as racists but as colonizers. Not every conflict was explicitly reducible to issues of land and property, but those issues were never absent as Jim Crow went on the defensive.[35]

3

FRANTIC RESISTANCE MISSISSIPPI AND THE DECOLONIAL ZEITGEIST

There have been hints made that the segregated system might be maintained for some time to come.
—Rep. Arthur Winstead, 1954

The political trends that troubled conservative Mississippians were part of a global movement toward decolonization. Colonialism and racism lost much of their legitimacy during and after World War II. The war exposed the fallibility of European empires, and the United Nations (UN) and its Educational, Scientific, and Cultural Organization (UNESCO), both established in 1945, discredited the racial ideologies that underpinned colonialism. French and British efforts to fashion a more benign, "developmentalist" colonialism after the war proved unsuccessful, and by the late 1950s, imperial retreat seemed inevitable. But if the zeitgeist was decolonial, settler states were the outliers. Increasingly viewed as pariahs for their commitment to racial hierarchy and minority rule, white settlers dug in against the "wind of change." Perhaps nowhere were they more unyielding than in the two "Souths": southern Africa and the American South. From Jackson to Johannesburg, whites doubled down rather than give up their political supremacy, convinced that racial equality posed existential threats.[1]

In Mississippi, a constellation of factors shaped white resistance to decolonial change. The Cold War, which coincided with decolonization, led white supremacists to conflate the breakdown of segregation with communism. Long-held sexual fears and demographic anxiety raised the stakes still further, as whites viewed miscegenation as an inevitable outcome of integration. "Intermarriage," warned the Rev. J. David Simpson of Newton County, "will surely come to pass if free social inter-mingling between the races displaces segregation." Although in retrospect, their fears were identifiably settler-colonial—that is, they revealed the depth of psychic conflict that resulted from building a society on stolen land with stolen labor—white Mississippians' consciousness of their own role as settler-colonizers was inchoate at best. They acknowledged ties to the global white settler community, yet their affinity for settlers in Southern Rhodesia and South Africa was based on what they considered a shared sense of racial embattlement, not a common history of land theft. "The global forces of *integration* are pressuring South Africa today," wrote Tom Ethridge, a Jackson columnist from Kemper County, "but [if] her government falls, it seems inevitable that the same ruthless forces will turn against Mississippi." In fact, white Mississippians seem to have so completely naturalized the theft and occupation of Indian land that, with few exceptions, they missed the settler-colonial connection entirely. For most, the primary site of contestation was the political and economic basis of white supremacy: Jim Crow.[2]

To be sure, Jim Crow could serve settler-colonial ends. By shutting nonwhite people out of the political process in a state where access to land and government payments was deeply political, Mississippi's leading whites gave themselves a distinct territorial advantage. Black and native people lacked the means to advocate effectively for themselves and their place on the land. Indeed, Black political activism in the Jim Crow era could lead to eviction. Hence, whites held control over a disproportionate share of the land. In 1950, a total of 20,710,770 acres—over two-thirds of the state's area—were in farmland. White land accounted for 16,118,273 of those acres, or 77 percent, in a state where whites were only half of the farm population. By the end of the decade, whites farmed 85 percent of the 18,674,821 available acres while representing 60 percent of the farm population. Reversing the trend would have required a level of Black and native participation in state, local, and farm elections that Jim Crow had long forbidden.[3]

Few whites dared speak out against Jim Crow in east-central Mississippi, but Black and Choctaw residents worked within the bounds of the possible to make the system more bearable. The Mississippi Band of Choctaw Indians (MBCI), as the politically reconstituted Mississippi Choctaws called themselves, spent much of the 1940s and 1950s attempting to achieve economic security. While Choctaws faced discrimination in their encounters with settler society, civil rights were not their primary concern. Instead, economic issues—especially land claims—predominated in the meetings of the new Tribal Council. As council member Jim Gardner put it, "Land is the biggest problem." In the late 1940s, the Tribal Council pursued financial compensation through the Indian Claims Commission for land lost to settlers. As the claims case stretched into the 1950s, Choctaws took other measures to escape poverty. At the same time, Black Mississippians attempted to secure voting rights and school desegregation. But such campaigns had little immediate impact in east-central Mississippi, and sporadic NAACP activity was no match for an organized, determined apartheid state. Moreover, farm elections would remain lily-white affairs until the late 1960s. As white Neshoba County resident Florence Mars recalled, the attitude of ruling whites was one of "frantic resistance."[4]

I

Few of the daily indignities of US settler colonialism abated in the decade-and-a-half after World War II. Whites in east-central Mississippi made sure that nearly every aspect of nonwork life remained racially segregated. As Florence Mars remembered, "Without segregation it was thought the races would mix and the great white southern civilization would be ended." Theirs was a fear of extermination—a demographic "war of numbers"—that, however irrational in Mississippi, resonated across the settler world. Black residents had long since carved out separate local economies of necessity, sharing social space with whites only where it could not be avoided. Choctaws faced many of the same forms of discrimination as Black residents and kept to themselves, as well. The superintendent of education in Noxubee County noted that Choctaws living there would attend neither white nor Black schools. In Neshoba County, Choctaws generally could not use the same public facilities as whites. Those living near the Pearl River community could shop at a small grocery store owned by Choctaws Nicholas and Cleddie Bell. White-owned restaurants tended not to serve them, and they were not allowed to sit in the main section of the movie theater. If they so desired, they could eat at Black-owned restaurants or sit in the balcony of the theater with Black patrons, although many Choctaws preferred to remain distant from their Black neighbors.[5]

Suffusing this segregated world, especially in the 1940s and 1950s, were cultural forms that glorified settler conquest. Western-themed films, television programs, dime novels, and comics repackaged the old frontier myth for mass audiences (and were nearly as popular in southern Africa as in the US). In east-central Mississippi, local marching bands performed Western-themed halftime shows, complete with "Indian and cowboy chases." Newspapers printed children's letters to Santa Claus requesting cowboy suits, toy rifles, gun belts, and Indian tents. Children's birthday parties featured "cowboy and Indian tablecloth and napkins." The blue-ribbon entry in the leadline horse show at the Central Mississippi Fair featured young white children dressed as "settlers" and riding in a wagon with a "gun to kill 'Indians or wild beasts.'" Symbols of ethnic cleansing so saturated popular culture that it was difficult for nonwhite people not to internalize them. As writer James Baldwin noted, it "comes as a great shock to see Gary Cooper killing off the Indians, and although you are rooting for Gary Cooper, that the Indians are you."[6]

The case of Pearl River Choctaw Claude Allen is illustrative of what Kenyan writer Ngugi wa Thiong'o called colonialism's "cultural bomb." Allen recalled that as a youth in the 1950s, he watched Western-themed TV programs and that "the white man was it, you know. He was making things happen." Like the other Choctaw children, he "used to play cowboy instead of Indian . . . and we used to be chasing the Indians." Allen, like Baldwin, became disillusioned with the celebration of settler violence as he arrived at a deeper understanding of American racism. Allen realized that he was "the Indians" when he was barred from a swimming pool to which his white friends were admitted. "I realized that I was dark complected and all that," Allen remembered. But that epiphany also made him determined to "stand up for [his] rights" and embrace his Choctaw identity. Similarly, brothers Medgar and Charles Evers of Newton County took in "cowboy pictures" as young men, but they soon realized that "[white men] who depend on violent means to secure their ends are cowards."[7]

As popular culture seemed to confirm that "the white man was it," so, too, were Choctaws and Black residents denied representation in local leadership. Local government was all-white as a matter of course, despite a reservoir of capable Black leaders in the region. Some counties lacked Black agricultural agents. As late as 1960, Kemper County had neither an extension agent nor a home demonstration agent serving the Black community; five counties in the region had one or the other, while only three had both. The Bureau of Indian Affairs (BIA) Indian agency, located in Philadelphia, employed some Choctaws, but only in nonleadership positions (mostly as chauffeurs or janitors). The agency's main office consisted of white Mississippians—an arrangement that was unpopular with Choctaws. Even BIA officials occasionally commented on the absurdity of allowing white racists to staff an Indian agency. In July 1949, for instance, Assistant Commissioner of Indian Affairs John H. Provinse wrote that the Philadelphia agency had "become too completely staffed with Mississippians, some of whom retained a southern prejudice against people of dark skin—whether Indians or Negroes."[8]

One of the few somewhat encouraging developments of the period was the Tri-Racial Goodwill Festival, which occurred annually from 1948 through 1951 in Leake County. Conceived by the Presbyterian reverend D. M. Mounger, a white man, the festival brought white, Black, and Choctaw residents together to "celebrate the harmony and good relationship of the three races." Although it is not entirely clear that Choctaws viewed themselves as a third race, per se, their active participation in the festival nevertheless signaled their support for antidiscrimination efforts. Each year the festival featured a white, Black, and Choctaw speaker from the area, and Choctaws entertained patrons with games of stickball. Attendance was apparently quite good, but, as BIA tribal relations officer Marie L. Hayes noted after attending the festival in 1951, "the Negroes were entirely segregated to one side of the field, while Indians and whites mingled together on the other side of the field." Moreover, press for the event depicted it as a way to "celebrate Leake County's 100 years of freedom from lynchings, race riots and major disturbances." The organizers might not have cared to remember, but two Black men, Joseph Leflore and Charles Johnson, died at the hands of Leake County lynch mobs in 1899 and 1902, respectively.[9]

Despite Rev. Mounger's good intentions, the Tri-Racial Goodwill Festival showed just how far Mississippians were from an honest reckoning with the past (or, for that matter, a clear assessment of the present). Such a needlessly self-congratulatory event obscured the degree to which peaceful relations between white, Black, and Choctaw residents were still predicated on the threat of violence. What might have happened, after all, if the segregated groups had mixed and racist social taboos had been tested? This sort of affair was anathema to "goodwill" and "harmony." What these Mississippians had was not peace but, rather, pacification. As historian Theda Perdue points out, the event was the sort of thing that white Southerners would condone only if they could control the staging. But if the festival was a wrongheaded celebration of a misremembered past, it was also the closest east-central Mississippi would come to reconciliation for many years.[10]

II

As mired as the region was in a culture that normalized white-settler supremacy, some residents began to challenge the status quo in unprecedented ways after World War II. Brothers Medgar and Charles Evers returned from military service in 1946 determined to grow Black political power in the state. They were not naïve about the risks involved. As young men in the 1930s, they had attended a campaign rally for the reactionary senator Theodore Bilbo, who famously advocated getting rid of Black Americans by sending them to Liberia. Seated at the front of what must have been a mostly white crowd, the brothers drew Bilbo's attention. "You see these two Negroes down here," Charles Evers recalled Bilbo saying, "if you don't keep them in their place, some day they'll be in Washington trying to represent you—taking my place and the rest of the good white people's place." For Bilbo, as for settlers the world over, Black power meant that whites would, quite literally, be *replaced*. The Evers brothers had lived in Mississippi long enough to know how hysterically whites reacted when faced with such fears. But in case they had forgotten, they found a stark reminder in the lynching of family friend Willie Tingle just months later. Tingle was dragged, hanged, and shot in half, his bloody clothes left in the pasture for weeks "to remind us Negroes what happened when we got too fresh."[11]

Yet Medgar and Charles Evers were not easily intimidated, and service in World War II further convinced the brothers that they deserved to live as first-class citizens in their home state. Returning in the wake of the *Smith v. Allwright* decision, they drove to the same courthouse where Bilbo had spoken a dozen years earlier, pushed past whites attempting to block the doors, and registered to vote. Although the two did not find out until later, white supremacists visited their parents nightly after the brothers registered. "Tell your sons to take their names off the books," they had warned. "Don't show up at the courthouse [on] voting day." Such personal threats mixed with Bilbo's frequent, unsubtle reminders to white Mississippians of the "best way to keep the nigger from voting." On primary day, July 2, 1946, the two brothers—accompanied by four other Black veterans—walked from Medgar Evers's home to the courthouse to find a mob of armed white men. They recognized familiar faces in the crowd, including Andy May, a local druggist and family friend, who nevertheless joined in the taunting, a pistol bulging from his hip pocket. Unwilling to engage in a gunfight in the streets of their hometown, the group of veterans returned home without voting. "We'll get them next time," Medgar reassured his brother.[12]

In the meantime, the Evers brothers attended classes at Alcorn College in the lower Delta and, as they had for most of their lives, followed US news coverage of events in colonial Africa. Particularly intriguing to them was a conflict unfolding in East Africa that involved some of the same issues of land and labor that Black Mississippians faced. Not yet ready to give up its empire after World War II, Britain attempted a second colonial occupation. But in Kenya, an explosive situation was developing in the White Highlands. In response to wartime demand and the flow of capital from Britain, settler farmers had mechanized and intensified their farming operations and had begun expelling Kikuyu squatters. Given how profitable the settlers had finally become, the Labor government now depended on them to help Britain rebuild its economy after the war. At the very same time, the government eased restrictions on independent African farmers who had long been prohibited from growing certain cash crops. The growth in peasant production, among other factors, meant that the lands to which the expelled squatters hoped to return were no longer available to them. Urban alternatives were not forthcoming either, as industry could not absorb the number of unemployed, and, soon, a movement called Mau Mau used violent measures to achieve its goals of land and freedom. After a brutal counterinsurgency campaign, the British finally relented, and Jomo Kenyatta, the formerly imprisoned leader of the Kenya African National Union (KANU) party, became prime minister and then president of an independent Kenya.[13]

For Mississippians like Medgar and Charles Evers, Kenyatta was an inspiration. "We learned all we could about Kenyatta," Charles Evers remembered, "in the papers, from friends, reports on the shortwave radio." They respected him for having traveled widely, studied at the London School of Economics, and then returned to his native Kenya to fight for his people, despite the obvious risks. The brothers felt similarly about their own home. Indeed, they, too, had traveled the world only to return to Mississippi, as Medgar Evers recalled, "to make a positive contribution." The other part of Kenyatta's appeal was, of course, the dread with which white Mississippians regarded him. "The white people were saying how terrible Kenyatta was," Charles later wrote, "but it was the way the white people told about the cowboys and the Indians—and we were for the Indians and we were for Kenyatta."[14]

As they read more about developments in Kenya, the brothers became emboldened. "Why not really cross the line," they wondered in the early 1950s. "Why not create a Mau Mau in Mississippi?" Many Mississippians, after all, faced enclosure and displacement, the very issues at the heart of Mau Mau. But ultimately, they never followed through on the idea. According to Charles Evers, "We bought bullets, made some idle Mau Mau plans, but Medgar never had his heart in it, and over time we dropped it." (Medgar and his wife, Myrlie Evers, did, however, name their first child Darrell Kenyatta Evers.)[15]

Whatever the similarities, Mississippi was not Kenya, and the Evers brothers determined early on that the most effective way to grow Black power was through the franchise. "The way whites guarded that ballot box," Charles Evers reasoned, "we knew voting was the key to power." Their decision to focus on voting rights reflected the tenor of the times. As Mary Dudziak and others have argued, Cold War anticommunism "narrowed the scope of civil rights discourse." Modest civil rights reform became a Cold War imperative between the 1940s and the 1960s as international criticism of US racial discrimination undercut American credibility abroad. But measured support for liberal aims like desegregation and voting rights were as far as the federal government would go. Moreover, in the Deep South, it was hardly safe to press for even limited reforms, to say nothing of a "Mau Mau in Mississippi." The defeat of the CIO's Operation Dixie pushed Black Mississippians out of the House of Labor for at least a generation, precluding interracial unionism as an avenue for reform. Like their Choctaw neighbors, the Evers brothers and other Black activists witnessed the steady circumscription of the politically possible, even as globally decolonization began to appear inevitable.[16]

In 1951 Charles Evers and his wife, Nan, moved to Neshoba County, where, after a brief stint teaching social studies in Noxapater (in nearby Winston County), Charles took over a funeral home in Philadelphia. He made extra money bootlegging, as Neshoba was then a dry county. Over the next few years, he also began selling burial insurance, opened a hotel and lounge, started a taxi service, and worked as a deejay at WHOC, Philadelphia's local, white-owned radio station. Evers's business acumen distinguished him from other east-central Mississippians, but it was his activism that especially drew the ire of area whites. Both Evers brothers had worked for the NAACP while at Alcorn, opening new Mississippi branches and reviving old ones. They had also made the acquaintance of Theodore Roosevelt Mason (T. R. M.) Howard, a wealthy Mound Bayou physician, businessman, and leader of the Regional Council of Negro Leadership, who encouraged them to fight for voting rights. By 1953, in addition to branch work, Charles Evers was leading the NAACP's voter registration efforts in Mississippi.

The Evers brothers had their work cut out for them. Early twentieth-century Black political organizing in east-central Mississippi was covert and sporadic where it existed at all. The Universal Negro Improvement Association (UNIA), whose members adhered to the Black nationalist, self-help-oriented teachings of Jamaican immigrant Marcus Garvey, established short-lived branches in Scott and Lauderdale Counties in the 1920s. But in the first third of the century, the NAACP did not have a significant presence in the region. Outside Meridian, where the organization established a strong foothold, Depression-era groups in Carthage (Leake County), Lake (Newton and Scott Counties), and Kosciusko and McCool (Attala County) lasted only briefly if they became registered branches at all. Neshoba County did not contain a NAACP branch when Charles Evers arrived, although a few residents had tried to form one in the late 1930s without success. Branch lists from the late 1940s and 1950s show modest membership in Bluff Springs and Louisville, in Kemper and Winston Counties, while most other branches were in larger cities or the Delta. But Neshoba County whites feared that with Charles Evers now operating out of Philadelphia, their community might be next.[17]

Neshoba County had not allowed nonwhite residents to vote in significant numbers in the twentieth century. Circuit clerks reported that the number of Black registrants in the county declined from eight to four between 1948 and 1960, and none of those voted in the 1950s. Outside of Lauderdale County, whose seat was Meridian, east-central Mississippi's Black population was almost completely disfranchised. In the early 1950s in Noxubee County, where Blacks outnumbered whites three to one, there were no Black voters registered. From the radio booth at WHOC, Charles Evers encouraged area Black residents to pay their poll taxes and register to vote if possible. He also attempted to establish a local Negro Voters League, although, as the figures suggest, he made little headway. Fear of economic reprisal was an especially powerful deterrent, as most Black residents worked for white landlords.[18]

There is no clear consensus on when or where Choctaws could vote. There can be little doubt that the poll tax effectively disfranchised some, although it is impossible to know how many. In spring 1948, tribal leader Will Jimmie complained that "Indians still couldn't vote" but did not specify the primary obstacle. In the early 1950s, almost no Choctaws voted in east-central Mississippi, although they had less difficulty doing so in other parts of the state. No serious voting rights campaign developed among the Choctaws in the 1940s or 1950s. In fact, as we shall see, the crackdown on nonwhite voting and the economic consequences of political agitation became more intense as the years progressed. Whites maintained a death grip on the levers of formal political power in east-central Mississippi, just as they did in the rest of the state.[19]

III

As Black Mississippians began to challenge Jim Crow in new ways, the drive for Choctaw self-determination was also gaining momentum. The changes that came to Indian Country after World War II had deep roots. In the late nineteenth and early twentieth centuries, federal Indian policy had been assimilationist. The 1887 General Land Allotment Act (Dawes Act)—the legal basis for assimilation—came amid a series of land cessions that collectively lopped tens of millions of acres away from the Indian land base. The act itself allotted reservation lands to individual Indians and cleared the substantial surplus for sale to settlers. The goal, as Vine Deloria Jr., has characterized it, was to "make the Indian conform to the social and economic structure of rural America by vesting him with private property." The results were disastrous. By the 1920s, the assimilation campaign had left Indians economically dependent and politically powerless, a fact that the Indian Citizenship Act of 1924, which forced US citizenship on "all non-citizen Indians born within the territorial limits of the United States," did little to change. Indians had lost most of their land by the onset of the Great Depression.[20]

In the 1930s and 1940s, Commissioner of Indian Affairs John Collier reversed the policy of assimilation. Collier was an anthropologist and a socialist, and time spent among the Pueblo Indians of New Mexico in the 1920s helped convince him of the need to reform federal Indian policy. A complex individual, he sincerely desired to help Indians even as he harbored romantic notions of who they were and what they represented. He was also a close student of colonial Africa and detested the abuses of European rule on the continent. Indeed, Collier once wrote an essay entitled "The American Congo," in which he compared the US government's treatment of Indians to European colonialism in Central Africa. On the other hand, he admired "liberal imperialist" writers like Julian Huxley, who believed in resurrecting and rehabilitating African cultures. In Huxley's popular *Africa View* (1931), Collier found a template for American Indian cultural renewal and "indirect rule" that he thought would foster "improvement of a type harmonious with native capacity." The Indian Reorganization Act of 1934 (IRA, also known as the Wheeler-Howard Act), of which Collier was the chief architect, applied Huxley's ideas about Africa to Indian Country. The IRA ended the old assimilation and allotment policies, restored remaining surplus lands to tribal ownership, permitted Indians to form tribal governments and adopt constitutions and bylaws, and established a revolving fund for economic development. It defined "Indians" as "all persons of Indian descent who are members of any recognized Indian tribe now under Federal jurisdiction, and all persons who are descendants of such members who were, on June 1, 1934, residing within the present boundaries of any Indian reservation, and . . . all other persons *of one-half or more Indian blood.*" Imperfect though it was, the IRA represented a new beginning for federal Indian policy.[21]

Choctaws in Mississippi took advantage of the IRA right away, although the process was not without hiccups. In the early 1930s, most Mississippi Choctaws were still squatters or sharecroppers and lived in a scattering of isolated communities. Their governments were small and informal. In February 1934, four months before the Indian reorganization bill passed, the local Office of Indian Affairs superintendent, Archie C. Hector, formed the Tribal Business Committee, composed of Choctaws from the various communities, to consider the IRA. Soon, however, a group called the Mississippi Choctaw Indian Federation formed under Choctaw leadership and with some members who also served on the Tribal Business Committee. Asked to weigh in, John Collier sided with the committee, as he considered Hector's "careful guidance" indispensable to the implementation of the IRA in Mississippi. Insulted by the suggestion that Choctaws could not form a legitimate government without agency assistance, members of the federation rallied a formidable coalition of federal and state officials and local leaders to their cause. Even as the dispute unfolded over what form the IRA government would take, the OIA official sent to oversee the establishment of the government abandoned the process altogether. Only after a decade—and, importantly, news that the Shell Oil Company was interested in oil leases on Choctaw lands—did all the pieces come together. As Katherine M. B. Osburn has observed, the ordeal afforded the Choctaws an opportunity to cultivate important relationships with political leaders and become more adept political players in the region.[22]

In April 1945, Choctaws approved a new constitution and Tribal Council, and the Mississippi Band of Choctaw Indians (MBCI) became a federally recognized tribe. After naming and defining the jurisdiction of the MBCI, the constitution defined membership in the tribe to include "Choctaw Indians of one-half (1/2) or more Indian blood, resident in Mississippi, January 1, 1940, as shown by the census rolls at the Choctaw Indian Agency, Mississippi," and made tribal revision of the rolls subject to the approval of the Secretary of the Interior. Members also included any "child of one-half (1/2) or more Choctaw blood born to any enrolled member of the band after January 1, 1940, resident in Mississippi." The Tribal Council had the power to pass rules—again, subject to the Interior Secretary's approval—regarding future membership and the revocation thereof, provided that "no person of less than one-half degree of Indian blood shall be admitted to membership." The emphasis on blood had a long history. In the nineteenth and early twentieth centuries, the Dawes Commission had used blood quantum to draw up rolls for land allotment. Choctaws' (and other Indians') later use of the language of blood often represented the selective appropriation of settlers' synecdochical vocabulary of racial purity for claim-making purposes. That blood quantum was, ultimately, unknowable and, thus, unreliable as an indicator of race (itself an absurdly problematic category) did not detract from its status as the official currency of claim-making in US settler society.[23]

The MBCI constitution also stated that the tribe's governing body would be the Tribal Council, composed of sixteen members elected every two years. Three members would come from each of the larger communities of Bogue Chitto, Conehatta, and Pearl River; two from each of the smaller communities of Red Water, Standing Pine, and Tucker; and one from Bogue Homo (located in Jones County). From those members or from the band at large, the Tribal Council would elect a chairman, vice chairman, and secretary-treasurer. The Tribal Council's powers included negotiating with the local, state, and federal governments; hiring legal counsel; vetoing tribal land transactions; advising the Secretary of the Interior on appropriation estimates or federal projects for the MBCI; appropriating tribal funds for the benefit of the MBCI; supervising and managing tribal economic affairs; passing and enforcing rules and regulations (subject to the Interior Secretary's approval) on tribal resources; and proposing amendments to the MBCI constitution and bylaws. Amendments must have the support of a majority of Choctaw voters and the approval of the Interior Secretary. Choctaw men and women aged twenty-one years and older could vote in tribal elections, for which the Tribal Council would set the rules.[24]

The MBCI Tribal Council was not an autonomous government, and the Mississippi Choctaws did not have full self-determination in the traditional sense. Most important decisions were still subject to the approval of the US government, and, as we shall see, agency personnel, local government, and white landlords still held a considerable amount of de facto power over Choctaws' lives. But there is no doubt that the Indian New Deal represented an important political milestone for the Mississippi Choctaws. The new constitution empowered the democratically elected Tribal Council to make claims against the government for lands—promised in Article 14 of the Treaty of Dancing Rabbit Creek—long ago denied or purloined by settlers and speculators. Tribal Council meetings, held at least four times per year, provided an open forum for discussing deep-seated economic and health-related problems as well as more mundane tribal business. Finally, the new government afforded every Choctaw adult, regardless of gender, class, or literacy level, an equal voice in tribal affairs.

IV

One of the most pressing issues for the new Tribal Council was the pursuit of land claims. New developments in federal Indian policy (discussed below) led to the establishment of an Indian Claims Commission (ICC) in 1946, which purported to streamline the claim-making process. Indians could now, in theory, seek compensation for past wrongdoing on the part of the government. While there was no way that cash settlements could make up for centuries of colonialism—and despite the federal government's postwar efforts at belt-tightening—proponents of the ICC believed that it would allow the government to save time and money in the long run. When President Truman signed the Indian Claims Commission bill into law on August 13, 1946, he affirmed that the government stood "ready to correct any mistakes we have made," even though he privately worried that establishing the ICC might mean "unloosening a Frankenstein." He need not have worried in the case of the Mississippi Choctaws.[25]

In spring of 1947 the MBCI Tribal Council appointed a committee to look into the land claims issue, and council members spent most of the next meeting discussing the 1830 Treaty of Dancing Rabbit Creek, which had promised land to Choctaws remaining in Mississippi, apportioned according to age and marital status. They decided to hire an attorney to help them secure land or (more likely) financial compensation. The Tribal Council was still searching in early 1948, when council member Baxter York reminded the group that they needed someone who had connections and was "an honest man. It is hard for a man to be honest all the way thru ... A lawyer outside of [Neshoba and Leake] counties is the right man and if we don't watch out we will run into a wasp next [sic]." York's observation would prove sadly prescient. It was difficult for the Choctaws to find an outsider with Washington connections, and people were beginning to get restless. As Will Jimmie pointed out, "We have been messing with this matter a long time. We hear there are lots of people falling dead, and I want to see this thing going down the road before I die."[26]

Ultimately, the Tribal Council settled on local attorney William T. Weir, who secured the assistance of J. A. Riddell of Meridian and Robert C. Handwerk of Washington, DC. They filed their claim with the ICC in 1949, but disturbing rumors soon suggested that Weir and Riddell were attempting to turn a profit by charging people claiming Indian ancestry $100 apiece to be allowed in on the suit. No proof ever materialized, but it would not be the last time that the Choctaws learned of crooked dealings on Weir's part. Hearings began in Meridian in March 1953 and continued in Washington, DC, in October, after having been postponed twice at Weir's request. The government claimed that it had paid the Choctaws their due and, further, that the Mississippi band did not constitute a legitimate tribe (which, if true, would have meant that they could not use the ICC). The ICC overruled the government's motion to dismiss the Choctaws' claim on those grounds and, later, ruled that the government owed the group $417,656. That was considerably less money than the Choctaws felt they were owed, but when the government appealed to the US Court of Claims, the latter denied even that amount, directing the ICC to dismiss the Choctaw petition altogether. Newspapers across Mississippi reported that the Choctaws' claim had been tossed out, but, somehow, most of the MBCI seem not to have known, and Weir claimed to still be working on the case.[27]

As the Choctaws awaited news from Washington about their claim, the Tribal Council had to contend with issues of extreme poverty in Mississippi. When mechanization and the other farm trends of the postwar period eliminated the need for much hand labor in east-central Mississippi, Choctaws went where they could find work. Since most had only ever farmed for a living, there was a tendency to seek out what farm work was available, even if it meant moving a considerable distance for weeks or months at a time. For instance, it was typical for Choctaws to remove to the Delta to pick cotton. Some returned after the season was over, while others remained, mostly concentrated between Natchez and Vicksburg. In Tribal Council meetings in the late 1940s and 1950s, removal to the Delta was generally discussed as a problem. The fact that dozens of families had to look for work outside of east-central Mississippi threatened the future stability of long-established Choctaw communities. Moreover, when Choctaws left the state to sharecrop in Tennessee or to pick fruits and vegetables in Florida, as they sometimes did, they risked giving birth to children who were not legally Choctaw.[28]

Another problem that accompanied even temporary labor migration was truancy. Many families that left for the Delta took their children with them so that they, too, could help with the harvest. Among the topics for discussion in a fall 1948 Tribal Council meeting was the "problem of Indians going to the Delta and picking cotton and taking their children out of school." By 1950 the issue had become serious enough to prompt local Indian agency personnel to plead with landowners not to use child labor. In a piece for the *Neshoba Democrat*, the agency invoked Article 26 of the Universal Declaration of Human Rights, which asserted that all children had the right to an education. The writers also cited the amended Fair Labor Standards Act, which prohibited the employment of children under age sixteen for agricultural labor during school hours. Too often, Mississippi farm employers were in flagrant violation. "Since October 23, the attendance in the Choctaw Indian schools has been 65% lower than expected," the article stated. "Some 250 Indian children under 16 years of age have been picking cotton in the surrounding counties and in the Mississippi Delta. These children should be in school." Limited evidence suggests that while Choctaw families continued to migrate for farm work, children did begin attending public schools in the counties where their parents worked.[29]

The Tribal Council also dealt with the pressing issue of housing, which involved questions of resource management and tribal sovereignty. Though the Indian agency had built or refurbished 202 houses on tribal land before 1945, the postwar years brought a housing shortage in the various Choctaw communities. In Pearl River, the largest of the communities, the need was particularly acute. At its Fall 1947 meeting, the Tribal Council discussed the need for "homes or emergency shacks" in Pearl River. Eight families were in immediate need, five of which were the families of GIs. In Red Water, Standing Pine, Conehatta, Bogue Chitto, Tucker, and Bogue Homo, thirty-four families needed houses; of those families, twenty-four contained GIs. In what would turn into a years-long process of establishing control over tribal forest resources, one council member recommended selling timber for the money to hire builders or simply using the lumber to build houses themselves. But, in what some considered a weakness of the IRA government, the Bureau of Indian Affairs required that the Choctaws employ a trained forester before doing any cutting. Will Jimmie, of the Tribal Council's Natural Resources Committee, remarked that "the government had them all tied if they could not cut their own timber." He was not wrong; the structure of indirect rule that Jimmie complained about was the US government's version of a technology of colonial governance to which plenty of colonized peoples around the world were still subjected. While building and repairs occurred piecemeal in the 1940s and 1950s, the MBCI did not establish full control over its timber until the early 1960s.[30]

In the decade-and-a-half following World War II, the Tribal Council discussed and debated a wide variety of topics and welcomed dozens of outside observers. Council members represented the seven principal Choctaw communities in a governing body that adapted the tribe's cultural distinctiveness to the changing times. Of course, cultural renewal hinged on economic survival, and Tribal Council meeting minutes reflect the pride of place given to issues of land and labor, particularly as mechanization proceeded and farm work became harder to find. With fewer opportunities to do the sort of work that had shaped their culture for over a century, the tribe increasingly sought new ways to survive and flourish as Choctaws. And it did so against the backdrop of epochal political changes emanating from Washington.[31]

V

The years 1953 and 1954 witnessed two important shifts for US empire. First, Congress registered its approval of a change in federal Indian policy that had been brewing for almost a decade. The change involved terminating the trust relationship between the federal government and Indian tribes—or, as US officials often put it, getting the government "out of the Indian business." It also effectively repudiated the Indian New Deal. Then, the Supreme Court of the United States handed down its decision in *Brown v. Board of Education of Topeka, Kansas*, a consolidation of cases regarding public school segregation. The *Brown* decision reversed the Court's 1896 decision in the case of *Plessy v. Ferguson*, which had effectively sanctioned Jim Crow. As Chief Justice Earl Warren opined on May 17, 1954, "the doctrine of 'separate but equal' has no place" in public education. While many Indians objected to termination and most Black Americans celebrated *Brown*, both reflected a postwar tendency toward assimilation rather than pluralism. Such a tendency could have positive expressions—such as desegregation—even as its basic logic owed to a narrow nationalism born of Cold War fears.[32]

Terminationist sentiment gained momentum immediately after World War II. Indians' exemplary wartime service seemed to many US officials to signal their readiness to assimilate into "mainstream" society. The Indian Claims Commission emerged to facilitate final cash settlements in the lead-up to full divestment. Adding urgency were growing concerns that reservations were backward or even "socialistic environments." Mainstreaming American Indians would, in the terminationist view, drag them out of poverty and strike a blow against communism. It would also silence foreign critics of American settler colonialism who viewed reservations as "concentration camps." Hence, the same Cold War calculus that was circumscribing Black protest rendered Indian assimilation a political imperative.[33]

The Indian Affairs task force of the Truman-appointed Commission on Organization of the Executive Branch of the Government (often referred to as the Hoover Commission, as its chair was former US president Herbert Hoover) endorsed assimilation in its 1948 report:

> Assimilation is recognized as the dominant goal within the Bureau of Indian Affairs. . . . The sentiment of Congress also is solidly behind the goal of assimilation. But if Indians, officials and legislators were all opposed to assimilation, it would still have to be accepted as a controlling policy. The basis for historic Indian culture has been swept away. Traditional tribal organization was smashed a generation ago. Americans of Indian descent who are still thought of as "Indian" are a handful of people, not three-tenths of one percent of the total population. Assimilation cannot be prevented. The only questions are: What kind of assimilation, and how fast?

The task force report reflected fundamental misunderstandings about Indians' capacity to adapt to change over time *as Indians*. Nevertheless, as historian Paul C. Rosier has argued, it supplied "a programmatic and philosophical blueprint for the termination of Native sovereignty." Five years later, in August 1953, House Concurrent Resolution 108 (HCR 108) signaled congressional support for termination.[34]

The Mississippi Band of Choctaw Indians had formed its IRA government later than most, just as terminationist sentiment was taking hold in

Washington. There was a lot at stake for the MBCI in the new policy, especially considering the services its members stood to lose if the BIA pulled out of segregated Mississippi. Tribal relations officer Marie L. Hayes informed council members a few weeks before HCR 108 that there would be "no material change," but, somewhat contradictorily, that termination meant "full independence for all Indians as citizens, sharing benefits and responsibilities." In October 1953 extension director Tom Hatch assured the MBCI that Congress was only terminating services for tribes that were ready. "They haven't said when we should get out of Mississippi," Hatch declared, "but it will depend on the way you get along and the way you help yourselves." A 1954 report prepared for the same Congress that passed the resolution seemed to confirm Hatch's prediction, listing the MBCI among the tribes that local BIA officials considered not yet ready for termination.[35]

That competency appraisal passed through plenty of hands between Mississippi and Washington, but what the 83rd Congress saw of it reflected both the assimilationist logic of the termination period and local BIA officials' naïveté regarding the long-term effects of racism. In it, officials blamed what they considered the Choctaws' lack of acculturation on the persistence of the Choctaw language and "old tribal customs," especially singling out Choctaw women's attire: "When a Choctaw woman goes to a community dressed differently from the other citizens, she naturally sets herself apart from the other group." The mainstream into which the US government expected Indians to assimilate would not countenance linguistic or sartorial deviation. Moreover, officials wrote that while Choctaws' poverty owed in part to factors beyond their control, they mainly lacked "the desire to improve and the vision to advance. . . . The fact that the Choctaw is timid and will not push out on his own causes him to fail to receive services to which he is entitled." Acknowledging that Indians in the South had to contend with "the racial barrier," they still suggested that Choctaws could overcome racism if they raised their own standards a bit higher. In the meantime, the report recommended delaying termination for the MBCI.[36]

Nevertheless, it soon appeared that the tribe would feel the effects of the broader termination drive in the loss of its hospital and, more insidiously, in the intensification of relocation efforts. The hospital, built for the

Choctaws in 1926, had met a critical need for a desperately poor people, and especially women and mothers. When councilwoman Cleddie Bell learned of plans to close it, she expressed her concern directly to the BIA Muskogee Area Office in Oklahoma. A week later, on January 12, 1954, the Tribal Council read a resolution by members of the Pearl River community protesting the closure. The resolution stated that since the establishment of the hospital, the overall and infant mortality rates had dropped; more expectant mothers were using the hospital for prenatal care; fewer Choctaws were using "Indian 'Doctors'"; more were being diagnosed and referred for tuberculosis; and MBCI members without means received free care, a service unavailable to Choctaws through local charities. The resolution carried.[37]

With no word on the hospital's fate over the next few months, Cleddie Bell led a push to petition the BIA for a full-time doctor to replace the contractor then in use. The contractor, the Tribal Council agreed, was not available as often as needed yet cost as much as a full-time doctor. Additionally, the council felt that over three thousand Choctaws were more than enough to warrant a full-time doctor. Even as they discussed this latest push, agency superintendent Paul Vance reminded the Tribal Council that Congress was then considering a bill to transfer Indian hospitals from the Bureau of Indian Affairs to the Public Health Service (PHS). In October 1954 the Tribal Council received word through Vance that the Muskogee Area Office had denied its request for a full-time doctor. By then, President Dwight D. Eisenhower had signed the transfer bill into law, and, while the new legislation meant that the Choctaws would keep their hospital, it produced a new set of problems that it would take the Tribal Council over a decade to iron out with the PHS.[38]

The other immediate effect of the shift in federal Indian policy was the increased emphasis the BIA placed on relocating Choctaws from the reservation to urban areas. As Douglas K. Miller and others have demonstrated, the Voluntary Relocation Program, which predated HCR 108 by a year, was designed to "emancipate" Indians from reservation life and transition them to year-round employment in urban centers like Chicago and Los Angeles while termination "quietly destroyed" the reservation system. If it was, perhaps, the clearest expression of the assimilationism at the core of termination, it was also a program that many Indians took advantage of to become more economically self-sufficient in rapidly changing times. Choctaws faced a difficult choice when considering whether to remove to an urban center or remain on the reservation. A move north or west would take them out of their home state, and if they gave birth outside of Mississippi, their children would not be considered Choctaw. Relocation officers would never have said so in their periodic sales pitches to the Tribal Council, but it was hard to imagine a more effective tool for deculturalization and forced assimilation.[39]

Yet, even as Cold War nationalism promoted the shift from New Deal–era tribalism to assimilation, contradictions appeared that linked the experiences of Choctaws with those of others under settler rule. Although Choctaws faced termination, BIA agents and local whites encouraged them to market a version of their ethnic identity to tourists. Thus, Choctaws were placed in the curious position of being asked to both smother and promote their Indian culture. In South Africa, Southern Rhodesia, and Kenya, the early postwar years witnessed similarly contradictory impulses. Especially in the former two, notions of "tradition" and "development" clashed, as both seemed indispensable to the settler project. Settler governments often leaned on "chiefs"—whose viability by then owed to their deference to the state—to contain and rule African populations. As they did so, though, these governments endorsed (even *invented*) a traditionalism that was at odds with the strong postwar push for development, modernization, and streamlining. As colonizers demanded that indigenous people be both traditional and modern—boxing themselves in by adopting notions of tradition and modernity that were mutually exclusive—they exposed the instability of settler rule in the era of decolonization. As Baptist missionary Victor M. Kaneubbe observed of the Choctaws in the 1950s, "their trad[ition] is wanted, but they are criticized for standing and sitting on the streets."[40]

VI

Of the two principal shifts in US empire in the mid-1950s, though, the greater pivot in Mississippi followed the *Brown* decision. On the one hand, the full implications of the decision remained in the realm of the abstract for some time. The Supreme Court would rule later on the specifics of implementation, but few whites genuinely believed that Mississippi schools would desegregate any time soon. The *Neshoba Democrat* editorialized that white and Black residents "have been getting along so well under the segregated system, and they do not see in the future any integration in the schools as both races desire to maintain separate schools." On the other hand, most whites, from officials down to ordinary folk, interpreted *Brown* as an exogenous assault on the Southern status quo. As might have been expected in a settler society, whites articulated their fears in terms of miscegenation. Florence Mars remembered that in the wake of the decision, it was "the fear of Negro men desecrating white women, that more than anything else stirred the emotions of the white population." Mars also recalled that whites considered miscegenation a tool—perhaps wielded jointly by the NAACP and the Soviet Union—intended to spread communism in the United States. Charles Evers agreed that "whites learned as kids that civil rights was a Communist front meant to pollute pretty white girls." In other words, white Mississippians were quite confident in their ability to avoid school desegregation, but they were also sure that the challenge posed by *Brown* was greater than the sum of its parts.[41]

Mississippi politicians had early hedged against a decision like *Brown* by gesturing toward the "equalization" of separate white and Black schools after World War II. In theory, this meant shoring up segregated education by reducing what most agreed were enormous disparities between white and Black schools. As a director of the planter-led Delta Council summed up the basic logic of equalization in the state, "Unless we help [Black schools] the Federal Government will come down and do it for us." But such efforts too often foundered because of local control over state-appropriated equalization funds. Still, in the late 1940s and early 1950s, a significant number of Black Mississippians supported genuine equalization within the segregated system, believing it to be the best available option. Once the Court ruled against school segregation in 1954, and as Black Mississippians increasingly backed integration, whites clung tenaciously to racial separation under the rubric of equalization. As a last resort, voters approved a constitutional amendment authorizing the state legislature to abolish Mississippi's public schools rather than integrate.[42]

Neshoba County's white educational leaders wrote equalization into their 1955 report on Philadelphia's separate municipal school district. They defended their continued support for segregation: "We believe that a continuation of segregation in Mississippi irrespective of whether it is maintained by law is not only possible but necessary for the best development of each group." Scrambling to address the deep disparities between white and Black education in Philadelphia, they hoped to provide Black elementary schools with a nine-month term, adequate transportation, a sewer connection, an auditorium and cafeteria, new furniture and modern equipment, proper instructional materials, and trained custodians. Black high school students would need at least one new school building with new furniture and modern equipment. Between the city and county districts, new building projects and significant renovations focused on the consolidated Booker T. Washington High School and George Washington Carver High School (both of which would be shuttered by 1970). Thus, bucking the unanimous opinion of the highest court in the land, local white officials expended an enormous amount of time, effort, and public money to hang on to school segregation.[43]

In Kemper County, whites pursued a similar course. "Let it be said here," declared L. O. Hopkins, superintendent of De Kalb Public Schools, in 1953, "that our more intelligent Negroes realize that the sad plight of their children will be aggravated many times, if they are forced to occupy the same classrooms with children of our race." In the event that the Supreme Court struck down school segregation, Hopkins proposed forming an integrated school board and giving the appearance of compliance with the ruling. "Of course, no center could be designated as a school for any particular race," he wrote to Senator John Stennis, "but separate school centers would be provided for the convenience of both races." Parents would have the right to request that the board transfer their child to a different school if they so desired, and segregation would continue in all but name. "The theory is that tradition and convention would carry out the desired solution," Hopkins explained. "After all, is there a more compelling influence than that of custom?" Black schools would, of course, have to be equalized in order for the plan to work; failing to do so would be "anti Christian." White educational leaders in Kemper County did indeed skirt *Brown* as long as possible before finally opening the private Kemper Academy in 1970.[44]

VII

As educational leaders dug in against change, Mississippi whites reacted to the progressive spirit of *Brown* with rank hostility. First came new codes of behavior. Florence Mars remembered that relations between white and Black residents became positively chilly after *Brown*. Where there had once been "easy interchange" between members of different racial groups (albeit mediated by the customary, one-sided obeisance of the Jim Crow era), there was now only fear and suspicion. Few whites attempted to challenge the new racial etiquette for fear of ridicule or worse. As Mars recalled, "The old relationship between white and Negro was over, at least for a long, long time." What Mars observed in Neshoba County had parallels in most other Southern communities. Pete Daniel writes that, after *Brown*, "most whites hardened their hearts against their black neighbors."[45]

Anxiety, as much as anger, filled whites after the Court's decision. They shared with settlers elsewhere a deep insecurity at the thought of exogenous interference in their way of life. The basis of that insecurity was complex, but its essence was an awareness that decolonization would empower the very people who had had to suffer for whites' privilege. The question that whites had posed to Lillie Jones—"If it ever gets to where you all will be over us, like we are you, would you turn us a favor?"—tormented many a settler. It is, then, no surprise that Mississippi whites began to make much of Medgar Evers's fascination with Mau Mau in those years—the *Jackson Clarion-Ledger* referring to him as "Medgar Evers, the Mau Mau admirer." Not for the last time, columnist Tom Ethridge drew comparisons between Mississippi and settler states in Africa. He alleged that "outsiders" were fanning "flames of unrest" in Kenya and South Africa, and that those same "meddlers" were the "spiritual comrades of NAACP zealots and kindred fanatics here in the United States." Furthermore, "Like Dixie, South Africa realizes that racial integration is certain to bring chaos, which must eventually lead to black control of government."[46]

Safeguarding segregation, thus, took on a new militancy in the mid-1950s. In the months after *Brown*, Mississippi voters approved a constitutional amendment further tightening voting restrictions, and in Sunflower County, a trio of prominent white men formed the White Citizens' Council. Composed of middle-class white supremacists, Citizens' Councils were a white-collar alternative to the Ku Klux Klan, defending segregation at every turn. In November 1956, the state issued a charter to the recently formed Neshoba County Citizens' Council. H. H. "Boots" Harpole of Philadelphia, who would enjoy a successful career with the state Public Service Commission and as an investigator in the Eighth Judicial District, was an early and active member. He also served on the executive committee of the fifth district of the Mississippi Association of Citizens' Councils. (Attending the annual district meeting with Harpole in 1957 was Philadelphia grocer Charles Mars, proving that the politics of the era could divide families as well as communities.) As a leading figure in the Association of Citizens' Councils, Harpole and a small delegation of fellow members met with Governor J. P. Coleman to urge the re-segregation of Veterans Administration hospitals in the state. He also appeared on state television to recruit "the ladies of the state who believe in segregation" for the Citizens' Council.[47]

Kemper County's Citizens' Council counted prominent agricultural and political leaders among its membership. Bob Hobson, who had served as the county's extension agent since 1953, assembled the temporary organization out of which a more permanent group would emerge. In May 1956 he wrote to Senator John Stennis that "in line with your advice," the Lion's Club had invited Citizens' Council founder and state secretary Bob "Tut" Patterson to deliver an address to drive membership. Soon, the group had a permanent slate of officers, including cattleman, Farm Bureau member, and state senator Murray Hailey as president; Ernest P. Bateman of the county board of supervisors as vice president; and J. G. Palmer as secretary-treasurer. Stennis, who hailed from Kemper County and knew the men personally, responded that the organization seemed "in good hands" and "will continue to be conducted on the very highest plane." He warned

Hobson that there would be "hard days ahead" and encouraged the new group to "think clearly and strongly and with foresight, and then act firmly at the proper time."[48]

Among the well-known community leaders in the Forest (Scott County) Citizens' Council were tax assessor, Lion's Club president, and Sunday school teacher Jimmy Fairchild; chancery clerk Ollie Williams; cattleman and Farm Bureau member Richard Ware; businessman and Rotary Club president J. V. Pace Jr.; and Farm Bureau member and Kiwanis Club president Wyatt Measells. In a 1957 appeal for membership, Williams touted the local group's pride in "our white blood and our white heritage of centuries." The Citizens' Council, Williams reminded readers of the *Scott County Times*, "is the South's answer to mongrelizers. We will not be integrated!" Newton County's Citizens' Council included among its officers James Thames and Milton McMullen, who served on the board of directors at Newton County Bank (Thames was the bank's vice president); former sheriff Hansel Reeves; Covert Jenkins, who would soon be mayor of Union; school official Wilson Taylor; and Jesse Ezell, president of the county board of supervisors. State Representatives Alton Phillips and William B. Lucas were both members of the Macon (Noxubee County) Citizens' Council. They urged more women to join their organization in January 1958, boasting that 379 locals (including twenty-one women) had already paid dues for the new year. It would probably be easier to list the prominent, white east-central Mississippians who were *not* members of their local Citizens' Council. The point is that ardent segregationists controlled every aspect of local life—from local government and banking to the administration of farm programs, including those that dealt with loans and acreage allotments.[49]

Citizens' Councils vigorously policed dissent in the years after *Brown*. In 1956, Neshoba Citizens' Council members decided to permanently rid the county of Charles Evers. For several years, Evers had drawn the ire of local whites because of his financial success and, especially, his exhortations to Black listeners of his radio program to pay their poll taxes and, if possible, register and vote. In February 1956, Evers attempted to start a chapter of the NAACP in Philadelphia, a step too far for the Citizens' Council. Council members applied economic pressure, making it difficult for Evers to turn a profit in any of his numerous business ventures. From raiding his hotel in the middle of the night to cutting off his credit and threatening his customers, the council nearly sank his small empire. Moreover, they informed WHOC operator Howard Cole that the businessmen in the Citizens' Council would pull their ads if Evers was allowed to continue his show. Evers saved Cole the embarrassment of having to fire him. "They were going to ruin him," he recalled, "and I left the station." Shortly after resigning as deejay, Evers cut his losses and moved to Chicago.[50]

While the Citizens' Council and local law enforcement would have been enough to preclude a grassroots civil rights movement in most counties, the new Mississippi State Sovereignty Commission soon joined the effort to preserve the racial status quo. The Sovereignty Commission was a taxpayer-funded agency established in 1956 to "do and perform any and all acts and things deemed necessary and proper to protect the sovereignty of the State of Mississippi . . . from encroachment thereon by the Federal Government." In practice, that mandate included everything from pro-segregation propaganda to developing a statewide network of white and Black informants to keep the white power structure apprised of challenges to white supremacy. Sovereignty Commission investigator Leonard C. Hicks first visited Neshoba County on July 10, 1957. While in Philadelphia, he contacted the sheriff, police chief, ex-police chief, Black county agent (L. W. Payne), and a Black peanut salesman named Riley. Hicks found what he considered a "reliable" Black informant in local sexton Ace Whitehead, who promised to alert the Sovereignty Commission of "any strange people or any NAACP activities." Two years later, Neshoba County sheriff George W. Harrington informed Sovereignty Commission agent Zack J. Van Landingham that there had been no sign of NAACP activity since Evers's departure and that "race relations are excellent."[51]

Underpinning such organized resistance—and belying Harrington's characterization of the racial climate—was the seeming impunity with which white supremacists could kill nonwhite individuals. Indeed, the post-*Brown* 1950s were a time of great trepidation for many Black Mississippians. Neither the murders of voting rights activists George W. Lee and Lamar Smith in the western Mississippi towns of Belzoni and Brookhaven, respectively, nor the well-publicized murder of young Emmett Till in Money had resulted in convictions. In Neshoba County, on the night of October 25, 1959, Philadelphia police officers Richard Willis and Lawrence Rainey attempted to arrest a thirty-year-old Black man named Luther Jackson, a Kemper County native who had recently been working in Flint, Michigan. The officers thought that Jackson and his passenger, Hattie Thomas, had been drinking in their car, which was stalled in a quiet residential area. Rainey alleged that Jackson attacked him, after which he fired his pistol into Jackson's stomach, fatally wounding him. Although Hattie Thomas survived to dispute that version of events, Rainey never faced charges. A few years later, he was elected sheriff, from which post he helped organize the 1964 murder of three civil rights workers.[52]

There was very little organized movement for civil rights or economic justice in east-central Mississippi before the 1960s. The reason is simple: over the course of the 1950s, such activism had become suicidal in Mississippi. White reaction to *Brown* and to local voter registration efforts effectively silenced dissent, white and Black, for years. After T. R. M. Howard fled for his life to Chicago in 1955, the only major organization left to challenge Jim Crow in the state was the NAACP, which primarily pursued voting rights and, especially after *Brown*, desegregation. In 1959, C. R. Darden, Lauderdale Countian and president of the Mississippi State Conference of NAACP Branches, asserted that public school integration was "the one and only channel through which equality in education, economics and political freedom may be attained." Meanwhile, Black Mississippians—politically marginalized and on the hook for the tax dollars needed to fund the spurious school equalization campaign—were disproportionately being forced from the land.[53]

Pursuing a strategy roughly opposite that of the NAACP, the MBCI Tribal Council hoped that land ownership and economic advancement would improve Choctaws' political and social standing. But in January 1959, the Tribal Council discovered that its claims case had been dismissed three years earlier. Chairman Emmett York complained that William T. Weir, the tribe's attorney, had known and never bothered to inform them. "If we didn't go to Washington and stir this up," York stated, "we wouldn't never know that it had been dismissed. We would be sitting here waiting for our money." Not yet prepared to give up on the claim, the Tribal Council began pursuing other avenues. Even as it did so, well-to-do white farmers continued to benefit from land consolidation and generous state assistance. There seemed to be no stopping them.[54]

In Mississippi, as in other settler states, reaction tended to trump decolonial change. Whatever reforms nonwhite Mississippians expected just after the war largely did not materialize; overt racial hostility escalated, particularly after *Brown*. Likewise, the notion that colonialism and racism were losing legitimacy did not seem to matter in Kenya, where settler tyranny dramatically worsened before finally collapsing. There, as would soon be the case in Southern Rhodesia, the image of settler men and women going about their daily affairs with a pistol at their hip became common. In South Africa, the 1948 ascendance of D. F. Malan and the National Party ushered in apartheid, the rigid system of segregation and white settler privilege that would last for nearly half a century. The 1953 formation of the Central African Federation, which included both Rhodesias and Nyasaland, served the interests of settlers, although its leaders were forced to declare a state of emergency in 1959 amid popular unrest. The onset of the Cold War and settlers' rabidly anticommunist posture further shored up white minority rule in places like South Africa and its mandate, South West Africa, and in Southern Rhodesia, Angola, and Mozambique, where the state was strong or ruthless enough to survive popular protest. In other words, in the 1940s and 1950s, most settler states—Mississippi included—dug in for the long haul.[55]

While frantic white resistance was the rule south of Mason-Dixon (and made frequent appearances north of it), the US government responded only haltingly. President Eisenhower nearly apologized after sending the 101st Airborne Division to Little Rock, Arkansas, to protect the first nine Black students at that city's Central High School. For the president, federal intervention was, as Thomas Borstelmann has observed, "a matter of preserving domestic order, not promoting racial justice," white violence a "strictly political rather than moral problem." Long indifferent to Southern white supremacy, the president's approach to racial confrontation was to denounce "extremists on both sides." In September 1957, the same month as the Little Rock crisis, Eisenhower signed a civil rights bill into law that the *Nation* correctly identified as a "sham." Although otherwise toothless, the Civil Rights Act of 1957 established a Civil Rights Division in the Justice Department and an independent Commission on Civil Rights. In its sprawling first report, the latter agency registered the scope of the problem that the US government was trying its best to ignore: "The colored peoples of Asia and Africa, constituting a majority of the human race, are swiftly coming into their own. The non-colored peoples of the world are now on test. The future peace of the world is at stake."[56]

4

ENCLOSURE SETTLER AGRICULTURE IN THE 1950S

> *The small independent farmer, caught in a squeeze between falling farm prices and rising production costs, is being forced to plow his last furrow, sell out to the big operator and move to town to look for a job.*
> —Jackson Clarion-Ledger, 1955

As conservative white resistance hardened, the transition to capital-intensive agriculture remade rural life. In the quarter-century after World War II, the number of farms in east-central Mississippi dropped by about two-thirds, from 30,644 to 10,811. Meanwhile, the average farm size more than doubled, from 82 acres to 168 acres. The number of tenants (including sharecroppers) plummeted from 14,071 to 663. Farming became the province of those who could afford the machinery and chemicals to stay competitive. Those who could not had little choice but to leave the land along with the tenants that mechanization and its accompanying trends had rendered superfluous. As one farmer in Attala County remarked, "If you don't have the best, you might as well close up." Such changes were particularly focused in the 1950s, the decade when the region's rural counties suffered declines in overall population that averaged around 15 percent, much of it due to outmigration. Many who did not leave moved from rural areas to county seats, where the labor market became saturated with ex-farmers. Anyone paying close attention could see an unemployment crisis in the offing. As scholars have rightly noted, it was as though the postwar South was reliving the nightmare of the English enclosure of several centuries earlier, which had, incidentally, produced much of the urban poverty for which settler colonialism became a pressure valve.[1]

Farmers and rural people with the most at stake in political decolonization were also most disproportionately affected by the new enclosure. To be sure, plenty of poor white farm families faced displacement in the 1950s. But Black families had never enjoyed the range of services that USDA agencies offered whites, and, what was more, they had never wielded the political power necessary to widen access to the resources that modern farming seemed to require. Thus, they were even less equipped to compete with well-capitalized whites. Nor did most Choctaw farmers fare well in the 1950s. While some farmed tribal land and had access to a separate extension service, they were very much in the minority. Most Choctaw farmers were sharecroppers on white-owned land where their labor was fast becoming redundant. Both Black and Choctaw farmers, once displaced, faced a local labor market that was not only saturated but also segregated. Employers restricted the most desirable positions to whites, while Black and Choctaw job-seekers competed over the few that remained.[2]

While many who benefited from enclosure were also opponents of political change, the process involved more than just petty retaliation for civil rights activism. It was but the latest in a series of socially, environmentally, and morally reckless developments whose consummation would be the complete industrialization of farming. And, although the market imperatives distinctive of capitalism had long intruded on Southern agriculture, the new enclosure movement ensured both their predominance and their permanence. Fading rapidly was the "live-at-home" ethos of the prewar period, embodied in small farmers producing enough for their own subsistence and a small surplus or money crop to sell. Farms became factories, and thousands of small Southern communities struggled to find their bearings.[3]

But it was not only the South that suffered. Farmers that left areas like east-central Mississippi often crowded into urban centers in search of factory work. Although the overall economy seemed healthy in the 1950s, bellwether industries like automobile manufacturing were evolving and could not absorb the latest wave of Southern migrants. As would become

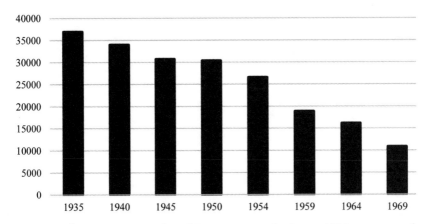

East-Central Mississippi: Number of Farms, 1920–1969. *Source*: US Department of Commerce, Bureau of the Census, *United States Census of Agriculture*, 1920, 1925, 1930, 1935, 1940, 1945, 1950, 1954, 1959, 1964, and 1969.

painfully clear in the late 1960s, crumbling husks of cities filled with unemployed workers—many of them Southern transplants with few marketable skills—were like powder kegs. Too late, observers would note the "southern roots of the urban crisis." Not surprisingly, similar problems confronted cities in other settler states, where displaced farmers sought employment in what one frustrated Southern Rhodesian job-seeker called "nonexistent industries." Different settler states had different ways of dealing with urban influx, but the overall trend was clear: agricultural modernization fed urban unemployment.[4]

Cold War nationalism stressed that the condition of human freedom was a capitalist economy. But the 1950s were a pivotal decade in Mississippi precisely because the internal contradictions of capitalism placed limits on the extension of basic human rights to all the state's people. The permanent phasing out of small-scale and subsistence farming in favor of large-scale, mechanized, and thoroughly capitalist operations produced a predictable set of social disruptions. With more land and subsidies accruing to fewer and fewer well-capitalized farmers, and with tenants and small landowners thrown into a state of flux, nonwhite people found themselves particularly vulnerable at a time when the political stakes were high. Growing inequality—sown in Mississippi and elsewhere by the push to modernize, mechanize, rationalize, and automate—combined

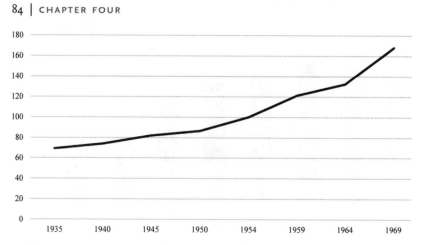

East-Central Mississippi: Average Size of Farms (Acres), 1920–1969. *Source*: US Department of Commerce, Bureau of the Census, *United States Census of Agriculture*, 1920, 1925, 1930, 1935, 1940, 1945, 1950, 1954, 1959, 1964, and 1969.

with settler reaction to undermine the prospect of bottom-up change just as the decolonizing world was at its most optimistic.

I

The gospel of agricultural modernization had some of its most effective evangelists in the Extension Service. Since 1918, the Extension Service had played a critical role in the lives of east-central Mississippians. It was the same agency that would guide many of the changes in rural life and work in the 1950s. Known as the educational arm of the USDA, the Extension Service made itself indispensable to rural people through its state-level personnel—county agents and home demonstration agents. County agents worked directly with farmers, disseminating the latest scientific information and showing farmers how to use it. In 1950, Neshoba County agent C. S. Norton and his assistants logged 280 days devoted to work with adult farmers, 17 days with 4-H clubs, and 670 individual visits to 610 different farms, in addition to various group farm tours and training and demonstration meetings. They published 48 newspaper articles, prepared 5 radio talks, and distributed 8,012 informational bulletins. County agents also tried to ingratiate themselves with local leaders in order to grow the reach and influence of the Extension Service. Such relationships would be increasingly important as the agency's modernizing agenda winnowed its clientele down to a profitable few.[5]

The administrative structure of the Extension Service placed limits on who had access to the agency's expertise. In Mississippi, as in most of the South, the Extension Service was thoroughly segregated. White farmers enjoyed a full range of services, while Black farmers, on average, received far less. Although there was a white agent in every county, only thirty-six of the state's eighty-two counties had a black agent in 1950; ten years later, there was hardly any improvement. Neshoba County illustrates the problem clearly enough. It had been among the fortunate minority since E. J. Johnson was appointed to the position of Black county agent in 1924. The next year, Will E. Perryman took Johnson's place and, over more than a decade, worked to grow the adult and 4-H programs "as near as possible" to what whites enjoyed in the county. From the early 1940s until 1969, the Black county agent was a well-credentialed Lauderdale County man named L. W. Payne. While some other counties in the region also had Black agents, neither of the neighboring counties of Leake or Kemper did. It was not uncommon for agents like Perryman and Payne to stretch themselves thin crossing county lines to address the needs of Black farmers in such underserved areas.[6]

A 1965 report issued by the US Commission on Civil Rights revealed long-standing inequality in extension work among white and Black farmers, even in counties (like Neshoba) with a Black agent. *Equal Opportunity in Farm Programs* was based on extensive state- and county-level research and interviews with agricultural leaders across eleven Southern states. The study found that in Mississippi counties with both white and Black agents, the white agent was invariably in charge of "coordinating the entire extension program." The Black agent was nominally under his supervision, regardless of credentials or experience. White county agents had readier access to the sources of information to which all extension personnel should have been privy. They enjoyed larger, better equipped offices and full staffs. White agents could also take advantage of a fuller range of in-service training with subject-matter specialists; Black agents took what they could get. For instance, in Mississippi there was thought to be no in-service training available to Black agents in the important fields of cotton or pasture and forage. If a white subject-matter specialist had the time, they might choose to meet with Black agents, or not. Despite L. W. Payne's educational background, the study confirmed that he was among a class of extension personnel routinely "denied adequate training and cut off from vital information" in rapidly changing times.[7]

White county agents viewed white farmers as their "constituency." It followed, then, that in counties like Leake and Kemper that did not have Black agents, services rendered to Black farmers were extremely limited. The white agent in Kemper County told researchers that he spent some time advising Black farmers, but the researchers observed that he disproportionately served the county's white minority. The absence of a Black agent in Kemper County meant that there were no 4-H clubs for Black children, as the white agent only served white children. If Black children received any instruction, it had to have been from agents like Payne in neighboring counties, but "this is not a regular part of [those agents'] program." Thus, in forty-six Mississippi counties, including two in east-central Mississippi, Black farmers were entirely at the mercy of white agents when it came to services and expertise that most agreed were necessary to stay afloat.[8]

Often referred to simply as "women's agents," the Extension Service's home demonstration agents worked with farm women on issues relating to "family welfare and happiness." In Neshoba County, they shared information on modern homemaking with over a dozen home demonstration clubs spread across the county. The agent and her assistants covered a diverse array of topics, including basic home improvement, kitchen planning, canning and freezing, home landscaping, gardening, poultry, first aid, budgeting, personality improvement, and public and world affairs. Like county agents, home demonstration agents made hundreds of home visits, conducted training and demonstration meetings, and communicated through circular newsletters, bulletins, and media appearances. As Mississippi extension director Clay Lyle saw it, they helped women "develop their better selves" and "become better informed citizens of Mississippi, their nation and the world."[9]

Of particular importance for home demonstration work in the 1950s was the surge of new appliances available to homemakers with means.

By 1950 the Rural Electrification Administration had connected about 95 percent of rural Neshoba County to the grid, and residents were buying labor-saving devices that few knew how to use. In 1952 home demonstration agent Esther L. Kerr reported "an increasing number of home freezers, particularly among the landowner farmers and town residents." After receiving repeated requests for assistance with freezing, Kerr held countywide demonstrations on "Freezing Foods" and "Using Frozen Foods." Agents also assisted with other appliances as the need arose. When one homemaker had the family's first gas heater installed in 1959, the home demonstration agent arrived just in time to help plan where the heaters might best be located. "It was found that [the homemaker] was putting one of the heaters on the wall where her sofa would be placed during the winter. She hadn't thought about that," the agent reflected. "This is just another case of poor planning." Like annual county agent reports from the period, home demonstration reports could contain more than a touch of unsubtle condescension.[10]

Yet despite the importance that farm families and extension personnel attached to home economics, Neshoba County did not have a Black home demonstration agent during the early postwar period. Home demonstration was every bit as segregated and unequal as farm extension. In counties without Black home demonstration personnel, it was up to white agents whether to break custom and provide service across the color line. While that might have occurred occasionally, there is virtually no record of it. As the Commission on Civil Rights confirmed, "especially when the two extension programs of 4-H and home demonstration clubs were discussed, most extension officials agreed that it was unusual to find a program for Negroes in a county without Negro workers." An integrated demonstration club would have invited (into the home, no less) a form of racial equality that whites were not yet ready to concede in any other facet of their lives.[11]

Finally, all agents had a hand in 4-H work. There were more than twenty 4-H clubs in Neshoba County in the 1950s, and extension personnel took pride in the hands-on training that the clubs afforded area youth. The main feature was the farm projects in which young people enrolled every year, including corn, cotton, swine, dairy, beef, poultry, and, increasingly, forestry. In fact, it was not uncommon for adult farmers to obtain some of the latest information second-hand, from their children who were working on extension-supervised club projects. Additionally, 4-H provided opportunities for young people to socialize through rallies, contests, camps, and dances. But, like the schools in which they were housed, 4-H clubs were segregated. In counties like Neshoba that had a Black agent, participation in Black 4-H programs was generally high, even though such programs did not have the resources of local white clubs. As the Kemper County example suggests, in places where there was no Black agent, young people relied on the good graces of extension personnel in other counties or simply went without.[12]

The segregated structure of the Extension Service was clearly inefficient. But more than that, it set up Black farm families for failure. In the highly competitive atmosphere of the 1950s, when Agriculture Secretary Ezra Taft Benson's motto was "Get big or get out," Black and white farmers received separate and unequal treatment not only from the Extension Service but also from the other agencies purporting to assist all farmers. The Farmers Home Administration (FHA), the Soil Conservation Service (SCS), and the Agricultural Stabilization and Conservation Service (ASCS)—agencies dealing with loans, soil exhaustion and erosion, and acreage allotment and price supports, respectively—all provided inferior service to Black farmers, if they served them at all. For instance, across the South, county ASC committees, which determined the allotment of cotton acreage and cost-sharing grants for conservation practices, entirely excluded Black farmers from decision-making. The Commission on Civil Rights described "the persistence of an entirely white structure in county after county where the economic welfare of Negroes is being decided in their absence."[13]

II

Extension personnel in the 1950s continued to hawk much of the same advice that they had given just after World War II. The return of cotton acreage allotments and marketing quotas in 1950 found agents encouraging growers to make every acre count. More production on less acreage meant continuing to replace hand-and-hoe labor with machines and chemicals.

Agent Norton encouraged farmers to "poison" their cotton with synthetic pesticides, suggesting a mixture of benzene hexachloride (BHC) and DDT or toxaphene. When the federal government lifted production restrictions during the Korean War, Neshoba County cotton farmers increased their acreage by a third and attempted to reduce labor costs still further to maximize profits. Norton brought in experts to demonstrate different types of pesticide sprayers and new pre-emergent herbicides, boasting in 1953 that "no chopping was necessary on any part except a sandy portion of the [demonstration] field." Acreage allotments returned for good in 1954, overseen at the local level by the new Agricultural Stabilization and Conservation (ASC) committees (formerly the Production and Marketing Administration, or PMA, and before that, the AAA), and between 1956 and 1958, cotton acreage declined even more as a result of the short-lived Soil Bank program.[14]

While some farmers continued to improve their production on reduced acreage after 1953, most took steps to abandon cotton. County agents continued to work with cotton farmers, preaching "higher yields per acre" and trying (often in vain) to explain how the new ASC committees worked, but they strongly encouraged the shift away from row-cropping. Norton wrote the same sentence at the end of his annual crop report until the end of the decade: "With the decreased emphasis on cotton and with cotton acreage allotments during the year, interest is shifting from row crops to livestock production." The *Neshoba Democrat* editorialized that "cotton no longer is the absolute monarch of the state's broad, fertile acres, nor the only pillar in its agricultural economy." The pattern that had begun in the late 1940s—the abandonment of cotton for livestock—showed no sign of abating in the 1950s. Between 1950 and 1959, the number of Neshoba County farms that derived more than 50 percent of their income from cotton declined from 1,448 to 490. Kemper County's agent, B. H. Dixon, wrote to Senator John Stennis that he was encouraging farmers to turn their attention to livestock and forestry—"We are doing everything we can to promote them as fast as conditions will permit."[15]

Another pattern that carried over from the 1940s was farmers' abandonment of animal traction for machines. Mississippi Extension Service director Clay Lyle reported that county agents helped thousands of farmers select tractors and other machines, trained them in tractor safety and responsible use, and held 4-H tractor-driving contests. Agent Norton assisted the local Ford dealer in holding tractor demonstrations, "displaying the latest type of machinery and its actual use on the farm," and 4-H club members and adult farmers participated in a county-wide tractor maintenance school. The widespread adoption of tractors meant that farmers no longer had to set aside acreage to take care of draft horses and mules, whose numbers in Neshoba County plunged from 6,863 to 1,358 between 1950 and 1959. As early as 1951, in their annual report on livestock, the agents in neighboring Newton County remarked that draft animals "are going out too fast to spend any time on." Additionally, as farmers transitioned away from cotton, some bought grain combines and corn pickers, renting them out to others for a fee. Dairy farmers bought everything from milking machines and coolers to balers, rakes, mowers, and hay conditioners. County agents assisted farmers in building equipment sheds to protect their new machinery.[16]

Such expenses made it harder for farmers to stay viable, though, to say nothing of their effect on the cost of entry for new farmers, who also had to consider the rising cost of land. In her studies of young white and Black Mississippi farm families, Dorothy Dickins noted that prospective farmers balked at the high cost of land and machinery. Choctaw landowner L. J. Henry acquired a tractor but could not afford to maintain it. Even renting machinery, rather than buying it, could be prohibitively expensive, although some farmers availed themselves of that option. In Neshoba County, farm expenditures on machine hire alone jumped from $62,155 in 1950 to $100,929 in 1959. "If you net enough from farming to maintain what most folks call a good standard of living," Clay Lyle observed in 1958, "you have a lot bigger investment than it took just a few years ago." He estimated that annual earnings of $2,500 would require a $14,000 investment for a cotton farm, $24,000 for a dairy-cotton farm, and $27,000 for a cotton-beef farm. The new capital-intensive farming could be daunting, as few had ever invested quite so much money at once. "Farm families are asking the Extension Service for more help in agricultural economics," Lyle reported. He described extension economists' role in helping farmers obtain and use credit and keep good records. The Extension Service now had to teach farmers how to survive in the unforgiving new environment that they had helped create.[17]

Staying afloat was no easy task, particularly with some local agricultural leaders unwilling to put forth the effort to keep small farmers in business. "I am not of the opinion that we should help the small farmer more than we do others," wrote agent B. H. Dixon of Kemper County, "because it might lead him to think that because he is a little farmer the Government is naturally going to take care of him." Devoting what Dixon considered undue attention to small farmers would lead most to "sit down and wait for such help and this we do not want them to do." Agent C. I. Smith wrote from Attala County that small farmers' struggle to survive was "a situation that cannot be helped." His only advice to such farmers was to "obtain larger farms or to obtain some public work . . . to help increase the family income." The first bit of advice was, of course, useless, as most career farmers were not "little" by choice. So, many had to find outside employment even as they continued to manage their farms.[18]

Choctaws had an especially hard time staying viable. In 1955, T. J. Scott, a local man who had worked for decades with the Indian Agency in Philadelphia, informed Senator James Eastland that Choctaws were increasingly unable to make a living farming. Even the non-sharecroppers—Choctaws who lived on small plots of land that the government had purchased decades earlier—were struggling. Their land was generally not very fertile, and they could not obtain credit to buy fertilizer. Eastland forwarded Scott's letter to Commissioner of Indian Affairs Glenn Emmons, who conceded that the "agricultural program at this reservation has always been a marginal one." He added that the non-sharecropping Choctaws' farms were simply too small to be viable. "Agriculture, like industry, has become big business," Emmons wrote. And "it is not possible for a farmer to make an adequate living on a farm of the size of most Choctaw assignments." Unless they could afford to expand, their only option would be to leave farming and "seek employment where [they] can receive a living wage." Emmons's suggestion that struggling Choctaws leave the land was in line with his agency's goal of relocating Indians from reservations to towns and cities where they might integrate into what one scholar called "'mainstream' systems of settler-state power."[19]

Those farmers who could afford to do so followed the advice of county agents and foresters, who sometimes suggested tree farming as an extra source of income. Agents Norton and Payne sent every landowner in Neshoba County a yearly reminder to register for tree seedlings, which were available through the local forestry office. Farmers could plant trees on unused acres, receive assistance from trained foresters in growing and maintaining their tree farm, and, after a few years, sell their timber at a competitive price. While cotton and livestock represented the first- and second-largest sources of income for local farmers throughout the 1950s, timber was a close third.[20]

But the cruel irony of extension work in the 1950s was that success meant a certain amount of failure. Propping up the largest and most profitable farmers and displacing the rest had been the Extension Service's unofficial goal at least since H. J. Putnam's 1946 memo on "problem" tenant farms. "The disappearance of farm families from Mississippi farms . . . should not be looked upon with regret," Putnam had declared, "but with extreme satisfaction." Big farmers "should be able to earn more as some of their labor is lost to industry or dislocated because of the introduction of labor-saving equipment." If mechanization displaced tenants by replacing them with machines and chemicals, it also forced out small landowners who could not take advantage of economies of scale. They could not afford both machines and the additional acreage necessary to make the machines pay for themselves. A dozen years after Putnam's memo, Clay Lyle surveyed the thinning ranks of Mississippi farmers, noting that the strong were surviving while "many small farmers are moving into more profitable non-farm employment." Both men's confidence in the employment prospects of ex-farmers, if sincere, was misplaced.[21]

III

The Farmers Home Administration joined the Extension Service in reducing the number of farmers by restricting who could get access to land. Acquiring more land was a key to survival in the 1950s, and the purpose of the FHA was to provide farmers with loans and technical assistance toward that end. But the program was administered at the county level by three-person committees consisting of locals named by the state director. Before the 1960s, nearly all county committeemen were white, which meant that local prejudice influenced decisions about the eligibility of loan applicants. This helps further explain why, at a time when most small farmers struggled, nonwhite farmers lost more land (and lost it faster) than whites. In east-central Mississippi, the fifteen years after World War II were particularly devastating. Black and Choctaw farmers (owners, tenants, and croppers) worked 41 percent fewer acres in 1960 than in 1945. During the same period, white acreage as a share of overall farmland in the region rose by almost 10 percent, from 73 percent to 82 percent.[22]

That FHA county committeemen could sometimes act quite ruthlessly is evidenced by an incident that took place in Kemper County. In February 1957 a white woman named Inez Gunn informed her friend, Senator John Stennis, that the FHA was trying to take land from two of her Black neighbors. "The FHA in Dekalb are in the process of taking the land away from the boys ," by which she meant two adult men, brothers J. Y. and Turner Mosley. "I am sure you know them," Gunn wrote, calling them "good, honest, hard-working negro boys" that "never give us any trouble." The Mosleys had apparently borrowed money to purchase a farm a few years earlier and had since had "bad luck" in the form of hail and drought, which set them behind in their payments. Then, in 1956, their acreage was cut, making it even harder for them to catch up. When they attempted to rent some of their land to the government, they did not receive what they (or Gunn) considered a fair rental payment. Gunn's husband, Worthy, thought that "there must be someone behind this that maybe wants the place."[23]

The senator thanked Gunn and pursued the matter with Mississippi's state FHA director, T. B. Fatherree, a man he had known for years. Stennis disclosed that he not only knew who the Mosley brothers were, but that their land adjoined a farm that Stennis and his brother owned. Fatherree wrote back detailing how the two men's accounts were in arrears—J. Y. was behind $511.25 and Turner $976.64. He also reported that while Turner was attempting to run the farm with mostly family labor, J. Y. was then working for a gin operator and farmer named Legette (perhaps one of the same Kemper County Legettes investigated for peonage a half-century earlier). Glen Brown, a Kemper County FHA committeeman that Fatherree had consulted, felt that the Mosleys had "not paid as much as could reasonably have been expected." While Fatherree would look further into the matter, he argued that the brothers "should be expected to apply themselves diligently in the development of a well balanced farm program," as "the farms which we have assisted them in purchasing are capable of provided [sic] such income when properly used."[24]

Ultimately, under pressure from Stennis, state and county FHA personnel reached an agreement with the Mosleys that allowed them to stay on their land for the time being. If the incident was, as the Gunns presumed, a case of unscrupulous committeemen out to dispossess vulnerable farmers, they probably learned to make sure that the land they coveted did not adjoin that of a US senator. It remains unclear why Stennis chose to intervene on behalf of the two Black men, as he was not in the habit of doing so. Perhaps he felt a sense of duty to the Gunns, who were favored constituents from his home county. Interestingly, records show that Turner Mosley was married to a Black woman named Audrey Stennis. In rural Southern counties like Kemper, white and Black families with the same surname—especially one as uncommon as Stennis—often shared family ties that predated emancipation. In any case, the incident demonstrated just how easy it might have been for two Black farmers without the Mosleys' connections to be forced off the land. There can be no doubt that plenty of farmers whose names will never be known lost their land under similar circumstances.[25]

IV

In the 1950s the public face of the new Mississippi agriculture was a man named Howard Langfitt. Born and raised in Iowa, Langfitt was stationed in Jackson, Mississippi, during World War II. He permanently settled in the Magnolia State in 1945 with his wife, Gloria, in order to take the job of Farm Services director at Jackson's WJDX radio. When the new medium of television took hold in the mid-1950s, Langfitt launched a program on WLBT-TV called *Farm Family of the Week*. In it, he spotlighted Mississippi farm families that county agents had singled out for their embrace of modern farming techniques and lifestyle choices.[26]

The farm families that county agents referred to Langfitt fit a certain mold, and they were the sort that, at least in the short term, benefited from enclosure. The men were big landowners, white, and typically (though not always) from old, well-established Mississippi families. They had diversified from all or mostly row-cropping—generally cotton and corn—to livestock and feed crops, and they had happily abandoned mules and tenants for tractors and chemicals. As Langfitt liked to say, they were "completely mechanized farmers." Especially in east-central Mississippi, they were also tree farmers, raising timber "as a crop" and renovating their homes and building equipment sheds for their tractors with timber from their own substantial holdings. Additionally, the men were members of the Farm Bureau and sat on important boards and committees; some were members of the White Citizens' Council. Their wives were depicted as modern homemakers and owned the ultimate status symbol thereof—a deep freezer.

In 1955 Langfitt featured Neshoba residents Mr. and Mrs. J. A. Howle. The Howles had lived on their farm since 1915, and for most of those forty years, it had consisted of around 900 acres, although it was now only 535 acres, still well above the county average. They had begun growing only cotton and corn but had gradually phased in livestock (120 head of cattle and 65 brood cows), oats, and hay. Now, the only cotton that they grew was a 29-acre allotment that they shared with their grown sons, who would soon inherit the entire farm. All of the rolling land on the Howle farm was terraced and planted "on the contour," and Langfitt was sure to emphasize that J. A. Howle was a "completely mechanized farmer," using "proper insect control and fertilization for maximum yields." He and his sons were "partners in machinery, crops and cattle," a fact that gave the sons a leg up on other young farmers. Indeed, as Howle told Langfitt, if he had not been able to give his sons hundreds of acres apiece outright, they would have abandoned farming.[27]

Mr. Howle was secretary of the Neshoba Baptist Church Sunday School, served twenty-five years on the Neshoba County school board, and was the president of the county Farm Bureau before becoming director of the state bureau. For eighteen years he was a director of the Neshoba County Fair, an important site of Southern political campaigning. Howle was Soil Conservation District commissioner for four years and served three years on the county ASC committee, two terms as president of the Neshoba Community Club, five years on the local draft board, and twenty-five years as financial secretary for Woodmen of the World. Mrs. Howle still kept a garden and either canned her produce or kept it in her new chest-style deep freezer. She was a charter member of the Neshoba County Home Demonstration Club, a thirty-seven-year-old organization of which she had been president in 1952. She had also served as president of the Women's Missionary Union and taught the women's Sunday School class at Neshoba Baptist. The Howles were not a typical hill-country farm family, but they were the very epitome of the large, well-to-do, and well-connected sort of landowners most equipped to transition from labor-intensive to capital-intensive farming.[28]

Two years later, C. S. Norton introduced Howard Langfitt to Mr. and Mrs. R. B. Moore, a couple who lived about eight miles southwest of Philadelphia near the Waldo community. They had begun farming before World War II on rented land with a Farm Security Administration loan for supplies. Soon, they had acquired their own land. The Moores remembered that, at first, they had been "strictly row crop farmers, using mules to raise cotton." Sometime in the 1940s, though, they had begun raising dairy cows, and by 1957 they had nineteen. At that point, the Moores had quit growing cotton altogether. As Langfitt stated approvingly, "Mr. Moore has long since given up mule farming and is a completely mechanized farmer with all the equipment he needs except for combining and hay baling which he hires done." Following the advice of Norton, they also raised pine timber, some of which Moore used to build new equipment sheds and add-ons to the family home. Mrs. Moore had a "modern kitchen," complete with a deep freezer, and the family had enjoyed electricity since before the war. Like the Howles, the Moores were well-connected folk, and Mr. Moore was a member of the Farm Bureau and an ASC community committeeman.[29]

Extension agents in Winston County referred Mr. and Mrs. J. U. "Bud" Fulcher of the Rocky Hill community. The Fulchers had first met in the county AAA office back when Bud was in the farm implement business and his future wife was an office worker. They bought their first farm in

1950 and began row-cropping, but, as Langfitt stated, "they soon realized they must change their farm program is [sic] they were to make a decent living." They upgraded to a larger farm and a dairy operation and boasted a "modern dairy barn which will hold ten cows at a time and is completely modern in every way." While they still grew some cotton, they "did not crop anything on the shares." And, of course, Langfitt assured viewers that "Bud Fulcher is a completely mechanized farmer." In Newton County, Mr. and Mrs. W. K. Boutwell and their three young sons lived on a relatively large farm in the Liberty community, adjoining old family land. Mr. Boutwell told Langfitt that his "two big farming changes have been from cotton to pastures and from mules to machines." With milking equipment, two tractors, a combine, a pickup hay baler, and other "necessary" machines, Boutwell, too, was a "completely mechanized farmer." Predictably, Bud Fulcher and W. K. Boutwell played important roles in their respective communities—Fulcher as president of the Winston County Farm Bureau and Boutwell as an ASC committeeman. Langfitt also pointed out that Fulcher was a member of the local Citizens' Council.[30]

In collaboration with county agents, Langfitt used families like the Howles, Moores, Fulchers, and Boutwells to celebrate a model of farming that could pay dividends in the competitive environment of the 1950s. But this sort of farming, which involved meeting the rising cost of land and equipment and evicting one's tenants, was off-limits to many in east-central Mississippi. As ASC committeemen and Farm Bureau officers, the male heads of Langfitt's Farm Families of the Week were close to the levers of power that mattered to farmers in the area. Notably absent from the ranks of those farm families were Choctaws and Black Mississippians. Those same groups were also completely shut out of the ASC administrative structure. Indeed, ASC committees, the Farm Bureau, and, most explicitly, the White Citizens' Councils were all committed in their own ways to dispossessing nonwhite Mississippians and derailing progressive reform. Thus, to many Mississippians who saw Langfitt on WLBT (itself a bulwark of segregation) at the height of enclosure, *Farm Family of the Week* might have seemed as much of an assertion of white male supremacy as a show about farming.[31]

Howard Langfitt's farm family profiles give some idea of the sorts of

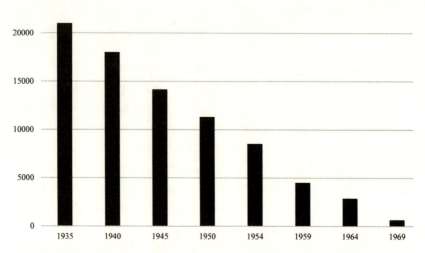

East-Central Mississippi: Number of Tenants, 1920–1969. *Source*: US Department of Commerce, Bureau of the Census, *United States Census of Agriculture*, 1920, 1925, 1930, 1935, 1940, 1945, 1950, 1954, 1959, 1964, and 1969.

Mississippians who prospered because of enclosure. Unfortunately, few such profiles exist of those forced to leave the land. That should not be terribly surprising, because displacement was an anticipated effect of the shift to capital-intensive farming, not an accident. Nevertheless, their presence was felt in nearby towns and cities and in the urban North and West. The clear first choice for most families forced out of farming was to relocate to the county seat. During the 1950s, when Neshoba County's population shrank by 18.7 percent, Philadelphia's increased by 12.2 percent. Similarly, in Newton County, the overall population decreased even as the populations of its county seat and largest city, Decatur and Newton, respectively, increased. But, like most other Southern towns, Philadelphia, Decatur, and Newton could not accommodate all of the ex-farmers who needed work. There were only so many jobs to be had, and in some local industries, mechanization and automation were threatening to shrink that number still further.[32]

Area lumber companies, for instance, complained of high labor costs and tough competition in the 1950s. A 1961 study found "a notable trend in increased use of mechanized and automatic equipment by Mississippi sawmills in recent years." These changes, by design, cut down on the number of workers needed such that, between 1949 and 1959, the number of sawmill and planing mill workers in the state plunged from 20,000 to 12,300. County agent C. S. Norton, who tracked the number of Neshoba County families employed in forest-related industries in his annual reports, estimated that around 150 fewer families were so employed in 1959 than in 1950. Thus, during a decade when more than 1,500 Neshoba County farmers left the land, the largest non-farm industry was eliminating jobs.[33]

Other non-farm work included contract construction, government work, and teaching, as well as glove-making at the Wells-Lamont factory. Wells-Lamont had opened its Philadelphia factory in 1945, and over the next fifteen years it employed between 350 and 500 workers at a time. Superintendent Ernest Bowton liked to hire women between the ages of sixteen and thirty-five to work the glove machines because they were the "most efficient." He seems not to have hired Choctaws, and, as Charles M. Tolbert's 1958 study reported, white workers at such factories could (and did) demand that even qualified Choctaws be denied employment. Bowton also deferred to local prejudice in only hiring Black workers in janitorial or shipping-and-receiving positions. Even with a third of the county's population barred from production work, turnover was low, and Wells-Lamont could only justify new hires in the event of an expansion, which tended to require a bond issue. Neshoba County's ex-farmers faced a glutted (and, for nonwhite workers, hostile) labor market at the worst possible time.[34]

Kemper County similarly struggled to provide non-farm employment. Between the late 1940s and mid-1950s, the county's government and business leaders aggressively courted Northern industries but mostly faced disappointment. In early 1946 a Northern clothing manufacturer had seemed interested in locating a factory in the county seat of De Kalb. The company hoped to employ around two hundred women between the ages of eighteen and forty-two; cheap, tractable labor was both the main selling point of Kemper County and the primary concern of the company. The De Kalb Lions Club had been so sure of a positive outcome that the weekly *Kemper County Messenger* had published employment applications. But, addressing the De Kalb Lions Club in September 1946, local booster Andrew McLeary cited labor strife as the reason the company would not be making any moves after all. Other interested manufacturers, of which there were rumored to have been several, had also withdrawn. The next year, there were hopes that a furniture company would locate a factory in De Kalb and employ as many as two hundred local men. But, in a pattern that would continue for that isolated rural community, nothing materialized. In the immediate postwar years, Kemper County never did attract a big plant capable of absorbing its growing population of displaced farmers.[35]

In Scott and Leake Counties, a growing poultry industry absorbed some displaced farm labor. But until the 1960s, poultry plants hired mostly white women and no Black workers for processing jobs. Black workers were not hired until whites were lured away by higher-paying factory jobs (such as at the new Sunbeam factory in the Scott County seat of Forest, which also resisted hiring Blacks) or until a white-led walkout at a poultry plant led management to bring in Black workers as strikebreakers.[36]

While agricultural leaders never wrote much about the plight of ex-farmers in the region, both farm extension and home demonstration reports reflect the unforeseen ways in which the shifting fortunes of farmers impacted extension work. Beginning around 1957, home demonstration agents reported declining attendance at club meetings as women sought outside employment at area factories to supplement the family income. Sometimes, these were younger women from farm families attempting to afford farm equipment and home appliances. Other times, they were from families who had had to give up farming and move into town. Grandmothers and other older relatives, enlisted to take care of their working daughters' children, also missed club meetings. White and Black extension agents reported that ex-farmers often called on them to make home visits within the city limits to assist with lawns and vegetable gardens. Agents across Mississippi received similar requests, and M. S. Shaw, the state leader of county agents, began to emphasize the new importance of "suburban and urban extension work." In 1959 he acknowledged that "since the Extension program is so well established, there is a growing demand in large towns and cities of our state for Extension Service." But, in practice, ex-farmers living in town were generally no longer the concern of county agents.[37]

Some observers of enclosure and its attendant effects saw trouble ahead for Mississippi. "For those who hope for an expanding industry and commerce which will absorb underemployed labor and other resources in agriculture," noted University of Mississippi economics professor Randolph G. Kinabrew in 1957, "this is a time of concern about how well Mississippi is realizing its economic potential." Perhaps it should not be surprising that within the same fact-finding report on economic growth and development prepared for the Mississippi State Senate, other contributors based their findings on the common assumption that "the national labor force will continue to be essentially fully employed." But at a time when virtually every industry was finding new ways to streamline and cut labor costs, that was a dangerous assumption.[38]

V

Some ex-farmers who could not find work in the region's smaller towns and cities relocated to Meridian, Jackson, or the Gulf Coast, while others moved to northern and western cities like Detroit, Chicago, and Los Angeles. Non-Southern newspapers from the late twentieth and early twenty-first centuries are dotted with the obituaries of men and women who left east-central Mississippi in the 1950s and early 1960s. Many were born in the 1920s or 1930s and would have reached adulthood when the cost of entry for farming was rising and tenancy was declining. While most left little in the way of a paper trail, James N. Gregory's work mapping the Southern diaspora with census data has afforded a rough picture of where they settled. By 1960 there were 215,217 native Mississippians in Illinois, 78,911 in California, 71,828 in Michigan, 65,143 in Missouri, 43,716 in Ohio, and 34,863 in Indiana. Mississippi Choctaws settled almost exclusively in the Midwestern states of Illinois, Indiana, and Ohio.[39]

In the mid-1950s, as termination was gathering steam, plenty of Choctaw families took advantage of the government's Voluntary Relocation Program. To say that they did so voluntarily, of course, would be to ignore the constrained choice that characterized life in Mississippi. By 1955 the BIA had placed around seventy Choctaws in Chicago, and two-thirds of those had chosen to stay; the other third, presumably, had returned home to Mississippi. Some early placements involved seasonal work in Chicago canneries, but the BIA intended most placements to be permanent. To that end, relocation officers who made periodic pitches to the Tribal Council and Choctaw community meetings asked that whole families commit to move, rather than simply male heads of household. Placing entire families in an urban setting away from the reservation increased the chances that relocation would stick. After all, the broader purpose of the program, as one scholar has put it, was "to ultimately preclude [Indians'] futures as Indian people, all in an effort to prune federal expenditures, support Cold War cultural consensus, and solve [the government's] perpetual 'Indian problem.'" Indians, of course, had their own reasons for relocating—namely to find secure employment while continuing to live *as Indians*.[40]

In September 1956 the Choctaw Agency in Philadelphia announced that Glenn J. Durham, a former vocational rehabilitation worker in the Veterans Administration, would serve as a full-time relocation officer for the Choctaws. Durham would attempt to place more Choctaws in permanent jobs in the Midwest. He would also cultivate contacts in the Mississippi and Florida state employment services whose representatives had contacted the agency in hopes of securing a few hundred migrant Choctaw workers to pick tomatoes and other truck crops. "They are anxious to have Choctaw people," Durham told the Tribal Council in October, "because they know they are good workers." Charlie Denson, for one, had occasionally traveled to Florida to pick oranges in Haines City and cut celery in Belle Glade and had established good relationships with his employers. Those present acknowledged that whether Choctaws moved to the Midwest or worked seasonally in Florida, the Tribal Council would soon have to decide whether to amend the MBCI constitution to extend membership to children born outside of Mississippi.[41]

At the same time, more than one hundred Choctaws moved to a crossroads community along the Mississippi River in western Tennessee called Golddust. They followed Willie Bell and his family, who left Philadelphia in 1953 to grow cotton and corn on halves for a white Golddust landowner named M. C. Cook. "We left the reservation," Cubert Bell later recalled, "because we thought if we could get away from the low income area and raise crops, we could make a better living." While few regretted the move, it seems to have been a mixed blessing. There was less overt racial hostility there than in east-central Mississippi, and the demand for hand labor was not as depressed. But it would soon become clear that Choctaw sharecroppers could only outrun mechanization for so long. Even tiny Golddust would succumb to the agricultural revolution that was sweeping the South.[42]

Non-Choctaw migrants who left Mississippi faced much uncertainty, even in the supposedly dynamic postwar era. The notion that the 1950s were a time of great prosperity in the United States survives in popular memory if not in scholarly consensus. To be sure, inequality was down. As Claudia Goldin and Robert A. Margo demonstrated, the wage structure was narrower from the 1940s through the 1960s than before or since—a development they referred to as the "Great Compression." Inequality fell in the 1940s and increased only slightly in the 1950s and 1960s before rising sharply again in the 1970s. Jefferson Cowie similarly referred to this period, which he associated with the New Deal order, as the "Great Exception," an "extended detour" from the normal pattern of inequality. Even Thomas Sugrue, who traced the deindustrialization of Detroit to the 1950s, acknowledged that, while it might not have been a "golden age of capitalism," some workers "attained the dream of economic security and employment stability."[43]

But despite being situated in the middle of such a "great" period, the 1950s witnessed their share of worrisome economic trends, two of which would have an especially direct impact on Mississippians. Of course, the first trend—the concomitant rise in productivity and decline in labor demand on farms—produced a veritable army of displaced farmers with narrow skillsets. The second trend, as Sugrue pointed out, was the decline in unskilled or low-skill jobs in the urban centers where large numbers of ex-farmers migrated. A mixture of decentralization and automation meant that the production-line jobs that many migrants sought on arrival in cities like Detroit were fast disappearing. In addition to recessions in 1949, 1953–1954, and 1957–1958, these trends made the 1950s a difficult decade for the Southern diaspora. As one Detroiter warned would-be migrants in 1958, "this is one of the poorest damn places in the country for your future."[44]

Decentralization involved the movement of factories from city centers to suburban or exurban areas, and it was well underway by the 1950s. The problems that such moves entailed for blue-collar workers—especially nonwhite workers—were many. As United Auto Workers (UAW) president Walter P. Reuther explained to the US Commission on Civil Rights, newly built plants outside the city center generally drew their workforces from neighboring suburban communities. Since post–World War II infrastructure projects focused on the automobile, not mass transit, commuting from the city to the new suburban plants could involve driving an hour or more both ways. White workers could avoid the long commute by relocating to a new suburban neighborhood near the plant, but, as Reuther told the commission, "even when the Negro gets a transfer, he can't find housing." Housing discrimination, thus, kept many nonwhite workers in crumbling cities (whence few could afford to commute) while it kept many suburban neighborhoods and workforces lily-white. "Decentralization has played havoc with hundreds of communities across the country," Reuther asserted.[45]

But it was not decentralization alone that troubled observers like Reuther. It was also the underlying causes, one of which was automation. The subject of much study and debate in the 1950s, automation threatened to do to industry what mechanization was then doing to agriculture. Some observers thought that the United States was "stumbling blindly into the automation era." As the *Nation* magazine editorialized in 1958, "The working force is expansive, while the latter-day industrial technology is contractive of man-hours," yet "nobody looks ahead to the sixties and seventies except to envision ever-rising levels of prosperity." Automation was eliminating production line jobs at a troubling clip, and the overall composition of employment was shifting in favor of white-collar work—not the sort of work for which ex-farmers tended to be qualified. "No matter how skilled a farmer might have been as a farmer," the House Subcommittee on Unemployment and the Impact of Automation would soon confirm, "in most cases he became an unskilled city worker when he moved to town and either replaced an unskilled city worker or added to the accumulation of unskilled workers." The influx of ex-farmers due to mechanization and other such forces came just as the ranks of unskilled and low-skill workers were thinning due to automation.[46]

The flight of factories from cities derived in part from the fact that automation required an "uninterrupted flow of production," which older multistory plants could not facilitate. Wide-open floor plans for new single-story, automated plants required land areas far larger than anything available in city centers. Such expanses could only be found in the developing suburbs. Again, as Reuther pointed out, nonwhite workers were at a disadvantage:

> So the problem, as I see it, is that Negroes will be housed in the major urban centers, and if industry escapes those centers and goes out in the rural areas where there is no housing, and if they draw their workers from the areas where they are located and there are no Negroes living there, it means the Negroes are going to be excluded from employment in new factories, and it is not easy.

Displaced Mississippi farmers who migrated to Northern cities in the 1950s thus encountered not a "golden age" but, rather, the beginning of decades of economic restructuring.[47]

Clint Collier had grown up near the Dixon and Waldo communities in western Neshoba County. His father and mother, John and Lena, born just after Reconstruction, owned a small farm on the Carthage road that John had bought for $400 in the first decades of the twentieth century. After stints in the US Navy and in government work, Clint Collier arrived in Detroit in the mid-1950s by way of Washington, DC, and Cleveland, Ohio. Immediately upon reaching Detroit, he regretted leaving his government job. The auto industry had its benefits, but Black workers rarely had equal access to them. Moreover, since the industry was highly sensitive to shifting demand and other unpredictable factors, production came in spurts, and layoffs were common. "In the automobile industry, I fell out of that because they would work you six months and lay you off six months," Collier remembered. Automobile makers would "hire you back when they were going to sale and going to have a good sale." Because Black workers (and rural migrants more broadly) were generally newer employees, they did not have enough seniority to weather the hard times. As Collier recalled, "I didn't have much seniority and kept getting out, off and on." Discrimination made getting rehired harder for Black workers than whites, and especially for older Black workers. Collier attested that "my age was running up. See, I got afraid of my age . . . [and] they wanted youth, youth, youth, youth." So, in 1956, anticipating the reversal of the Great Migration by a decade or two, Collier returned to Mississippi to work as a teacher in Leake County.[48]

Arraner Stephens Spivey, a Black resident of Attala County born in 1908, remembered that while some outmigrants experienced success in the North and West, "it was bad for them to leave their homes." And, having lost their land in Mississippi, "not many, just a very few" who left in the post–World War II years ever returned: "very few will come back home." She could only remember one Attala native—a construction worker named Henry Kimbrough—who actually came back to Mississippi. Kimbrough and his wife had tried their luck in Chicago but eventually returned, as they still owned a home in Kosciusko. Eventually, they were able to build "a nice home on the Trace" (the Natchez Trace Parkway, near Kosciusko). But Spivey stressed that their story was not the norm.[49]

Among the thousands of other families that left east-central Mississippi during this period were some extraordinary musical talents. Otis Rush was born in 1935 and raised on a farm outside of Philadelphia. He moved to Chicago in 1949 to find work in the stockyards and soon found his voice as a renowned blues artist. In his popular 1959 single, "Double Trouble," he sang,

> It's hard to keep a job,
> laid off and having double trouble.
> But hey, yeah, they say you can make it if you try.
> Yes, some of this generation is millionaires,
> but it's hard for me to keep decent clothes to wear.

Born in 1933 and also raised on a Neshoba County farm, "Big Ike" Darby left in the 1950s, relocated to Mobile, Alabama, by way of New Orleans, Louisiana, and enjoyed regional fame as a rhythm and blues singer, artist manager, and record store owner. Charlie Musselwhite, a Kosciusko native, made it to Chicago by way of Memphis, Tennessee, and landed a recording deal with Vanguard Records. Musselwhite has since become a legend of blues harmonica. Artists such as Rush, Musselwhite, and

Darby—like their Delta counterparts Muddy Waters, B. B. King, and Little Milton, to name just a few—left behind a Mississippi that seemed to have no place for them.[50]

Much of the world was in motion in the 1950s. A wave of rural people flooded urban areas that would have little to offer them. The world-historical importance of that wave is difficult to overstate. As Eric Hobsbawm argued, the "most dramatic and far-reaching social change of the second half of this century, and the one which cuts us off for ever from the world of the past, is the death of the peasantry." He also pointed out that "when the land empties the cities fill up." In most settler societies, what Hobsbawm called the "peasantry" had actually been entangled in the capitalist economy to varying degrees since the late nineteenth or early twentieth centuries. But there is no denying that, by the end of the 1950s, a postwar agricultural revolution was driving most of them off the land for good. White elites, who benefited from that transition, entered 1960—which UN Under-Secretary-General Ralph Bunche optimistically dubbed the "Year of Africa"—having significantly undermined the bargaining positions of colonized peoples. Their communities, however, reaped the whirlwind.[51]

MISSISSIPPI'S 1960

5

> *The peoples of the world ardently desire the end of colonialism in all its manifestations.*
> —United Nations General Assembly, 1960

Settler states were models of defiance in 1960, a year otherwise known for the triumph of anticolonial nationalism. From Sharpeville to Jackson, white supremacists thumbed their noses at a world that increasingly viewed them as outcasts. In east-central Mississippi, political standpattism mixed with economic desperation. The unemployment crisis induced by the new enclosure movement now threatened the stability of local communities that had, since before World War II, sought unsuccessfully to "balance agriculture with industry." As the entire region suffered, nonwhite Mississippians lost their economic footing in ways that made it especially risky to press for political change. Agents of the US Commission on Civil Rights privately characterized political organizing among rural Black Mississippians as "hopeless" because of the certainty of economic reprisal. Choctaws faced a similarly desperate situation and were no closer to realizing their land claims. Ruling whites would soon appeal to the federal government for economic assistance, even as they refused to incorporate nonwhite workers into the labor market on an equal basis and mobilized every available resource to fight even the smallest threats to white supremacy.[1]

I

The indirect effects of mechanization and enclosure were difficult to ignore by 1960. Population shifts—whether to the county seat or to large cities—left rural communities abandoned, country churches shuttered, and schools consolidated. Some small towns and communities disappeared from the map entirely, as surely as had Choctaw towns like Tala and Kunshak Chito a century earlier. Struggling bus and passenger rail lines discontinued or scaled down service, leaving residents to rely almost exclusively on private automobiles. Patterns of consumption changed, as farmers increasingly bought food at supermarkets rather than raise it at home. As Kemper County home demonstration agent Bessie McCoy observed, "Families find it cheaper to buy their fryers than to grow them." And, of course, those who had been forced out of farming had little choice. Popular entertainment was also changing. The days of the rural juke joint were numbered, and semi-pro baseball, which had once penetrated even the most isolated areas of the Deep South, all but collapsed. The Cotton States League, a once-popular Class-C league with team names like "Planters," "Millers," and "Ginners," had folded for good in 1955, citing lack of attendance. Everywhere was change.[2]

Of even greater long-term significance was the collective effect that agricultural and lifestyle changes had on the natural environment. While waste and resource depletion had long attended settler societies, the new pattern of living that followed what Paul Conkin called the "revolution down on the farm" multiplied and routinized such problems. The deleterious effects of the sort of commercial farming that took hold after World War II are well-documented. Fossil-fuel dependence, carbon emissions, the destruction of biodiversity, and the use of large amounts of land to support concentrated animal feeding operations are among the factors that most concern contemporary scientists. These changes coincided with a new standard of living for farmers and non-farmers alike that included increased energy use and placed too little emphasis on resource conservation.[3]

Top of mind for Mississippians in 1960 were the more immediate, localized, and social effects of agricultural change and the ways in which local leaders responded. As observed, mechanization and enclosure set people in motion and disrupted local economies. For many who remained on the farm, capital requirements—both for farming and to satisfy the demands of a rising standard of living—shot through the roof. Neshoba County agent C. S. Norton's 1960 annual report highlighted problems with the local Balanced Farm and Home (BFH) Program, a facet of extension work that helped a select group of farmers methodically plan their farm operations and home improvement projects. The high cost of farm living was thinning the ranks of the program's white member families, whose "resources were too limited to afford them the income they had a right to expect." Norton explained that "in all cases they exhausted their source of borrowing before they could put in the enterprises necessary for a livable income. They had too little collateral to match what they needed to borrow."[4]

Mississippi's Black county agents were afforded far less training in administering BFH Programs. Neshoba County's L. W. Payne was unable to implement such a program for Black farmers until 1960, five years after the county's white extension personnel began theirs. By then, getting started was exceedingly difficult. "The Balanced Farm and Home Program in Neshoba County is not too good," Payne wrote of the Black program's first year. "It isnt [sic] what we would like for it to be." Whereas the county's white agents had assisted nearly eighty BFH families, Payne mentioned only four. Aside from further demonstrating the racial inequality imbedded in USDA agencies and programs, both 1960 reports inadvertently show the capacity of modern farming to disrupt rural communities. That a significant number of white BFH families—with whom Norton and his assistants worked directly for 101 days of the year, and on whom significant resources were expended—could not stay solvent is an especially damning indictment of the new model of farming that government agencies and farm organizations had spent fifteen years pushing.[5]

Yet, as farmers struggled to adapt to the new environment, agricultural leaders continued to peddle the same bankrupt advice. Paradoxically, they encouraged farmers to follow proper production-control measures (acreage allotments meant to boost prices) while stressing higher yields per acre, which threatened to negate the production controls. In February

1960, citing new federal legislation, Senator John Stennis cautioned Mississippi cotton farmers to protect their acreage allotments. Farmers were now required to plant or "release" at least 75 percent of their allotment in order to keep it. Releasing acreage meant signing it over at the county ASC office to be reassigned to other farmers. Farmers could choose to release their entire allotment and—as long as they agreed to plant one-tenth of it every third year—keep it. If a farmer failed to plant or release their allotment, they risked losing it, which in turn reduced the overall allotment for the county and state. "Everyone loses if cotton isn't planted on all available acres," declared M. S. Shaw, associate director of the Extension Service. "More cotton harvested means more money passing through local trade channels. If you are a farmer who grows something other than cotton, or a part-time farmer with a job in town, you'll probably get your share of increased local prosperity."[6]

After the campaign waged by Stennis and the Extension Service, Neshoba County led Mississippi in releasing acreage to the state ASC: 1,211 local farmers planted 8,526 of 15,900 allotted cotton acres, while 1,244 farmers released their acreage. Having helped lead the production-control effort, the Extension Service then did an about-face and, as county agent Norton explained, "emphasized higher yields of cotton through better land selection, use of good planting seed, a balanced fertilizer program, proper weed control, an efficient insect control program . . . and harvesting and handling methods for higher grade of cotton." And, of course, Norton continued to facilitate contacts between farmers and implement and chemical dealers. At the end of a season marred by drought, farmers realized an average of 0.7 bale per acre (6,000 bales from 8,526 acres), up from 0.63 bale per acre in 1959 (6,900 bales from 10,900 acres). Higher yields per acre—the result of greater capital investment—very nearly made up for the higher number of acres released, meaning that cotton farmers did not gross much more than the year before (and, quite possibly, netted less).[7]

Norton was not alone in dispensing what seems to have been counterproductive advice. Area agents provided innumerable ways for farmers to put themselves out of business by attempting to obsolesce the labor of others. Associate county agent Lex C. Mason of Newton County used his column space in the *Newton Record* to tout a new pre-emergent herbicide and spray kit, reminding farmers that "a lot of the work in cotton can be eliminated." He assured the skeptical that a "cotton farmer with a good allotment can pay for the spray rig in a couple of years." Later in the year, Mason profiled Edward Scoggin, "a good example of the dairy industrialist in Newton County." He wrote approvingly that Scoggin had purchased an all-new parlor with overhead feeding, a bulk tank, and a pipe line with an automatic washing device—a setup that "can be operated by one man very efficiently." In a county where unemployment (10 percent), underemployment, and declining population (14 percent since 1950) were directly related to mechanization and enclosure, the Extension Service encouraged beleaguered farmers to risk their solvency by purchasing equipment meant to reduce labor still further. In every scenario, someone lost; in some, everyone lost.[8]

Attala County agent J. F. Buchanan's assessment is worth quoting at length, as it is unusually frank and perfectly sums up the situation in which farmers there found themselves in 1960:

> Very few of the younger persons are coming back to the farm. Most of the older persons are gradually leaving the farm due to the fact that their children have gone to the cities to jobs in offices and factories in other sections of the state and nation. This group of older farmers cannot keep the pace of mechanization for many reasons. If they are to stay on the farm, they will have to mechanize most of their operations. At their age they do not want to go into debt to secure the necessary machinery that it takes these days to make a decent living farming. Therefore, they are faced with the closing down of the farm, selling out in most cases, and going to town. What is being done with those farms? . . . They are going to persons who have more money than they actually need, and they put the place in trees. In some cases I feel sure that a lot of these [farms] are being bought up by large corporations for growing timber.

Attala County's Black extension agent, James E. Williams, was equally forthright: "The year 1960 found most Negro farm families faced with the challenge of change in order to survive an economy that is rapidly changing, technologically and socially."[9]

Still, other agricultural leaders had little patience for naysaying. USDA bureaucrat Bert Newell dismissed complaints about modern farming as nostalgia. Newell's November editorial in *Agricultural Situation*, the monthly publication of the Agricultural Marketing Service, also bears quoting at length:

> I'm not moaning about all of these changes. I can do without the kind of romance that went with the good old days when we thawed the pump out with a kettle of boiling water and shocked wheat in the broiling sun. Mechanization has done tremendous things for the efficiency of farming, but, of course, it has created some problems, too. The cotton picker can harvest an awful lot of cotton in a day and save a lot of labor. Of course, it doesn't sing hymns as it picks, and it gathers a lot of trash along with the lint that old uncle Joe would have considered a disgrace to any good cotton picker. Now, this created a problem, and it took quite a piece of doing to improve the gin so that it would take out the trash. . . . So it goes. I wonder what the next 5 or 10 years will bring.
> . . . Won't somebody try to write a little poem puttin' some romance into "bedding down" the tractor and getting antifreeze in the radiator?

But Newell must have known that skepticism of capital-intensive farming was not totally rooted in a romantic view of the past, but, rather, in the frustrations of farmers who were being left behind.[10]

When the results of the 1959 farm census became available in the fall of 1960, agricultural leaders at every level had confirmation that their guiding philosophy was not only thinning the ranks of farmers but also sowing economic insecurity across entire regions. Moreover, they knowingly presided over the near elimination of Black landownership, as modern farming continued to disproportionately benefit well-heeled whites and sideline Black farmers altogether. And it should have been clear to anyone paying close attention that the purposeful destruction of tenancy was leading to the hyper-exploitation of seasonal wage workers. For instance, in July 1960, a Choctaw man named Riley Phillip told the Tribal Council that the white woman for whom he had been chopping cotton simply refused to pay him. Phillip had visited the woman on multiple occasions in unsuccessful attempts to get his money. The problem was ultimately left in the lap of superintendent Paul Vance, a white Mississippian who only kept his post at the Indian Agency because of his marriage to the niece of the influential Senator James Eastland. The outcome was never recorded, but the circumstances bespeak an increasingly desperate lot for the region's remaining nonwhite farmers.[11]

In sum, by 1960 nearly every aspect of life in east-central Mississippi reflected the disruptive effect of making farming—hitherto the region's primary industry—almost entirely the province of an elite handful of white men. The collapse of white and Black BFH farm families seemed to show how little viability depended on factors like effort and planning, and how much capital investment and social connections now mattered. The conflicted role of agricultural leaders, who stressed both production control measures and higher yields per acre through greater capital investment, suggested their lack of a clear objective beyond, perhaps, facilitating the growth of agribusiness. Expertise had clearly fallen out of alignment with the needs of local communities. Had the region enjoyed a more diverse economy, and had its leaders truly cared about poor and nonwhite farmers, the transition away from small, labor-intensive farming would have been less traumatic. But as local leaders spent the year unsuccessfully attempting to woo businesses south, desperation gripped east-central Mississippi.

II

On February 4, 1960, the Wells-Lamont glove factory in Philadelphia announced that for the first time in its history, it would have to stop production. The company blamed the two-week closure on the wider effects of the recently settled steel strike of 1959, the longest in history up to that point. It also cited lower sales of gloves due to uncharacteristically warm weather in the North over the last several months. The closure was scheduled to last from February 12 to 29, after which the work week would be cut from forty to thirty-two hours in many departments. "Throughout the 15 years of Wells-Lamont's operations in Philadelphia, the plant has shown steady growth and progress," the *Neshoba Democrat* reported, "and officials said this slack-off right now would in no way hamper the future expansion plans of the factory." Although the company and the newspaper attempted to downplay the seriousness of the moves, they did not bode well for the community. Competing for work at places like Wells-Lamont were ex-farmers, part-time farmers, and women whose families still farmed but needed another source of income to meet rising costs. The temporary closure and permanent cutbacks showed that even those fortunate enough to find such work faced the whims of markets and the unpredictable business cycle.[12]

Additionally, there had still been no serious moves to open up hiring in local industries to nonwhite applicants. For instance, around the time of the Wells-Lamont announcement, the board of supervisors set a bond issue election for the county's share of a proposed Hill-Burton hospital project. The Hill-Burton Act of 1946 had provided for federal aid in the construction and operation of hospitals for communities in need. Notwithstanding its bold mandate, in 1960 the act's provisions still permitted segregated service. So, when Neshoba County residents wrote the *Democrat* to ask about the new hospital's hiring policies—specifically whether Black caregivers would serve white patients—the answer reassured nervous whites. One letter of inquiry from an anonymous Neshoba resident read as follows: "Define an open staff hospital as to segregation. . . . Can a colored physician practice in an open staff Hill-Burton Hospital and can he admist [sic] patients as any other physician?" The editor admitted that, technically, Hill-Burton hospitals might employ qualified Black physicians. But, "the second part of the question can be answered by asking a question. Has that taken place in the present hospital, which is an open-staff institution?"[13]

Although staffing the new hospital would likely involve hiring a number of qualified outsiders, it was still the most promising development in an otherwise disappointing drive to bring more jobs to the area. On paper, east-central Mississippi was a promising destination for capital flight. Except in Meridian, the region had very few labor unions, and outside of the border town of Union, Neshoba County had none. Philadelphia's mayor, Clayton Lewis, and Chamber of Commerce industrial committee chairman Wilbur Franks Cole had recently logged 2,400 miles in an attempt to drum up contacts in various Midwestern industries, including two furniture manufacturers, a fabricator of metals, a small appliance manufacturer, and a wood fabricator. Cole's committee had also written countless letters to Midwestern furniture manufacturers in attempts to lure them south. Neither effort was particularly successful. Polite rejections were the most common response. "We could not possibly be interested in locating a plant in your area, for the reasons that I will not take up time to explain now," one furniture company wrote the chamber. "However, if we had such a plant in mind we certainly would be attracted by what you have to offer."[14]

The Choctaw Tribal Council also recognized the importance of attracting new industries, dependent as most Choctaws still were on disappearing forms of agricultural employment. The tribe attempted to work in tandem with the Chamber of Commerce to market the region and its Choctaw workforce. At its April 1960 meeting, the Tribal Council learned that a furniture manufacturer had expressed interest in locating nearby and using Choctaw labor. But with nothing concrete, and citing "a large amount of unemployment among the members of the MS Band of Choctaw Indians resulting in an average income below that of non-Indians of this section," the Tribal Council resolved to set aside $100,000 in tribal funds to attract industry. By the fall, with the mayor and the Chamber of Commerce offering land and resources to sweeten the deal, it seemed that the Chicago-based company Dresher Manufacturing might locate a plant in Philadelphia. Wages would be minimal, and nobody could be sure that the company would follow through on hiring Choctaws. Additionally, with superintendent Paul Vance inserting himself as the tribe's representative in some important meetings with Dresher, the Tribal Council was not always privy to negotiations. Nevertheless, the deal promised some relief from crippling unemployment.[15]

But only days after their regularly scheduled October meeting, the Tribal Council called a special meeting. Paul Vance had received notification that the Dresher deal had fallen through. The company's savings on labor and timber would not be enough to offset the cost of shipping from the Deep South to major markets. Moreover, being in the sixth month of a recession made Dresher think twice about risking an unsuccessful move. The tribe had little choice but to pursue other prospects that it had forsaken in order to woo Dresher. The outcome was unfortunate for the Choctaws, but it was also discouraging for the local government. Philadelphia had offered six acres near the railroad and was willing to assist in the blacktopping of roads and parking lots and the laying of additional water lines. Still, it had been unable to close the deal.[16]

The hunt for new industries in east-central Mississippi was all the more important because outmigration was becoming less rewarding. Nationwide trends that boded poorly for ex-farmers in the 1950s became the cause of much official concern in 1960. The US labor force was growing rapidly, yet proportionately fewer production-line and other low-skill workers were needed, which meant that workers with fewer skills had trouble finding jobs. As one analyst put it, the trouble was now not so much the *rate* as it was the *anatomy* of unemployment. As opposed to frictional unemployment (which was generally short-term and less worrisome), structural unemployment (which could reflect changes in technology and productivity) was cancerous. It could affect entire regions. As an area's dominant industry experienced decline or required fewer workers, the resulting decline in incomes hurt other industries like service and construction. Outmigration to escape such conditions made the area unattractive to new investment. In a sign of the times, the Labor Department adopted a new area classification in its monthly reports: "areas of substantial and persistent labor surplus."[17]

The industries in which structural unemployment was greatest were coal, textiles, and automobiles. In bituminous coal mining, increased competition from other fuel sources and rising production costs prompted large-scale mechanization after World War II. The result was increased output per man-hour and, predictably, mass displacement of mine workers. The textile industry, often cited as the first victim of deindustrialization, had been facing a long period of decline in the North, interrupted only briefly by World War II. Between 1945 and 1960, some 670 mills closed. And jobs in automobile manufacturing and related industries had been disappearing for much of the 1950s due to automation, decentralization, and relocation. The industrial North had, in short, become an unreliable pressure valve for Southern surplus labor. If east-central Mississippi wanted its people to have jobs, leaders would have to use the region's perceived strengths—principally cheap labor—to lure them south. But that process was arduous and time-consuming, and hope remained elusive.[18]

In December, the *Neshoba Democrat* editorialized that "just as surely as night follows day, efforts are being made each day to push us to the front in the very competitive field of finding new industries." But, the reporter lamented, promising talks too often gave way at the eleventh hour, and opportunity bypassed the region. "Whatever the reason for passing us by, the fact still remains that we must have 'industrial halitosis.'" Of course, as former-governor and "practical segregationist" J. P. Coleman had reminded Mississippians in his farewell address at the beginning of the year, rabid white reaction would almost certainly work at cross purposes with industrial development: "you cannot attract industry to a state which is in domestic turmoil." In that regard, Mississippians did not help their own case in 1960.[19]

III

If 1960 was the "Year of Africa" and, by extension, a time of optimism for people living under colonial rule, it also revealed the limits of decolonization. As James H. Meriwether argues, "The year swung between glorious heights and shocking depths." Settler states remained unmoved by moral suasion, and only in Algeria and Kenya, sites of brutal counterinsurgency operations, did white rule seem seriously threatened. Whites in South Africa (and South West Africa), Southern Rhodesia (then a part of the Central African Federation), Angola, and Mozambique clung to power and privilege as tightly as white US Southerners, although, as Jean Allman has pointed out, "they did so as pariahs." Indeed, Mississippi columnist Tom Ethridge complained that "settlers everywhere are being jeered as 'diehards and extremists.'"[20]

As world opinion turned against them, settlers showed their true colors. On March 21, South African police in the township of Sharpeville fired into a crowd peacefully protesting the country's pass laws. They killed sixty-nine protestors and wounded over two hundred, having shot many of them in the back. The ensuing outrage on the part of Black South Africans led the government to ban anti-apartheid political organizations, including the African National Congress and the new Pan-Africanist Congress. Forced underground, these organizations abandoned gradualist approaches and began to espouse armed resistance. Addressing a crowd in the Transvaal days after the massacre, Prime Minister Hendrik Verwoerd stubbornly dismissed external criticisms of the apartheid regime: "We don't intend to be perturbed about what is done and said in the outside world in all ignorance."[21]

The Sharpeville Massacre was celebrated by settlers across what Gerald Horne called the "White Atlantic." On April 12, the Mississippi House of Representatives voted 77–8 to commend South Africa's "firm segregation stand." The resolution cited "a definite parallel between events in that country and recent disorders in the southern states of the United States," praising South Africa's "steadfast policy for segregation and the staunch adherence to their traditions in the face of overwhelming external agitation." Also in the direct aftermath of Sharpeville, the official organ of the Citizens' Council began publishing articles written or sourced by white South African journalist John R. Parker. One such piece advertised a group called the Society of the Two Souths, a pen-pal service founded in the Transvaal to forge direct links between whites in South Africa and the US South. Such tangible connections were probably limited, but they demonstrate a shared sense of connection between two groups who saw themselves as similarly besieged.[22]

In Kenya, whites reacted to shifting political winds with characteristic paranoia. "I'm never without a gun at night," one Kenyan settler declared that summer after British divestment became inevitable. "One never knows what one will find waiting when one gets home. It's rather like carrying an umbrella in case of rain." Denouncing the "bloody wind of change," another settler, Jim Hughes, said that he would "start a revolution if I could get 1,000 gutsy blokes together," or, perhaps he would move to South Africa "and fight along side them there for the survival of the white race." Others saw the writing on the wall and quietly determined to move elsewhere. Bobs and Audrey Hopcraft told a reporter that they would be leaving because "with independence will come multi-racial schools," and their daughter simply "isn't going to one." In June, a group of settlers calling themselves the Pioneer Society met in Nairobi to discuss emigrating to South America, Honduras, Australia, or New Zealand after land in the White Highlands was made available to Africans (their take on what would become known as "white flight" in the United States). Such whites would not seriously consider the possibility of living among native people as equals. As one settler woman later remembered, "Of course, we couldn't stay on in Kenya after Mau Mau."[23]

Mississippi, though, like South Africa, was a place where whites seemed firmly in control, despite world opinion. On June 7, Ezekiel C. Smith of the US Commission on Civil Rights met with Medgar Evers in Jackson to get the names of individuals across the state who might be willing to share first-hand information on Black disfranchisement. In the first three years of its existence, the commission had done only limited work in the state, and in sixteen counties it had not yet made a single local contact. Evers, along with Mr. L. S. Alexander and Mrs. G. N. Bates, both of the Mississippi Teachers' Association, provided letters of introduction to Black citizens who would share their personal experiences with Smith. Such individuals knew that they were risking their lives by associating with the Commission on Civil Rights, a group to which reactionary whites were openly hostile. Nevertheless, in county after county, Smith found courageous informants whose testimony shed light on local conditions.[24]

In Kemper County, Smith met Elijah Tillis, a teacher whose work put him in touch with many Black farm families. "It is the feeling of Mr. Tillis," Smith wrote of their meeting, "that there is an overriding fear in the Colored people that if they tried to register to vote they would suffer either from economic reprisals or bodily harm." Tillis told Smith that most of Kemper County's Black farmers were sharecroppers who feared swift retaliation from their landlords for attempting to participate in the political process. Black residents who were not farmers—those most likely to assume leadership roles in the community—still feared that others they referred to as "Uncle Toms" would betray them to whites.[25]

Twenty miles north, in the Noxubee County town of Shuqualak, Smith spoke to John Bryant, a dry-cleaning presser and school janitor. Bryant had previously lived in cities like Washington, New York, and Chicago, where he had been a registered voter. But when he and his wife had moved south to Mississippi to take care of her ailing mother, Bryant had run into a wall of white repression. When he tried to talk to local Black residents about registering to vote, whites told Bryant to leave the county, physically threatened him, and, on at least one occasion, had him arrested. He reported facing constant surveillance by informants white and Black. Like Kemper County, Noxubee was a farming county where Black sharecroppers eschewed formal politics for fear of eviction and Black teachers and other community leaders largely avoided taking any risks that could jeopardize their employment.[26]

The report that Smith submitted to the commission on June 29 outlined a pattern of economic intimidation in county after county. "White land owners . . . have effectively 'Bottled Up' the Colored people in the predominantly farming areas," Smith wrote. "Economically the Colored people are almost entirely dependent upon the White people." In addition to the "economic squeezes" that kept most Black Mississippians out of politics, Smith cited the threat of violence and the failure to properly fund Black education as reasons for the "lack of dynamic, effective and intelligent leadership among the Colored people." There were, of course, capable individuals in every county, several of whom had bravely shared their stories with Smith. But white racism (and the reasonable suspicion that some in the Black community were spies for the State Sovereignty Commission) severely limited the degree to which they could organize for activism.[27]

Smith's report painted a picture of bigotry that might have seemed hyperbolic but for a conflagration in Neshoba and Newton Counties just weeks later. Local whites became incensed about a proposed new divinity school for Black students—Bay Ridge Christian College—to be established six miles north of Union in a predominantly white section of the county. The school's founder and president, the Reverend Horace Germany, and four other faculty, one of whom was Black, had drawn their ire for meeting on an integrated basis. Germany was originally from the area, although he had attended seminary in Anderson, Indiana, and held a pastorate in Muncie, Indiana, from 1948 to 1952. He told members of the Commission on Civil Rights that he had "studied to be a Missionary in Africa but decided he should do his missionary work among the poverty stricken Negroes of his home State of Mississippi." He returned to Union and bought properties adjoining his family's land until his holdings covered an expanse that had previously been farmed by fifteen separate families.[28]

Germany intended Bay Ridge Christian College to be a place where Black students could obtain both religious and vocational instruction, "so that they can go back among their people," the Commission on Civil Rights reported, "and help them improve their standard of living." He was not affiliated with any civil rights advocacy organizations, nor did he "preach integration," a fact that he had hoped would help him assuage the local White Citizens' Council, whose members he knew well. But after addressing a council meeting in 1959, he had received threats on his life, home, and cattle. Mississippi attorney general Joe Patterson refused to intervene or offer protection, and the atmosphere was so hostile that Ward Bonnell and Robert Amidon of the Commission on Civil Rights had to tell locals that they were traveling salesmen "selling school fixtures and supplies" in order to obtain directions to Germany's farm to conduct their interview. Unfortunately, one of the filling stations where they stopped was operated by O. C. McNair, a member of the Citizens' Council. While McNair gave the men directions, he made it clear that Germany would not be allowed to run a "nigger school" in the area.[29]

Neither the warnings of hostile whites nor the presence of State Sovereignty Commission investigator A. L. Hopkins—tasked with collecting the tag numbers of Germany's visitors and intercepting his book orders—seemed to dissuade the minister. Nor did Governor Ross Barnett's refusal to accept the college's charter fee. So, on August 13, a crowd of two hundred whites told the faculty to disband the college and get rid of its "out-of-state colored people." Five days later, a few "drunks" attacked Germany as he was getting into his car in Union. Two days after that, just across the county line in Newton County, a thousand whites assembled in protest around New Ireland Baptist Church to approve a resolution accusing Germany and his faculty of seeking "nothing but personal monetary gain and to precipitate, aggravate, and contribute ill will and hatred between the colored and white races of this community." The Bay Ridge Christian College had, apparently, disrupted the "peaceful coexistence of white and colored people in this community, who in the past have had harmonious relations." Presiding over the mass meeting, the pastor of New Ireland, the Reverend J. P. Bush, was joined atop a flatbed trailer by a beleaguered Germany and a small coterie of area ministers who opposed the college. Among them was a young Primitive Baptist preacher named Edgar Ray Killen, who would later gain notoriety for his role in the 1964 murder of three civil rights workers.[30]

Incredibly, that massive show of disapproval was not enough to scare Germany away. The final straw came on Friday, August 26. While Germany was loading bricks into a truck in Union, a mob of whites, angry over his steadfast refusal to disband the college, severely beat him. Germany recalled that the group had included some familiar faces, including Citizens' Council members, and that constable W. T. Reeves had appeared at the scene only to be sent away by the mob's leader. (Reeves later denied knowledge of the incident, as did the man that Germany fingered as the leader, and local reporters placed "beating" in quotes in their accounts.) Recovering in an undisclosed hospital in Meridian, Germany sent word to news outlets that he would finally be abandoning the project, as local whites had made it impossible to continue. The campaign to expel the Bay Ridge Christian College demonstrated the veracity of Ezekiel Smith's grim assessment of the state in 1960. The prospect of a few dozen Black students migrating to the area and attending classes in a heavily white section of Neshoba County had been enough to mobilize the State Sovereignty Commission, the White Citizens' Council, and a thousand or more ordinary residents. In retrospect, it appears as a dress rehearsal for the more deadly response to Freedom Summer four years later.[31]

As the battle over the Bay Ridge Christian College had been heating up, the Mississippi Band of Choctaw Indians received the latest in a string of bad news about their land claim. Realizing in January 1959 that its case had been dismissed years earlier, the Tribal Council had searched for an attorney who still thought that it had a chance. (The council's only hope at this point was an act of Congress.) A sympathetic out-of-state attorney named Sydney C. Reagan agreed to take them on, but, per their constitution, the tribe's choice of counsel had to meet the approval of the Secretary of the Interior. Reagan hoped to put the matter before the 86th Congress, but the extended approval process took up precious time, and, on June 2, 1960, he wrote Chairman Emmett York to withdraw his offer to represent them. On October 11, two days before the Dresher Manufacturing deal fell through, the tribe learned that normally sympathetic Representative Arthur Winstead did not think that the claim had a chance in Congress. Finally, when the Tribal Council gathered again on December 29 for its last meeting of the year, its members learned that Deputy Commissioner of Indian Affairs Rex Lee had encouraged them to put the matter to rest. At this point, Lee had telegraphed, "no further recourse of the tribe seems possible."[32]

East-central Mississippi's toughest challenges—enclosure, "industrial halitosis," and white-supremacist extremism—came to a head in 1960. Those issues were, of course, intimately linked—solving one meant to some degree addressing all three. But farm leaders continued to chart a contradictory course, while local boosters attempted to attract industry and investment without disturbing a time-honored social order built on racism and colonialism. The set of well-heeled white men that moved between the White Citizens' Council, the Farm Bureau, and state and local agricultural committees found their interests served by the direction of change since 1945, but others were not as fortunate. Every county in east-central Mississippi made the list of distressed rural areas to be included in proposed redevelopment legislation that would ultimately pass during the Kennedy administration. The distress was, of course, disproportionately felt in the region's Black and Choctaw communities—a stubborn fact of the settler-colonial status quo that would bedevil the civil rights activists of the 1960s.[33]

CONCLUSION

> There is nothing in the evidence offered by the book of the American republic which allows me really to argue with the cat who says to me: "They needed us to pick the cotton and now they don't need us anymore. Now they don't need us, they're going to kill us all off. Just like they did the Indians." And I can't say it's a Christian nation, that your brothers will never do that to you, because the record is too long and too bloody. That's all we have done. All your buried corpses now begin to speak.
> —James Baldwin, 1965

On September 20, 1967, Kemper County agricultural leaders publicly counted the ballots cast by white and Black farmers in the recent ASC election. Three winners in each community would serve as delegates to a county convention that would select the county's ASC committee, which assigned acreage allotments and government supports. Before the mid-1960s, these elections had favored landed and formally educated farmers, and they were whites-only affairs. But civil rights groups like the Student Nonviolent Coordinating Committee (SNCC) and the Congress of Racial Equality (CORE) recognized their importance and helped Black farmers get on the ballot and get their votes counted. One of those community-level contests would have involved the land discussed in this book's opening section, where, more than a century earlier, enslaved people had encountered the charred ruins of Choctaw homes (a scene that encapsulates the imbrication of land and labor exploitation at the heart of our story). In that and every other community election in Kemper County, the Black farmers that ran lost. Some blamed bad luck—others, white intimidation. One landowner apparently forced four of his tenants to mark their ballots while he watched to ensure that they did not select a Black candidate. At any rate, integrated elections notwithstanding, whites retained control over who remained on the land.[1]

To be sure, a lot had happened in seven years. Black Mississippians had mounted an irresistible challenge to the racial status quo. President Lyndon Johnson had signed the Civil Rights Act (1964) and the Voting Rights Act (1965) into law, seemingly dealing a deathblow to Jim Crow. Yet dispossession remained a central feature of Southern life, as it had been for over a century. The Black farmers voting in Kemper County's 1967 ASC election were the lucky few still on the land; the majority were small landowners. But in under a decade, more than half of them would be gone. Tenants and sharecroppers disappeared even faster, thrown away by landlords who no longer needed them. As journalist Robert Sherrill observed of the rural South in the 1960s, "The same people who were considered 'good ol' darkies' a few years ago are now considered deadwood, hardly worth keeping alive." One landowner he interviewed called field hands "as useless as a mule." In one sense, such social disintegration represented change—the transition from an economy that used and abused people to one that simply abandoned them. Yet it is not hard to see how the disposal of human beings had always been at the center of the settler-colonial project, wherever it happened to unfold. The enclosure movement of the mid-twentieth century was, in that sense, simply a new chapter in a very old story, of which Mississippi was as much a part as settler states elsewhere.[2]

Without arresting the ongoing colonization discussed in this book, redevelopment, civil rights reforms, and antipoverty programs in the 1960s could have only mixed results, depending largely on white Mississippians' ability to undermine their intended purpose. In May 1961, President John F. Kennedy signed into law the Area Redevelopment Act, meant to aid depressed regions like the rural South. As historian Gregory S. Wilson has explained, the Area Redevelopment Administration (ARA) was intended to provide a domestic version of the sort of redevelopment aid that the US government was then extending to foreign countries to promote what it called "modernization." While the vision, scope, and funding of the ARA were somewhat limited, the program's creation prompted a slew of aid applications from distressed Mississippi counties to the state's Agricultural and Industrial Board. Applications came in the form of documents called overall economic development programs (OEDPs), which explained a county's history, problems, needed adjustments, and goals. Each county in east-central Mississippi submitted an OEDP that emphasized the adverse effects of rural change, including unemployment, underemployment, and outmigration.[3]

On August 21, 1962, the Neshoba Rural Area Development Association submitted its OEDP. Under "Problems and Needed Adjustments," it reported that farm income had decreased since 1940, as had the number of farmers. Yet there was not enough non-farm employment to fully absorb the labor surplus. Later that year, the Newton County OEDP reported that "one of the greatest causes of [underemployment] is the decreasing need for labor on the farm. With modern equipment being used on the farms, one man can do the job that in previous years required ten." Moreover, small farmers "cannot compete with the larger farmer with the high cost of machinery." And "underemployment is exceptionally high in the non-white races." Kemper County reported that "many farm workers have been made idle by crop reduction programs, by mechanization and by conversion to grassland farming," and that the "need for industrial development . . . is more acute now than it has ever been." Describing a similar situation, Leake County also reported that industrial development "is an acute problem" and that "sufficient employment opportunities have not been available in the past to hold the County residents."[4]

On the surface, white Mississippians' appeals for federal intervention in their local economies seem inconsistent with their insistence on states' rights and home rule. But the gatekeepers of redevelopment aid at the state and local levels were generally the same people who had always called the shots. For instance, the month after the creation of the ARA, none other than the Extension Service announced that it was "ready to help Mississippians increase and improve employment opportunities in rural areas through aid offered by the Area Redevelopment Act." Federal intervention would not, then, threaten the status quo because aid would flow through white elites to struggling whites, not people of color. There can be little doubt that while white Mississippians were not of one mind about federal aid (after all, Representative Arthur Winstead voted against the Area Redevelopment Act), they believed that they could use it to further their own objectives. Indeed, writing from Jackson in 1963, SNCC field secretary Joan Bowman reported that Black workers were "*as a matter of course and by design* discriminated against in all of the state's institutions . . . even in the federal programs of area redevelopment and job retraining." William L. Taylor of the Commission on Civil Rights reported that an ARA program to train tractor drivers was scuttled at the local level for fear that trainees would attend integrated classes. It is, then, no wonder that the Southern Regional Council saw "little cause for optimism regarding rapid change in the status of Negroes in the near future."[5]

The student activists that descended on Mississippi en masse in the Freedom Summer voter registration campaign of 1964 encountered a society already torn by the race and class tensions of enclosure. When white terrorists burned down Mt. Zion Church in the Longdale section of Neshoba County, one of a few remaining bastions of Black landownership in the area, Michael Schwerner and two other civil rights workers, James Chaney and Andrew Goodman, drove up from Meridian to investigate. (Back in Meridian, where a New Jersey industrialist was visiting, the Chamber of Commerce urged local newsmen not to cover the church burning for fear that negative publicity would scare away investment.) The June 21 murder of Chaney, Goodman, and Schwerner moved Neshoba County, as a *New York Times* reporter put it, "from obscurity to notoriety." Soon, a Choctaw man found the activists' burned-out station wagon in the Bogue Chitto swamp. Months later, investigators found their bodies in a dam that local landowner Olen Burrage was building to contain a stock pond. In the meantime, their martyrdom had helped force the passage of long-awaited civil rights legislation.[6]

But neither the Civil Rights Act nor the Voting Rights Act could work miracles. As researchers from the Bureau of Labor Statistics concluded in 1966, "The changes taking place in American institutions could bring about the most important condition of all—that of equality among Americans of varying color, origin, or creed," but, they warned, "the measures taken and the changes they have made so far are not nearly enough." The evidence that civil and voting rights were not enough was clear in east-central Mississippi. The OEDP for the Mississippi Band of Choctaw Indians, submitted in 1966, reported that "no openings have existed for Choctaws who have been driven out of farming. Most of these forced out were thus driven onto welfare rolls." In 1967 the Neshoba County ASC and FHA committees were still lily-white, although other counties in the area had begun allowing a single (token, and functionally powerless) Black FHA committeeman. And while some nonwhite residents now found work at local factories, they were the exception. Charles Henson, a Black worker at US Motor, lamented that probably eighteen of seven hundred employees at his plant were Black in 1967. Only five were Choctaw.

Without steady nonagricultural employment, plenty of families' living conditions actually worsened in the years after the civil rights movement. A team of physicians that toured six Mississippi counties including Neshoba in May 1967 reported encountering "children whose nutritional and medical condition we can only describe as shocking." These were the families of "able-bodied" (though unemployed) fathers deemed ineligible for welfare. "Welfare and food programs," the physicians wrote in disgust, "are in the hands of people who use them selectively, politically, and with obvious racial considerations in mind."[7]

A decade later, the picture had changed, but only slightly. The Mississippi Advisory Committee of the Commission on Civil Rights, which now included Choctaw chief Calvin Isaac, underscored the persistence of grinding poverty felt disproportionately (though by no means exclusively) by nonwhite Mississippians: "Economic change appears to lag far behind the cosmetic change in social attitudes." Industry had still not absorbed the bulk of displaced farmers. Discrimination in hiring still plagued the state and local governments; upper- and mid-level public-sector workers were still overwhelmingly white and male. Moreover, the threat of federal government reprisal for noncompliance with civil rights laws had diminished since the 1960s. "Although Federal court rulings, Federal troops, Federal civil rights laws, and Federal dollars have been critical factors in altering attitudes and behavior in this State," the committee members wrote, "meaningful change is as difficult to see as the progress of a glacier that advances at the rate of inches each millennium." Clint Collier, a Black Neshoba County resident and the son of farmers, reckoned that redistribution of wealth was probably the only solution, but "when you start talking about that you become communist then . . . and you are in trouble."[8]

Nor had USDA agencies meaningfully cleaned up their act. The Commission on Civil Rights revisited the issue of discrimination in USDA farm programs in a 1982 report titled *The Decline of Black Farming in America*. In it, they confirmed that their 1965 report, *Equal Opportunity in Farm Programs*, had been ignored, leaving Black farmers "disproportionately vulnerable to seemingly neutral gross economic and agricultural trends and policies." A shocking 94 percent of the nation's Black-owned farms had been lost since 1920. While class action lawsuits have, in recent years, addressed discrimination complaints from the 1980s to the 2000s, no remedy appears forthcoming for earlier land loss and displacement. Nor does antidiscrimination doctrine truly get to the core of the problem of ongoing colonization, as Alyosha Goldstein observes. Antidiscrimination jurisprudence, Goldstein argues, "remains incapable of addressing the mutability and multidimensionality of white supremacy and other normative social hierarchies that are underwritten by . . . economies of dispossession." Maldistribution of land—achieved through dispossession and displacement and normalized as progress—cuts across settler societies and mocks liberal reformism. And it will likely continue to do so as long as Americans insist that they have a race problem, not a colonization problem, failing to see that the former connotes the latter.[9]

Although the Mississippi Choctaws were unsuccessful in their postwar pursuit of treaty claims, they experienced a remarkable resurgence in the last quarter of the twentieth century. Against long odds, using the Economic Opportunity Act of 1964 and its Community Action Program, the Choctaws mounted an economic comeback of sorts. The so-called Choctaw Miracle, which truly took off in the 1980s and 1990s, brought new plants and, eventually, resort hotels, casinos, and golf courses to the reservation, meaning new jobs for the area. The tribe is now among the state's largest private employers. As Daniel Cobb points out, their ability to use federal antipoverty initiatives to effect tribal renaissance depended on circumventing local institutions entirely. Aid flowing directly to the Choctaws enabled them in part to overcome the legacy of land loss.[10]

But with the exception of the Choctaw Miracle, Mississippi remains very much in the mold of the not-quite-post-colonial settler state. It is not alone. The white supremacist regimes in southern Africa collapsed between the 1970s and the 1990s, but in Zimbabwe and South Africa, as in Mississippi, land justice has yet to arrive. While those African countries have experimented to varying degrees with expropriation without compensation, glaring inequality persists. Fortunately, critiques of the structures that sustain such inequality are growing louder and more persuasive. And thinking comparatively about settler societies and the ways in which they operate can lead to the encouraging conclusion that, as Brenna Bhandar writes, "The repertoire of legal techniques used to appropriate land and the philosophical rationales underlying them are not, necessarily, infinite in number," meaning that, hopefully, "racial regimes of ownership ... *can be dismantled.*" But if the past is any guide, structural change will not come easily.[11]

NOTES

INTRODUCTION

1. Source Material for Kemper County, 11–12, WPA Files online. A portion of the original source material contains spellings that reflect the compiler's version of their subject's dialect. In the text, I have rendered it in standard English. In the source, it reads "dem Indians mouning fur dey homes."

2. Jean M. O'Brien, "Tracing Settler Colonialism's Eliminatory Logic in *Traces of History*," *American Quarterly* 69, no. 2 (June 2017): 250; Hagar Kotef, *The Colonizing Self: Or, Home and Homelessness in Israel/Palestine* (Durham, NC: Duke University Press, 2020); Federal Writers' Project, *Mississippi: The WPA Guide to the Magnolia State* (Jackson: University Press of Mississippi, 2009). For the effects of agricultural modernization on Southern society, see Gilbert C. Fite, *Cotton Fields No More: Southern Agriculture, 1865–1980* (Lexington: University Press of Kentucky, 1984); Pete Daniel, *Breaking the Land: The Transformation of Cotton, Tobacco, and Rice Cultures since 1880* (Urbana: University of Illinois Press, 1985); Jack Temple Kirby, *Rural Worlds Lost: The American South, 1920–1960* (Baton Rouge: Louisiana State University Press, 1987); Donald Holley, *The Second Great Emancipation: The Mechanical Cotton Picker, Black Migration, and How They Shaped the Modern South* (Fayetteville: University of Arkansas Press, 2000); Paul K. Conkin, *A Revolution Down on the Farm: The Transformation of American Agriculture since 1929* (Lexington: University Press of Kentucky, 2008); D. Clayton Brown, *King Cotton in Modern America: A Cultural, Political, and Economic History since 1945* (Jackson: University Press of Mississippi, 2011); and Adrienne Monteith Petty, *Standing Their Ground: Small Farmers in North Carolina since the Civil War* (New York: Oxford University Press, 2013). On the "generalization" of the tools of empire, see Walter Johnson, *The Broken Heart of America: St. Louis and the Violent History of the United States* (New York: Basic Books, 2020), 8.

3. Pete Daniel, "African American Farmers and Civil Rights," *Journal of Southern History* 73, no. 1 (February 2007): 3–38; N. B. Mitchell to James O. Eastland, January 2, 1949, Folder 3, Box 33, Issue Correspondence, Constituent Files, James O. Eastland Collection, University of Mississippi, Oxford, MS; Nicholas Lemann, *The Promised Land: The Great Black Migration and How It Changed America* (New York: Knopf, 1991), 49–50. See also James C. Cobb, *The Most Southern Place on Earth: The Mississippi Delta and the Roots of Regional Identity* (New York: Oxford University Press, 1992), 204–208.

4. Numan V. Bartley, "The Southern Enclosure Movement," *Georgia Historical Quarterly* 71, no. 3 (Fall 1987): 438–450; Margaret D. Jacobs, "Seeing Like a Settler

Colonial State," *Modern American History* 1, no. 2 (July 2018): 258. A rare exception, Adrienne Monteith Petty includes Native Americans in her examination of small farmers in North Carolina. See *Standing Their Ground*.

5. See Patrick Wolfe, *Settler Colonialism and the Transformation of Anthropology: The Politics and Poetics of an Ethnographic Event* (New York: Cassell, 1999); "Settler Colonialism and the Elimination of the Native," *Journal of Genocide Research* 8, no. 4 (December 2006): 387–409; and *Traces of History: Elementary Structures of Race* (Brooklyn: Verso, 2016). For incisive (yet genuflective) critiques of Wolfe, see Robin D. G. Kelley, "The Rest of Us: Rethinking Settler and Native," *American Quarterly* 69, no. 2 (June 2017): 267–276; O'Brien, "Tracing Settler Colonialism's Eliminatory Logic"; and Stephanie E. Smallwood, "Reflections on Settler Colonialism, the Hemispheric Americas, and Chattel Slavery," *William and Mary Quarterly* 76, no. 3 (July 2019): 407–416.

6. Wolfe, *Traces of History*, 34; Jacobs, "Seeing Like a Settler Colonial State"; Theda Perdue, "The Legacy of Indian Removal," *Journal of Southern History* 78, no. 1 (February 2012): 3–36; Angela Pulley Hudson and Hatty Ruth Miller, "Unsettling Histories of the South," *Southern Cultures* 25, no. 3 (Fall 2019): 30–45; Andrew K. Frank and Kristofer Ray, "Indians as Southerners; Southerners as Indians: Rethinking the History of a Region," *Native South* 10 (2017): vii. See also James Taylor Carson, "'The Obituary of Nations': Ethnic Cleansing, Memory, and the Origins of the Old South," *Southern Cultures* 14, no. 4 (Winter 2008): 6–31. Malinda Maynor Lowery laments the "process of writing [Indians'] existence out of the popular story of the South, which has come to be dominated by the stories of black and white southerners and the twin pillars of the Civil War and civil rights," in Malinda Maynor Lowry, "The Original Southerners: American Indians, the Civil War, and Confederate Memory," *Southern Cultures* 25, no. 4 (Winter 2019): 19. See also Jodi Byrd, *The Transit of Empire: Indigenous Critiques of Colonialism* (Minneapolis: University of Minnesota Press, 2011); and Gina Caison, *Red States: Indigeneity, Settler Colonialism, and Southern Studies* (Athens: University of Georgia Press, 2018).

7. Gerald Horne, *From the Barrel of a Gun: The United States and the War against Zimbabwe, 1965–1980* (Chapel Hill: University of North Carolina Press, 2001); James C. Cobb, *Redefining Southern Culture: Mind and Identity in the Modern South* (Athens: University of Georgia Press, 1999), 211. For an excellent survey of the literature on the South in the world, see Tore C. Olsson, "The South in the World since 1865: A Review Essay," *Journal of Southern History* 87, no. 1 (February 2021): 67–108. My understanding of this rich topic owes especially to George Padmore, *The Life and Struggles of Negro Toilers* (London: Red International of Labor Unions Magazine for the International Trade Union Committee of Negro Workers, 1931); C. L. R. James, *A History of Pan-African Revolution* (Oakland, CA: PM Press, 2012); Raymond Arse-

nault, "White on Chrome: Southern Congressmen and Rhodesia, 1962–1971," *Issue* 2, no. 4 (Winter 1972): 46–57; George M. Frederickson, *White Supremacy: A Comparative Study in American and South African History* (New York: Oxford University Press, 1981); John W. Cell, *The Highest Stage of White Supremacy: The Origins of Segregation in South Africa and the American South* (New York: Cambridge University Press, 1982); Horne, *From the Barrel of a Gun*; Chris Myers Asch, *The Senator and the Sharecropper: The Freedom Struggles of James O. Eastland and Fannie Lou Hamer* (Chapel Hill: University of North Carolina Press, 2008), 253–278; Andrew Zimmerman, *Alabama in Africa: Booker T. Washington, the German Empire, and the Globalization of the New South* (Princeton, NJ: Princeton University Press, 2010); Daniel Geary and Jennifer Sutton, "Resisting the Wind of Change: The Citizens' Councils and European Decolonization," in *The U.S. South and Europe: Transatlantic Relations in the Nineteenth and Twentieth Centuries*, ed. Cornelis A. Van Minnen and Manfred Berg (Lexington: University Press of Kentucky, 2013), 265–282; Elizabeth Gillespie McRae, *Mothers of Massive Resistance: White Women and the Politics of White Supremacy* (New York: Oxford University Press, 2018), 185–216; and Elizabeth A. Herbin-Triant, *Threatening Property: Race, Class, and Campaigns to Legislate Jim Crow Neighborhoods* (New York: Columbia University Press, 2019). On transnational networks of activism, see especially Carol Anderson, *Eyes off the Prize: The United Nations and the African American Struggle for Human Rights* (New York: Cambridge University Press, 2003), and *Bourgeois Radicals: The NAACP and the Struggle for Colonial Liberation* (New York: Cambridge University Press, 2014); John Munro, *The Anticolonial Front: The African American Freedom Struggle and Global Decolonisation* (New York: Cambridge University Press, 2017); and Nicholas Grant, *Winning Our Freedoms Together: African Americans and Apartheid, 1945–1960* (Chapel Hill: University of North Carolina Press, 2017). On land reform, see Vann R. Newkirk II, "The Great Land Robbery," *Atlantic*, September 2019, available online at https://www.theatlantic.com/magazine/archive/2019/09/this-land-was-our-land/594742/; Mahmood Mamdani, "Why South Africa Can't Avoid Land Reforms," *New York Times*, June 17, 2019, https://www.nytimes.com/2019/06/17/opinion/south-africa-land-reform.html (accessed July 1, 2021).

8. For a description of the farm landscape of east-central Mississippi before World War II, see Federal Writers' Project, *Mississippi: The WPA Guide to the Magnolia State* (Jackson: University Press of Mississippi, 2009), 304–308, 464–469. On the capitalist transition in the countryside, and especially the descent into the "vortex of the cotton economy," see Steven Hahn, *The Roots of Southern Populism: Yeoman Farmers and the Transformation of the Georgia Upcountry, 1850–1890* (New York: Oxford University Press, 1983).

9. Cobb, *The Most Southern Place on Earth*; Clyde Woods, *Development Arrested: The*

Blues and Plantation Power in the Mississippi Delta (Brooklyn, NY: Verso 1998); Nan Elizabeth Woodruff, *American Congo: The African American Freedom Struggle in the Delta* (Cambridge, MA: Harvard University Press, 2003); Asch, *The Senator and the Sharecropper*; Jodi Byrd, "Variations under Domestication: Indigeneity and the Subject of Dispossession," *Social Text* 135, vol. 36, no. 2 (June 2018): 128–129.

10. Wolfe, *Traces of History*, 10–18, 82. For Choctaws' engagement with Mississippi's Jim Crow–era racial politics, see Katherine M. B. Osburn, "Mississippi Choctaws and Racial Politics," *Southern Cultures* 14, no. 4 (Winter 2008): 32–54; and Theda Perdue, "Southern Indians and Jim Crow," in *The Folly of Jim Crow: Rethinking the Segregated South*, ed. Stephanie Cole and Natalie J. Ring (College Station: Texas A&M University Press, 2012), 54–90.

11. Tribal Council Minutes, July 10, 1951. Black activists' almost exclusive focus on civil and voting rights began to change when student-activists ran local Black farmers in Agricultural Stabilization and Conservation Service (ASC or ASCS) elections, which decided who sat on the committees where money and acreage allotments were disbursed. But those campaigns were mostly unsuccessful and, in any case, too late to make a serious impact. For a discussion of Choctaws' avoidance of Black Mississippians, see Katherine M. B. Osburn, *Choctaw Resurgence in Mississippi: Race, Class, and Nation Building in the Jim Crow South, 1830–1977* (Lincoln: University of Nebraska Press, 2014), 20–21, 28–29.

12. For the relatively short career of the concept of decolonization, see Todd Shepard, *The Invention of Decolonization: The Algerian War and the Remaking of France* (Ithaca, NY: Cornell University Press, 2006), 3–10; and James D. Le Sueur, ed., *The Decolonization Reader* (New York: Routledge, 2003), 1–6.

13. On the USDA's role in ongoing settler colonialism, see Alyosha Goldstein, "The Ground Not Given: Colonial Dispositions of Land, Race, and Hunger," *Social Text* 135, vol. 36, no. 2 (June 2018): 83–106.

CHAPTER 1: LAND, LABOR, AND RACE IN THE PREWAR YEARS

1. "Keep the Labor," *Mississippi Union Advocate*, October 20, 1909, 8; James Belich, *Replenishing the Earth: The Settler Revolution and the Rise of the Angloworld* (New York: Oxford University Press, 2009), 21. On the importance of the labor question in the late-nineteenth-century world, see Amy Dru Stanley, *From Bondage to Contract: Wage Labor, Marriage, and the Market in the Age of Slave Emancipation* (New York: Cambridge University Press, 1998), 60–97.

2. C. A. Bayly, *The Birth of the Modern World* (Oxford: Blackwell, 2004), 439–444; Eric Foner, *Nothing but Freedom: Emancipation and Its Legacy* (Baton Rouge: Louisiana State University Press, 2007), 30–38. On southern Africa, see Alois S. Mlambo, A

History of Zimbabwe (New York: Cambridge University Press, 2014), 54–61; Sabelo J. Ndlovu-Gatsheni, "Mapping Cultural and Colonial Encounters, 1880s–1930s," in *Becoming Zimbabwe: A History from the Pre-colonial Period to 2008*, ed. Brian Raftapoulos and A. S. Mlambo (Harare: Weaver Press, 2009), 64–65; Charles van Onselen, *Chibaro: African Mine Labour in Southern Rhodesia, 1900–1933* (Johannesburg: Ravan Press, 1980), 74–127; David Johnson, "Settler Farmers and Coerced African Labour in Southern Rhodesia, 1936–46," *Journal of African History* 33, no. 1 (1992), 111–128; Robin Palmer, "The Agricultural History of Rhodesia," in *The Roots of Rural Poverty in Central and Southern Africa*, ed. Robin Palmer and Neil Parsons (London: Heinemann, 1977), 221–254. On eastern Africa, see Lord Hailey, *Native Administration in the British African Territories: Part I. East Africa: Uganda, Kenya, Tanganyika* (London: His Majesty's Stationary Office, 1950), 198–201. For African autonomy despite the settler onslaught, see Charles van Onselen, *The Seed Is Mine: The Life of Kas Maine, a South African Sharecropper, 1894–1985* (New York: Hill & Wang, 1997).

3. Katherine M. B. Osburn, *Choctaw Resurgence in Mississippi: Race, Class, and Nation Building in the Jim Crow South, 1830–1977* (Lincoln: University of Nebraska Press, 2014), 12–13; Claudio Saunt, *Unworthy Republic: The Dispossession of Native Americans and the Road to Indian Territory* (New York: Norton, 2020), 204–208; US Congress, House of Representatives, Committee on Indian Affairs, "Land Claims, &c. Under 14th Article Choctaw Treaty," May 11, 1836, 24th Cong., 1st Sess., 44, 51; Baxter York, interview with staff of Nanih Waiya, transcript, Noxapater, MS, April 8, 1974, Southern Indian Oral History Project, University of Florida.

4. US Department of Commerce, Bureau of the Census, *State of Mississippi, 1860*, available online at https://www2.census.gov/library/publications/decennial/1860/population/1860a-22.pdf; Map Showing the Distribution of the Slave Population of the Southern States of the United States, Compiled from the Census of 1860 (Washington: Henry S. Graham, 1861), available online at https://www.loc.gov/resource/g3861e.cw0013200/?r=-0.154,0.286,1.107,0.428,0. For the east-west transfer of enslaved people during the cotton boom of the nineteenth century, see Adam Rothman, *Slave Country: American Expansion and the Origins of the Deep South* (Cambridge, MA: Harvard University Press, 2005); Ira Berlin, *The Making of African America: The Four Great Migrations* (New York: Viking, 2010); Walter Johnson, *River of Dark Dreams: Slavery and Empire in the Cotton Kingdom* (Cambridge, MA: Belknap Press of Harvard University Press, 2013); and Edward E. Baptist, *The Half Has Never Been Told: Slavery and the Making of American Capitalism* (New York: Basic Books, 2014). Patrick Wolfe and Lorenzo Veracini are the theorists most associated with the rather rigid formulation of settler colonialism. Patrick Wolfe points out that "in principle, it is not good policy to incur reliance on a population that one is simultaneously seeking to eliminate, nor to promote the survival of the bearers of sovereignties that exceed

the settler import." Wolfe, *Traces of History: Elementary Structures of Race* (Brooklyn: Verso, 2016), 25. For excellent critiques of Wolfe, see Jean M. O'Brien, "Tracing Settler Colonialism's Eliminatory Logic in *Traces of History*," *American Quarterly* 69, no. 2 (June 2017): 249–255; and Robin D. G. Kelley, "The Rest of Us: Rethinking Settler and Native," *American Quarterly* 69, no. 2 (June 2017): 267–276.

5. *Meridian Daily Clarion*, October 21, 1865, 2; Jarret Ruminski, *The Limits of Loyalty: Ordinary People in Civil War Mississippi* (Jackson: University Press of Mississippi, 2017), 182. One of the many crimes of slavery in this settler-colonial context was the double theft of the same land—from its original owners *and* from those subsequently forced to work it for free, who ought to have inherited a piece of it. Relatedly, Richard White observes that "Southern redistribution, in essence, was about whether Southern whites could be treated as Indians and Southern blacks could be treated like white men." Richard White, *The Republic for Which It Stands: The United States during Reconstruction and the Gilded Age, 1865–1896* (New York: Oxford University Press, 2017), 44. See also W. E. B. Du Bois, *Black Reconstruction in America, 1860–1880* (New York: Free Press, 1998), 368–369.

6. On settler belonging, see Mark Rifkin, *Settler Common Sense: Queerness and Everyday Colonialism in the American Renaissance* (Minneapolis: University of Minnesota Press, 2014). On the ways in which Reconstruction-era land reform elided native peoples, see Kevin Bruyneel, *Settler Memory: The Disavowal of Indigeneity and the Politics of Race in the United States* (Chapel Hill: University of North Carolina Press, 2021), 45–75.

7. Harold D. Woodman, "Post–Civil War Southern Agriculture and the Law," *Agricultural History* 53, no.1 (January 1979): 319–321, 325; and *New South—New Law: The Legal Foundations of Credit and Labor Relations in the Postbellum Agricultural South* (Baton Rouge: Louisiana State University Press, 1995), 45–48. This transition has generated no small amount of scholarly attention. See especially Joseph P. Reidy, *From Slavery to Agrarian Capitalism in the Cotton Plantation South: Central Georgia, 1860–1880* (Chapel Hill: University of North Carolina Press, 1992); Julie Saville, *The Work of Reconstruction: From Slave to Wage Laborer in South Carolina, 1860–1870* (New York: Cambridge University Press, 1994); Steven Hahn, *A Nation under Our Feet: Black Political Struggles in the Rural South from Slavery to the Great Migration* (Cambridge, MA: Belknap Press of Harvard University Press, 2003); and Erin Stewart Mauldin, "Freedom, Economic Autonomy, and Ecological Change in the Cotton South, 1865–1880," *Journal of the Civil War Era* 7, no. 3 (September 2017): 401–424. Of the tenure arrangements in Newton County in the late 1930s, one Mississippian wrote that "the sharecropper . . . is so distinct and separate a class that he should not be classed with the cash renter." Source Material for Newton County, Agriculture, 2, WPA Files online.

8. J. Crawford King Jr., "The Closing of the Southern Range: An Exploratory

Study," *Journal of Southern History* 48, no. 1 (February 1982): 69. See also Steven Hahn, "Hunting, Fishing, and Foraging: Common Rights and Class Relations in the Postbellum South," *Radical History Review* 26 (1982): 37–64; Gilbert C. Fite, *Cotton Fields No More: Southern Agriculture, 1865–1980* (Lexington: University Press of Kentucky, 1984), 8–9; Foner, *Nothing but Freedom*, 61–65; Erin Stewart Mauldin, *Unredeemed Land: An Environmental History of Civil War and Emancipation in the Cotton South* (New York: Oxford University Press, 2018), 122–127; and Suresh Naidu, "Labor Mobility and Economic Development in the Post-Bellum U.S. South," working paper, 30, available online at https://eml.berkeley.edu/ffiwebfac/cromer/e211_spo8/naidu.pdf (accessed June 21, 2021). Voters in Newton County, which had fewer large planters, rejected stock laws at least twice in the late nineteenth century. See Alfred John Brown, *History of Newton County, Mississippi, from 1834 to 1894* (Jackson: Clarion-Ledger Company, 1894), 311–313.

9. The most comprehensive account of *chibaro* is van Onselen, *Chibaro*. For *chibalo*, see Ruth First, *Black Gold: The Mozambican Miner, Proletarian and Peasant* (New York: St. Martin's Press, 1983). Pete Daniel, *The Shadow of Slavery: Peonage in the South, 1901–1969* (Urbana: University of Illinois Press, 1972), 22–25; Douglas A. Blackmon, *Slavery by Another Name: The Re-Enslavement of Black Americans from the Civil War to World War II* (New York: Anchor, 2009), 227.

10. "A Peonage Case in State," *Jackson Daily News*, March 10, 1904, 8; "Charged with Peonage," *Jackson Weekly Clarion-Ledger*, March 17, 1904, 7.

11. R. C. Lee to Philander C. Knox, March 21, 1904, *Peonage Files of the US Department of Justice, 1901–1945* (Bethesda, MD: University Publications of America, 1989), microfilm, reel 3; R. C. Lee to William H. Moody, September 20, 1904, *Peonage Files*, reel 3; A. J. Hoyt to William H. Moody, March 16, 1906, *Peonage Files*, reel 3; R. C. Lee to William H. Moody, May 29, 1906, *Peonage Files*, reel 3; "Pickett Peonage Case Dismissed," *Macon Beacon*, September 15, 1906; William Cohen, *At Freedom's Edge: Black Mobility and the Southern White Quest for Racial Control, 1861–1915* (Baton Rouge: Louisiana State University Press, 1991), 284.

12. Tom Stephens to Franklin K. Lane, September 1, 1917, in *Survey of Conditions of the Indians in the United States: Hearings before a Subcommittee of the Committee on Indian Affairs*, 71st Cong., 3rd Sess., 1930, 7827–7828 (emphasis mine).

13. Osburn, *Choctaw Resurgence in Mississippi*, 36–56. The subjection of a multiracial rural proletariat to forced labor on taken land represented what historian Walter Johnson has characterized as the "generalization" of the tools of empire, now "deployed against the working class as a whole." The coercive tools of colonial invasion, in other words, were adapted to the labor control needs of elite settlers. Johnson, *The Broken Heart of America: St. Louis and the Violent History of the United States* (New York: Basic Books, 2020), 8–9, 71, 84.

14. County Correspondence, *Newton Record*, October 16, 1919, 4; Mississippi Forestry Commission, *Mississippi's Assessment of Forest Resources and Forest Resource Strategy* (Jackson: Mississippi Forestry Commission, 2010), 7–8.

15. File 50–41-3-1, *Peonage Files*. For more on McLendon's correspondence with the Justice Department, see Daniel, *Shadow of Slavery*, 147–148.

16. File 50–40-3-2, *Peonage Files*; Industrial Review, *Jackson Clarion-Ledger*, July 15, 1924, 2. Attala County resident Arraner Stephens Spivey, born in 1908, confirms that a road tax of about five dollars was typical. Those who could not pay the tax had to "work it out" with the local government. Arraner Stephens Spivey, interview by Preston Hughes, digital audio, unknown location, February 26–27, 2002, Center for Oral History and Cultural Heritage, University of Southern Mississippi.

17. "Labor Agent Given Flogging by Miss. Posse," *Richland Beacon-News*, November 16, 1929, 1; George Padmore, *The Life and Struggles of Negro Toilers* (London: Red International of Labor Unions Magazine for the International Trade Union Committee of Negro Workers, 1931), 50. Several Southern states had passed antienticement laws by the early twentieth century. These laws punished anyone enticing workers who were already under contract. See Oscar Zeichner, "The Legal Status of the Agricultural Laborer in the South," *Political Science Quarterly* 55, no. 3 (September 1940): 427–428.

18. US Congress, Senate, Subcommittee of the Committee on Indian Affairs, *Survey of the Conditions of the Indians in the United States: Hearings before a Subcommittee of the Committee on Indian Affairs*, 71st Cong., 3rd Sess., 1930, 7689.

19. As Richard White argues, "All [Southern whites'] latent fears of retaliatory violence against a system sustained by the lash and gun haunted them"; White, *Republic for Which It Stands*, 30; Lillie Jones, interview by Mike Garvey, transcript, Philadelphia, MS, December 11, 1974, USM; K. Stephen Prince, *Stories of the South: Race and the Reconstruction of Southern Identity, 1865–1915* (Chapel Hill: University of North Carolina Press, 2014), 211. On founding violence and preserving violence, see Walter Benjamin, "Critique of Violence," in *Reflections: Essays, Aphorisms, Autobiographical Writings*, trans. Edmund Jeffcott (New York: Schocken, 1986), 287–300; Jacques Derrida, "Force of Law: The 'Mystical Foundation of Authority,'" in *Acts of Religion* (New York: Routledge, 2002), 289–293; and Achille Mbembe, *On the Postcolony* (Berkeley: University of California Press, 2001), 25. On implications for settler-colonial theory, see Lorenzo Veracini, "Settler Collective, Founding Violence, and Disavowel: The Settler Colonial Situation," *Journal of Intercultural Studies* 29, no. 4 (November 2008): 363–379. For a comparison of racist violence in South Africa and the American South, see Ivan Evans, *Cultures of Violence: Lynching and Racial Killing in South Africa and the American South* (New York: Manchester University Press, 2009). On pre–World War II lynching and sexual fears, see Jane Dailey,

White Fright: The Sexual Panic at the Heart of America's Racist History (New York: Basic Books, 2020), 1–94.

20. Obie Clark, interview by Charles Bolton, transcript, Meridian, MS, September 30, 1997, USM; Clinton Collier, interview by Orley B. Caudill, transcript, Morton, MS, July 28, 1981, USM; Eric Norden, "The Playbook Interview with Charles Evers," *Playboy*, October 1, 1971, available online at https://www.playboy.com/read/the-playboy-interview-with-charles-evers. On the link between lynching and forced labor, see Cohen, *At Freedom's Edge*, 293–294. E. M. Beck and Stewart E. Tolnay point to a direct correlation between labor demand and racial violence. Importantly, the "lynching of a black for any offense [i.e., not just work-related issues] would have the effect of tightening or reinforcing white control over the entire black population." See Beck and Tolnay, "A Season for Violence: The Lynching of Blacks and Labor Demand in the Agricultural Production Cycle in the American South," *International Review of Social History* 37, no. 1 (1992): 12.

21. "Butchered with a Bowie," *Jackson Clarion-Ledger*, February 20, 1891, 1; "Lynching Near Meridian," *Natchez Weekly Democrat*, May 26, 1897; "Negro Lynched by a Mob," *Atlanta Constitution*, May 17, 1900, 2; "Paid the Penalty," *Jackson Clarion-Ledger*, August 30, 1901; "Four Negroes May Have Been Lynched," *Vicksburg Herald*, October 29, 1909, 1; "Angry Mob Hangs Negro Who Tried to Kill White Men," *Jackson Weekly Clarion-Ledger*, June 22, 1911, 7; "Ku Klux Klan Said to Have Been Revived in Neshoba County," *Biloxi Daily Herald*, November 10, 1902, 6; Clayton Rand, *Ink on My Hands* (New York: Carrick & Evans, 1940), 239–252.

22. Mary Lillian Peters (Ogden) Whitten, interview by Chester Morgan, edited by the interviewee, transcript, 1973, USM. For the connection between violence pre- and post-conquest, see Jason E. Pierce, *Making the White Man's West: Whiteness and the Creation of the American West* (Boulder: University Press of Colorado, 2018), 209–245.

23. Source Material for Noxubee County, Antebellum, 122, WPA Files Online; Source Material for Kemper County, Indians, 18, WPA Files Online; Edward W. Said, *Culture and Imperialism* (New York: Alfred A. Knopf, 1993), 288; Wolfe, *Traces of History*, 75–81; Richard N. Price, "The Psychology of Colonial Violence," in *Violence, Colonialism and Empire in the Modern World*, ed. Philip Dwyer and Amanda Nettlebeck (London: Palgrave Macmillan, 2018), 25–52. See also Hagar Kotef's "phenomenology of violence" in Kotef, *The Colonizing Self: Or, Home and Homelessness in Israel/Palestine* (Durham, NC: Duke University Press, 2020), 185–199.

24. "Negro Lynched at Scooba," *Choctaw Plaindealer*, July 25, 1924, 1; "Mob Lynches Scooba Negro as Assaulter," *Jackson Clarion-Ledger*, July 20, 1924, 1; "Soundly Whipped and Given Warning," *Jackson Clarion-Ledger*, March 31, 1927, 3; "Neshoba Murder Trial Date Set," *Jackson Clarion-Ledger*, February 10, 1940, 5;

"Neshoba Man Acquitted in the Death of Two Choctaw Indians," *Jackson Clarion-Ledger*, February 23, 1940, 1. Comprehensive maps of area race violence are at Monroe Work Today, http://www.monroeworktoday.org/explore/ and EJI Lynching in America, https://lynchinginamerica.eji.org/explore/Mississippi.

25. *Union Appeal*, June 23, 1921, 3; "Deemer Plant Closes Down," *Jackson Daily News*, June 26, 1921, 7.

26. Henry A. Wallace, "The Year in Agriculture," in USDA, *Yearbook of Agriculture, 1934*, ed. Milton S. Eisenhower (Washington, DC: Government Printing Office, 1934), 1–2; Paul K. Conkin, *A Revolution Down on the Farm: The Transformation of American Agriculture since 1929* (Lexington: University Press of Kentucky, 2008), 27, 56–63; Pete Daniel, *Breaking the Land: The Transformation of Cotton, Tobacco, and Rice Cultures since 1880* (Urbana: University of Illinois Press, 1985), 18–22; USDA, *Agricultural Statistics, 1936* (Washington, DC: Government Printing Office, 1936), 82.

27. Wallace, "Year in Agriculture," 28; Paul W. Bruton, "Cotton Acreage Reduction and the Tenant Farmer," *Law and Contemporary Problems* 1, no. 3 (June 1934): 287; "State Farmers Are Paid $9,924, 837 for Plowup," *Jackson Clarion-Ledger*, March 29, 1934, 9; F. J. Hurst, "Agricultural Extension Department Notes," *Union Appeal*, September 7, 1933, 2; Daniel, *Breaking the Land*, 108–109.

28. Fite, *Cotton Fields No More*, 139–162; Pete Daniel, "The Legal Basis of Agrarian Capitalism: The South since 1933," in *Race and Class in the American South since 1890*, ed. Melvyn Stokes and Rick Halpern (Providence, RI: Berg, 1994), 79–81; Arthur Krock, "Farm Act Is Swept Away," *New York Times*, January 7, 1936; Charles S. Johnson, Edwin R. Embree, and W. W. Alexander, *The Collapse of Cotton Tenancy: Summary of Field Studies and Statistical Surveys, 1933–35* (Chapel Hill: University of North Carolina Press, 1935), 51–52.

29. *Report of the Special Committee on Farm Tenancy* (Washington, DC: Government Printing Office, 1937), 6–7; National Emergency Council, *Report on Economic Conditions of the South* (Washington, DC: Government Printing Office, 1938); Ira Katznelson, *Fear Itself: The New Deal and the Origins of Our Time* (New York: Liveright, 2013), 170–171.

30. Clinton Collier, interview by Orley B. Caudill, transcript, Morton, MS, July 28, 1981, Center for Oral History and Cultural Heritage, University of Southern Mississippi.

31. "Mississippi Choctaws, Now Definitely Denied Rights in Oklahoma, Have Poor Lot," *Daily Oklahoman*, December 29, 1918, 35; John T. Reeves, *Additional Land and Indian Schools in Mississippi*, 64th Cong., 2nd Sess., March 16, 1917, H. Doc. 1464, 23–24; US Congress, House of Representatives, Committee on Investigation of the Indian Service, *Condition of the Mississippi Choctaws: Hearing before the Committee on Investigation of the Indian Service*, 64th Cong., Union, MS, March 16,

1917, 136–137, 153–157; Clara Sue Kidwell, "The Choctaw Struggle for Land and Identity in Mississippi, 1830–1918," in *After Removal: The Choctaw in Mississippi*, ed. Samuel J. Wells and Roseanna Tubby (Jackson: University Press of Mississippi, 1986), 88–89; Clayton Rand, "Neshoba County Fast Coming to Front in State," *Jackson Daily News*, September 28, 1919, 21.

32. Katherine M. B. Osburn, *Choctaw Resurgence in Mississippi: Race, Class, and Nation Building in the Jim Crow South, 1830–1977* (Lincoln: University of Nebraska Press, 2014), 65–75; Frank McKinley, Choctaw (Mississippi) 1920 Narrative Report, Central Classified Files, RG 75, NARA, available online at https://catalog.archives.gov/id/155867776 (accessed June 21, 2021); Baxter York, interview with staff of Nanih Waiya, transcript, Noxapater, MS, April 8, 1974, Southern Indian Oral History Project, University of Florida; Irvin M. Peithmann, *The Choctaw Indians of Mississippi* (Carbondale: Southern Illinois University, 1961), 5–10, Choctaw (Mississippi) Tribal File, 1959–1961, Records of the National Congress of American Indians, National Museum of the American Indian Archive Center, Suitland, MD; R. J. Enochs, Choctaw (Mississippi) 1927 Narrative Report, Central Classified Files, NARA. For a summary of the bungling and malfeasance with regard to Mississippi Choctaw land claims since 1830, see US Congress, Senate, Subcommittee of the Committee on Indian Affairs, *Choctaw Indians of Mississippi: Hearing before the Subcommittee of the Committee on Indian Affairs*, 76th Cong., 3rd Sess., 1940, 13–18.

33. Tabitha Kanogo, *Squatters and the Roots of Mau Mau, 1905–63* (Athens: Ohio University Press, 1987), 4–5, 35–68; Bruce Berman and John Lonsdale, *Unhappy Valley: Conflict in Kenya and Africa* (Athens: Ohio University Press, 1992), 245–246.

34. Christopher Youé, "Black Squatters on White Farms: Segregation and Agrarian Change in Kenya, South Africa, and Rhodesia, 1902–1963," *International History Review* 24, no. 3 (September 2002): 569–574; Robin Palmer, *Land and Racial Domination in Rhodesia* (Berkeley: University of California Press, 1977), 241–242; Pius S. Nyambara, "'That Place Was Wonderful!': African Tenants on Rhodesdale Estate, Colonial Zimbabwe, c. 1900–1952," *International Journal of African Historical Studies* 38, no 2 (2005): 282; Charles van Onselen, "Race and Class in the South African Countryside: Cultural Osmosis and Social Relations in the Sharecropping Economy of the South-Western Transvaal, 1900–1950," *American Historical Review* 95, no. 1 (February 1990): 100, 106; Colin Bundy, *The Rise and Fall of the South African Peasantry* (Berkeley: University of California Press, 1979), 232–236. Ian D. Ochiltree offers a comparative look at South African and US sharecropping, arguing that whatever the similarities, Southern planters made sharecropping serve Jim Crow, while many white South Africans distrusted sharecropping itself for the independence they thought it afforded Africans. See Ochiltree, "A Just and Self-Respecting System"?: Black Independence, Sharecropping, and Paternalistic

Relations in the American South and South Africa," *Agricultural History* 72, no. 2 (Spring 1998): 352–380.

CHAPTER 2: SEA CHANGE: SETTLER AGRICULTURE AFTER WORLD WAR II

1. John and Mack Rust, "The Cotton Picker and Unemployment," Folder 4, Box 22, Allen Eugene Cox Papers; James C. Cobb, *The Most Southern Place on Earth: The Mississippi Delta and the Roots of Regional Identity* (New York: Oxford University Press, 1992), 204.

2. Although World War II was undoubtedly a pivot point both politically and in terms of labor control, important scholarship points to the origins of an embattled segregationist movement in the late 1930s and even questions the central importance usually attributed to the war vis-à-vis civil rights. See Jason Morgan Ward, *Defending White Democracy: The Making of a Segregationist Movement and the Remaking of Racial Politics, 1936–1965* (Chapel Hill: University of North Carolina Press, 2011); and Kevin M. Kruse and Stephen Tuck, eds., *Fog of War: The Second World War and the Civil Rights Movement* (New York: Oxford University Press, 2012).

3. Meeting of the Delta Council Labor Committee, May 29, 1946, Folder 18, Box 22, Agricultural Extension L. I. Jones Collection; US Department of Commerce, Business and Defense Services Administration, *World Survey of Agricultural Machinery and Equipment: Africa and Australia-Oceania* (Washington, DC: Government Printing Office, 1960), 1–2, 13–15.

4. US Department of Agriculture, Bureau of Agricultural Economics, *Farmers View the Postwar World: A Survey of the Cornbelt, the Cotton Region of the Southeast, and the Central Valley of California*, September 25, 1944, 2–12. US Department of Agriculture, *What Peace Can Mean to American Farmers: Post-War Agriculture and Employment*, May 1945, 19–20, 24–28; Stuart Chase, "Production First," *Nation*, January 13, 1945, 41; Lizabeth Cohen, *A Consumers' Republic: The Politics of Mass Consumption in Postwar America* (New York: Alfred A. Knopf, 2003), 111–129; James H. Street, *The New Revolution in the Cotton Economy: Mechanization and Its Consequences* (Chapel Hill: University of North Carolina Press, 1957), 77–82. The *New Republic*'s Arthur P. Chew agreed: "Agriculture's hopes for continued full production depend on the nation's hopes for full employment, which rest in turn on the prospect for a peacetime demand to replace the wartime demand." Chew, "What's Ahead for Agriculture?," *New Republic*, September 17, 1945. See also US Department of Agriculture and State Agricultural Extension Services, *Facts about Cotton and Southern Farming: Background Information for Farm Leaders* (February 1946).

5. US Congress, House of Representatives, Committee on Agriculture, *Cotton:*

Hearings before the Subcommittee of the Committee on Agriculture, 78th Cong., 2nd Sess., 1944, 376–377, 505–511. Welch was transmitting the report of a fact-finding program conceived at the May 1945 meeting. See US Congress, House of Representatives, Committee on Agriculture, *Study of Agricultural and Economic Problems of the Cotton Belt*, 80th Cong., 1st Sess., 1947, 6–17.

6. "Assignment 17: Agriculture," May 13, 1937, Box 10772, WPA Files, MDAH; *Census of Agriculture*, 1940; C. I. Smith, C. S. Norton, and O. F. Parker, Annual Narrative Report, Neshoba County, MS, 1945, 3, 12, Box 170, Records of the Extension Service, RG 33, NARA; "Farm Agents Get First Hand Information on Cotton Pickers," *Neshoba Democrat*, December 22, 1944, 16; Henry Lesesne, "Cotton Mechanization No Longer Idle Talk As New Machines Take Over Work," *Jackson Clarion-Ledger*, December 16, 1945, 39; D. Clayton Brown, *King Cotton in Modern America: A Cultural, Political, and Economic History since 1945* (Jackson: University Press of Mississippi, 2011), 125–146. For landowners' and county agents' efforts to misrepresent farm labor requirements in the interest of large planters' labor control, see Nan Elizabeth Woodruff, "Pick or Fight: The Emergency Farm Labor Program in the Arkansas and Mississippi Deltas during World War II," *Agricultural History* 64, no. 2 (Spring 1990): 76–80.

7. "Farm Labor Shortage Proves Good Deal for Gholson Farmer," *Neshoba Democrat*, July 30, 1943, 10. Tragically, Skipper, who lived with mental illness, later shot his wife and Evie Jo's young daughter to death in their Kemper County farmhouse before turning the gun on himself. "Ex-Mental Patient Slays Wife, Child," *Jackson Clarion-Ledger*, January 10, 1968, 9. "Hill-dropping" eventually made thinning unnecessary. For a discussion of the lingering problem of chopping cotton, see Donald Holley, *The Second Great Emancipation: The Mechanical Cotton Picker, Black Migration, and How They Shaped the Modern South* (Fayetteville: University of Arkansas Press, 2000), 126–127. For more on the notion of the "second shift," see Arlie Hochschild, *The Second Shift: Working Families and the Revolution at Home* (New York: Viking, 1989); and Evan P. Bennett, *When Tobacco Was King: Families, Farm Labor, and Federal Policy in the Piedmont* (Gainesville: University Press of Florida, 2014).

8. "County Farmer Meets Labor Shortage with Farm Machinery," *Neshoba Democrat*, November 29, 1946, 16. My understanding of the relationships between race, inequality, and technological innovation owes to Neda Atanasoski and Kalindi Vora, *Surrogate Humanity: Race, Robots, and the Politics of Technological Futures* (Durham, NC: Duke University Press, 2019); Wendell Berry, "Horse-Drawn Tools and the Doctrine of Labor Saving," in *The World-Ending Fire: The Essential Wendell Berry* (Berkeley, CA: Counterpoint, 2017), 151–158; and Numan V. Bartley, *The New South, 1945–1980* (Baton Rouge: Louisiana State University Press, 1995), 126.

9. D. W. Parvin, *Development of the Dairy Industry in Mississippi* (State College: Mis-

sissippi State College, Agricultural Experiment Station, 1945); C. I. Smith, "Dairy Cow Is Simply a Processing Plant," *Neshoba Democrat*, January 12, 1945; J. C. Brister, "Dairying Is Profitable Project for Neshoba County Farmers," *Neshoba Democrat*, January 12, 1945; Joe Moore, interview by Pic Firmin, transcript, Gulfport, MS, May 2, 2003, USM; "Dairy Products Show Better Results Than Cotton Crops," *Jackson Clarion-Ledger*, July 24, 1946, 8; *Census of Agriculture*, 1950; "C. I. Smith Resigns County Agent's Job, Goes to Pet Milk Co.," *Neshoba Democrat*, February 9, 1945, 1. Steep grades constituted one of several problems (including coarse, sandy soil, short rows, and a mismatch between maximum tractor size and minimum horsepower needed to handle the required machinery) that plagued hill-country farmers who tried to mechanize row-cropping operations. See E. A. Kimbrough, *Case Studies of Small Tractors on Hill Farms of Mississippi* (State College: Mississippi State College, Agricultural Experiment Station, 1951). In 1946 agent C. S. Norton distributed a pamphlet to area farmers reminding them that "Good pasture is our cheapest and best milk-producing feed. It conserves our soil, and *requires less labor*" [emphasis mine]. C. S. Norton, Annual Narrative Report, Neshoba County, MS, 1946, Box 202, Records of the Extension Service, RG 33, NARA. For the broader transition from cotton to cattle in the deep South, see Brooks Blevins, *Cattle in the Cotton Fields: A History of Cattle Raising in Alabama* (Tuscaloosa: University of Alabama Press, 1998); and Karlyn Forner, *Why the Vote Wasn't Enough for Selma* (Durham, NC: Duke University Press, 2017), 104–109.

10. In a 1949 study of 170 Mississippi demonstration farms, the Extension Service determined that dairy-only farming was almost four times more profitable than cotton-only farming. This was despite dairy-only farmers having twice as large a capital investment in machinery and equipment (to say nothing of other factors) and more than 2.5 times more in expenses. Importantly, of those expenses, labor ("hired labor" and/or "cropper labor") accounted for 13 percent for dairy-only farmers versus 24 percent for cotton-only farmers. See T. M. Montgomery, "A Summary of 170 Farm Record Books Kept by TVA Unit Test Demonstration Farmers," in L. A. Olson, Annual Report, Mississippi Extension Service–Tennessee Valley Authority, 1950, Box 192, Records of the Extension Service, RG 33, NARA. J. C. Brister, "Dairying Is Profitable for Neshoba County Farmers," *Neshoba Democrat*, January 12, 1945, 1; "County Farmer Meets Labor Shortage with Farm Machinery," *Neshoba Democrat*, November 29, 1946, 16; C. I. Smith, C. S. Norton, and O. F. Parker, Annual Narrative Report, 1945, 6.

11. C. S. Norton, "Irby Majure's Farm Is Dream-Come-True," *Jackson Clarion-Ledger*, November 30, 1950; "Irby Majure Gives His Cows Symphonic Music While Milking," *Neshoba Democrat*, January 12, 1945, 3; "Good Pastures, Milk Cows and Hard Work Will Pay," *Neshoba Democrat*, August 5, 1949, 20.

12. "A Study of the Robert E. Payne Farm, File No. U 4–4, for the Period 1946 through 1950," in L. A. Olson, Annual Report, Mississippi Extension Service–Tennessee Valley Authority, 1950, Box 192, Records of the Extension Service, RG 33, NARA. Extension economist T. M. Montgomery summarized the program's goals in 1948: "The unit-test-demonstration program is one which is designed to show, by demonstration, that approved practices of soil conservation and the practice of following the latest farming methods as recommended by the Mississippi Experiment Stations will pay on practical farms. With the help of the county agent, the farmer works out a long-time farm plan." L. A. Olson, Annual Report, Mississippi Extension Service–Tennessee Valley Authority, 1949, Box 225, Records of the Extension Service, RG 33, NARA.

13. James E. Moak and Lawrence J. Kerr, *Economic Opportunities in Mississippi's Pine Lumber Industry* (State College: Mississippi Agricultural Experiment Station, 1961), 1–2; Lee M. James, *Mississippi's Forest Resources and Industries*, Forest Resource Report No. 4 (Washington, DC: US Department of Agriculture, 1951), 7–12; Turner Catledge, interview by William H. Hatcher, transcript, New Orleans, LA, September 14, 1971, Center for Oral History and Cultural Heritage, University of Southern Mississippi; Dick Allen, interview by Bobbie Jean Dickinson, transcript, Philadelphia, MS, September 6, 1988, Mississippi Forestry Association Records; Thomas A. DeWeese, interview by Linda Edgerly, transcript, Philadelphia, MS, November 28, 1979, Mississippi Forestry Association Records; Edward L. Demotte, "East Mississippi's Blue Line of Prosperity," *Jackson Clarion-Ledger*, April 30, 1953, 34.

14. C. S. Norton and Joe C. Fulton, Annual Narrative Report, Neshoba County, MS, 1948, 5–7, Box 204, Records of the Extension Service, RG 33, NARA; B. H. Dixon, "County Agent Notes," *Kemper County Messenger*, March 21, 1946, 1; C. S. Norton, Annual Narrative Report, Neshoba County, MS, 1947, 21, Box 211, Records of the Extension Service, RG 33, NARA.

15. Ladd Haystead, The Farm Column, *Fortune*, June 1945, 171. For a discussion of the contradictions of postwar agricultural policies, see Pete Daniel, *Lost Revolutions: The South in the 1950s* (Chapel Hill: University of North Carolina Press, 2000), 39–60.

16. Street, *New Revolution in the Cotton Economy*, 123–132; "Song of Dixie Darkies Will Fade Away if New Cotton Picker Success," *Jackson Clarion-Ledger*, February 17, 1935; "Mechanical Cotton Picker Demonstrated at Stoneville," *Greenwood Commonwealth*, August 31, 1936; "Crump Would Outlaw Picker," *Greenwood Commonwealth*, September 5, 1936, 1.

17. C. Horace Hamilton, "The Social Effects of Recent Trends in the Mechanization of Agriculture," *Rural Sociology* 4, no. 1 (March 1939): 11; B. O. Williams, "The Impact of Mechanization of Agriculture on the Farm Population of the

South," *Rural Sociology* 4, no. 3 (September 1939): 300–311; Margaret Jarman Hagood, "Discussion," *Rural Sociology* 4, no. 3 (September 1939): 313–314; Street, *New Revolution in the Cotton Economy*, 175–210; Eugene Butler, "Farm Labor," Folder 30, Box 12, Eugene Butler Papers, MSU; Oscar Johnston, "Will the Machine Ruin the South?," *Saturday Evening Post*, May 31, 1947, 37, 98; Dorothy Dickins, *The Labor Supply and Mechanized Cotton Production* (State College: Mississippi State College, Agricultural Experiment Station, 1949), 5. Arthur Raper acknowledged both sides and viewed mechanization as a mixed blessing in "The Role of Agricultural Technology in Southern Social Change," *Social Forces* 25, no. 1 (October 1946): 21–30. For an excellent encapsulation of this sudden shift in opinion, see Charles S. Aiken, *The Cotton Plantation South since the Civil War* (Baltimore: Johns Hopkins University Press, 1998), 128–132.

18. Robert Durr, "The Deep South Speaks," *Kansas City Plaindealer*, November 29, 1946. On the "labor vacuum" thesis, see Wayne A. Grove and Craig Heinicke, "Better Opportunities or Worse? The Demise of Cotton Harvest Labor, 1949–1964," *Journal of Economic History* 63, no. 3 (September 2003): 736–767; Woodruff, "Pick or Fight," 76–80.

19. H. J. Putnam, "The Influence of Size of Farms on Family Labor Earnings, Land Use, Etc.," November 5, 1946, unpublished report in C. M. Chaffee, Mississippi Narrative Progress Report on Agricultural Development through Test Demonstration, 1946, 15–16, Box 196, Records of the Extension Service, RG 33, NARA.

20. C. S. Norton, Annual Narrative Report, Neshoba County, MS, 1946, 17.

21. Douglas A. Blackmon, "The World War II Effect," *Wall Street Journal*, March 29, 2008; Title 18, U.S.C., §1581–1588; Risa L. Goluboff, "The Thirteenth Amendment in Historical Perspective," *Journal of Constitutional Law* 11, no. 5 (July 2009): 1457–1458; Michael J. Klarman, *From Jim Crow to Civil Rights: The Supreme Court and the Struggle for Racial Equality* (New York: Oxford University Press, 2004), 233–235, 286–289.

22. File 50–41–21, *Peonage Files*; File 50–41–27, *Peonage Files*.

23. File 50–41–20, *Peonage Files*; "Lauderdale County Man to Face Peonage Charge," *Jackson Clarion-Ledger*, September 14, 1943, 14; "Fined for Peonage," *Hattiesburg American*, September 30, 1943, 4.

24. Michael J. Klarman, "The White Primary Rulings: A Case Study in the Consequences of Supreme Court Decisionmaking," *Florida State University Law Review* 29, no. 1 (Fall 2001): 57, 65; Ira Katznelson, *Fear Itself: The New Deal and the Origins of Our Time* (New York: Liveright, 2013), 186–222.

25. Michael Honey, "Operation Dixie: Labor and Civil Rights in the Postwar South," *Mississippi Quarterly* 45, no. 4 (Fall 1992): 439–452; "Labor Drives South," *Fortune*, November 1946, 134–140, 230, 232, 234, 237; John Dittmer, *Local People:*

The Struggle for Civil Rights in Mississippi (Urbana: University of Illinois Press, 1994), 22–24.

26. Meeting of the Delta Council Labor Committee, May 29, 1946, Folder 18, Box 22, Agricultural Extension L. I. Jones Collection.

27. *Congressional Record*, 79th Cong., 2nd Sess., January 17, 1946, 90; US Congress, Senate, Committee on Labor and Public Welfare, *Antidiscrimination in Employment*, 80th Cong., 1st Sess., 1947, 653, 655; "Nondiscrimination in Employment," *CQ Almanac 1947*, 3rd ed., 06-651-06-652 (Washington, DC: Congressional Quarterly, 1948), http://library.cqpress.com.proxy.lib.fsu.edu/cqalmanac/cqal47-1398547; L. L. McAllister to James O. Eastland, February 13, 1946, Folder 1, Box 32, Issue Correspondence, Constituent Files, James O. Eastland Collection; Henry J. Dorsey to John C. Stennis, February 23, 1948, Folder 5, Box 1, Civil Rights, John C. Stennis Papers; John C. Stennis to Henry J. Dorsey, February 26, 1948, Folder 5, Box 1, Civil Rights, John C. Stennis Papers. See also Eileen Boris, "Fair Employment and the Origins of Affirmative Action in the 1940s," *NWSA Journal* 10, no. 3 (Autumn 1998): 142–151; David Freeman Engstrom, "The Lost Origins of American Fair Employment Law: Regulatory Choice and the Making of Modern Civil Rights, 1943–1972," *Stanford Law Review* 63, no. 5 (May 2011): 1071–1143; Jeffrey A. Jenkins and Justin Peck, "Building toward Major Policy Change: Congressional Action on Civil Rights," *Law and History Review* 31, no. 1 (February 2013): 139–198; and Katznelson, *Fear Itself*, 259–260, 395.

28. Robert J. Rosenthal, "Exclusions of Employees under the Taft-Hartley Act," *ILR Review* 4, no. 4 (July 1951): 556–570; National Labor Relations Act, 29 USC § 151 (1935); US Congress, House of Representatives, Committee on Education and Labor, *Labor-Management Relations Act: Report (to Accompany HR 3020)*, 80th Cong., 1st Sess., 1947, HR Rep. 245, 68–69.

29. "Congressman Arthur Winstead Announces for Reelection," *Union Appeal*, May 16, 1946, 1; "Bilbo, Winstead and Noble Win," *Union Appeal*, July 4, 1946, 1; Dittmer, *Local People*, 1–2; Joseph Crespino, *In Search of Another Country: Mississippi and the Conservative Counterrevolution* (Princeton, NJ: Princeton University Press, 2007), 104–105.

30. Gilbert C. Fite, *Cotton Fields No More: Southern Agriculture, 1865–1980* (Lexington: University Press of Kentucky, 1984), 218.

31. Dane Kennedy, *Islands of White: Settler Society and Culture in Kenya and Southern Rhodesia, 1890–1939* (Durham, NC: Duke University Press, 1987), 187; Clyde Woods, *Development Arrested: The Blues and Plantation Power in the Mississippi Delta* (Brooklyn, NY: Verso 1998), 163. For a somewhat different take on the politics of mechanization, see Nan Elizabeth Woodruff, "Mississippi Delta Planters and Debates over Mechanization, Labor, and Civil Rights in the 1940s," *Journal of Southern History* 60, no. 2 (May 1994): 263–284.

32. Klaus Deininger and Hans P. Binswanger, "Rent Seeking and the Development of Large-Scale Agriculture in Kenya, South Africa, and Zimbabwe," *Economic Development and Cultural Change* 43, no. 3 (April 1995): 512–513; William Beinart, "Soil Erosion, Conservationism and Ideas about Development: A Southern African Exploration, 1900–1960," *Journal of Southern African Studies* 11, no. 1 (October 1984): 52–83. For a brief overview of such trends, see A. W. Shepherd, "Capitalist Agriculture in Africa," *Africa Development* 6, no. 3 (July-September 1981): 5–21.

33. Paul Mosley, *The Settler Economies: Studies in the Economic History of Kenya and Southern Rhodesia, 1900–1963* (New York: Cambridge University Press, 1983), 30–33; John Lonsdale, "The Depression and the Second World War in the Transformation of Kenya," in *Africa and the Second World War*, ed. David Killingray and Richard Rathbone (London: MacMillan, 1986), 103–119; J. F. Lipscomb, *We Built a Country* (London: Faber & Faber, 1956), 79–81, 90–104, 101–102; L. Winston Cone and J. F. Lipscomb, *The History of Kenya Agriculture* (Nairobi: University Press of Africa, 1972), 81–115; Caroline Elkins, *Imperial Reckoning: The Untold Story of Britain's Gulag in Kenya* (New York: Owl, 2005), 23–28; Constance G. Anthony, *Mechanization and Maize: Agriculture and the Politics of Technology Transfer in East Africa* (New York: Columbia University Press, 1988), 46–62.

34. Stefan Schirmer, "Motives for Mechanisation in South African Agriculture c1940–1980," *African Studies* 63, no. 1 (July 2004): 3–28; Charles van Onselen, *The Seed Is Mine: The Life of Kas Maine, a South African Sharecropper, 1894–1985* (New York: Hill & Wang, 1997), 278–279. See also Bill Freund, "Forced Resettlement and the Political Economy of South Africa," *Review of African Political Economy* no. 29 (July 1984): 51; Charles van Onselen, "Race and Class in the South African Countryside: Cultural Osmosis and Social Relations in the Sharecropping Economy of the South-Western Transvaal, 1900–1950," *American Historical Review* 95, no. 1 (February 1990): 122–123. To a certain degree (constrained mainly by the nature of tobacco cultivation), settlers in Southern Rhodesia mechanized in the postwar decades, too, although the process does not seem to have been quite as sudden, nor the effects as clear-cut. In general, though, the pattern of mechanization on settler farms and older methods on African farms held, as did that of taking advantage of new machines, the postwar commodities boom, and plentiful labor to evict tenants and use wage workers when possible. See US Department of Commerce, Bureau of Foreign Commerce, Near Eastern and African Division, *Investment in Rhodesia and Nyasaland* (Washington, DC: Government Printing Office, 1956), 40–41; US Department of Agriculture, Foreign Agricultural Service, *Notes on the Agricultural Economies of the Countries in Africa, III: Eastern and Southern Africa* (Washington, DC: Government Printing Office, 1959), 16–17; Shepherd, "Capitalist Agriculture in Africa," 6–8; and Giovanni Arrighi, *The Political Economy of Rhodesia* (The Hague: Mouton, 1967), 32, 46–47.

35. Patrick Wolfe, *Traces of History: Elementary Structures of Race* (Brooklyn, NY: Verso, 2016), 2.

CHAPTER 3: FRANTIC RESISTANCE: MISSISSIPPI
AND THE DECOLONIAL ZEITGEIST

1. C. A. Bayly, *Remaking the Modern World, 1900–2015: Global Connections and Comparisons* (Hoboken, NJ: Wiley Blackwell, 2018), 154–155; D. A. Low and J. M. Lonsdale, "Towards the New Order, 1945–1963," in *History of East Africa*, vol. 3, ed. D. A. Low and Alison Smith (Oxford: Clarendon Press, 1976), 1–63; Frederick Cooper, *Decolonization and African Society: The Labor Question in French and British Africa* (Cambridge: Cambridge University Press, 1996); Jane Burbank and Frederick Cooper, *Empires in World History: Power and the Politics of Difference* (Princeton, NJ: Princeton University Press, 2010), 420–429; Jean Allman, "The Fate of All of Us: African Counterrevolutions and the Ends of 1968," *American Historical Review* 123, no. 3 (June 2018): 730–731; Elizabeth Gillespie McRae, *Mothers of Massive Resistance: White Women and the Politics of White Supremacy* (New York: Oxford University Press, 2018), 200–202; Immanuel Wallerstein, "What Hope Africa? What Hope the World?," in *After Liberalism* (New York: New Press, 1995), 57–93. For a discussion of settler resistance to imperial retreat, see Caroline Elkins, "Race, Citizenship, and Governance: Settler Tyranny and the End of Empire," in *Settler Colonialism in the Twentieth Century*, ed. Carolina Elkins and Susan Pederson (New York: Routledge, 2005), 203–222. The "two 'Souths'" formulation comes from Thomas Borstelmann, *The Cold War and the Color Line: American Race Relations in the Global Arena* (Cambridge, MA: Harvard University Press, 2001), 137.

2. J. David Simpson, "Non-Segregation Means Eventual Inter-Marriage," unpublished article, 1948, Folder 3, Box 32, Issue Correspondence, Constituent Files, James O. Eastland Collection.

3. Bureau of the Census, *Census of Agriculture*, 1959.

4. Mississippi Band of Choctaw Indians Tribal Council Meeting Minutes, July 10, 1951, MBCI Tribal Archive, Choctaw, MS; Florence Mars, *Witness in Philadelphia* (Baton Rouge: Louisiana State University Press, 1977), 59.

5. Mars, *Witness in Philadelphia*, 12; Frank Hurst to James O. Eastland, June 9, 1944, Folder 20, Box 30, State and Local Files, Constituent Files, James O. Eastland Collection; Philip Martin, *Chief* (Brandon, MS: Quail Ridge Press, 2009), location 1042; HP Davis, "Notes Re: Visit to the Choctaw Jurisdiction, Philadelphia, Mississippi, April 9 to 20, 1948," Folder 8, Box 152, Association on American Indian Affairs (hereafter AAIA) Records (microfilm). Some Choctaws seem to have believed that separating themselves from the Black community would re-

duce the chances that Choctaws would be similarly abused. Others held negative views of Black culture. See Charles Madden Tolbert, "A Sociological Study of the Choctaw Indians in Mississippi" (PhD diss., Louisiana State University, 1958), 125–129. "War of numbers" is how Josiah Brownell described the fear of replacement among white settlers in Southern Rhodesia in the mid-twentieth century. See Brownell, *The Collapse of Rhodesia: Population Demographics and the Politics of Race* (New York: I. B. Tauris, 2011).

6. Richard Slotkin, *Gunfighter Nation: The Myth of the Frontier in Twentieth-Century America* (New York: HarperPerennial, 1993), 10–16, 347; James Burns, "The Western in Colonial Southern Africa," in *The Western in the Global South*, ed. MaryEllen Higgins, Rita Keresztesi, and Dayna Oscherwitz (New York: Routledge, 2015), 11–23; "Decatur High School Band," *Newton Record*, September 18, 1958, 7; "Letters to Santa Claus," *Winston County Journal*, December 9, 1955, 1; "Mike Celebrates Sixth Birthday," *Winston County Journal*, July 13, 1956, 2; "'California or Bust' Is the Goal of These 'Settlers,'" *Kosciusko Star-Herald*, July 19, 1956, 1; James Baldwin, "The American Dream and the American Negro," *New York Times*, March 7, 1965, 32. In Africa, once the technology was widely available, the popularity of Western-themed films was not limited to settler states. See Ch. Didier Gondola, *Tropical Cowboys: Westerns, Violence, and Masculinity in Kinshasa* (Bloomington: Indiana University Press, 2016); and Abderrahmane Sissako, dir., *Bamako* (2006; New York: New Yorker Films, 2007), DVD. For a discussion of Western-themed toys in the context of settler colonialism, see Michael Yellow Bird, "Cowboys and Indians: Toys of Genocide, Icons of American Colonialism," *Wicazo Sa Review* 19, no. 2 (Autumn 2004): 33–48.

7. Ngugi wa Thiong'o, *Decolonising the Mind: The Politics of Language in African Literature* (London: James Currey, 1988), 3; Claude Allen, interview by Samuel Proctor, transcript, 3, Pearl River, MS, December 2, 1973, University of Florida Digital Collections, https://ufdc.ufl.edu/UF00007833/00001 (accessed September 25, 2019); Charles Evers and Neil E. Goldschmidt, interview by Robert Penn Warren, transcript, February 12, 1964, Who Speaks for the Negro? Collection, Vanderbilt University, https://whospeaks.library.vanderbilt.edu/interview/charles-evers-and-neil-e-goldschmidt (accessed September 26, 2019). By comparison, a man called Sipho Booi, born in Pondoland (Eastern Cape, South Africa), remembered being upset at having to play the Boer, rather than the British, when he and his friends played Boer War games. See Surplus People Project, *Forced Removals in South Africa: Vol. 2: The Eastern Cape* (Cape Town: Surplus People Project, 1983), 343.

8. Claude Allen, interview by Samuel Proctor, 3; John H. Provinse to Alexander Lesser, July 15, 1949, Folder 10, Box 249, AAIA Records (microfilm); Tolbert, "A Sociological Study of the Choctaw Indians in Mississippi," 125–129. Some coun-

ties in the region—Newton, Winston, and Attala, for instance—contained a Black extension agent and a Black home demonstration agent. Others—such as Leake and Kemper—contained neither. Even in counties that had such personnel, white agents received the literature and resources distributed by the USDA and could share it with Black agents or not. For a map of the distribution of agents by 1960, see W. E. Ammons, County Agent Leader Annual Narrative Report, Mississippi, 1960, Box 168, Records of the Extension Service, RG 33, National Archives and Records Administration (hereafter NARA). For Black leadership in the rural communities of Neshoba County, particularly as it pertained to schools and churches, see "Supplement to Assignment 10: Negroes," January 29, 1937, Box 10772, Work Projects Administration (WPA) Files, Mississippi Department of Archives and History (hereafter MDAH); Inez Calloway Johnson, *History of Longdale High School, 1949–1963* (Jackson, MS: I. C. Johnson, 1999), 1–3. For more on the Longdale School, see Carol V. R. George, *One Mississippi, Two Mississippi: Methodists, Murder, and the Struggle for Racial Justice in Neshoba County* (New York: Oxford University Press, 2015), 169–170. On Black leadership in Leake County, see Winson Hudson and Constance Curry, *Mississippi Harmony: Memoirs of a Freedom Fighter* (New York: Palgrave Macmillan, 2002).

9. "Tri-Racial Event Set for Thursday," *Jackson Clarion-Ledger*, October 26, 1949, 7; "Narrative Report of Visit of Tribal Relations Officer, Muskogee Area, to Choctaw Indian Agency, Philadelphia, Mississippi, October 22 to November 2, 1951," 21–22, Tribal File, Choctaw (Mississippi), 1947–1958, Records of the National Congress of American Indians (hereafter NCAI); "Tri-Racial Festival Marks 100 Years of Harmony," *Jackson Clarion-Ledger*, October 19, 1950, 7; *Westville News*, October 26, 1899, 1; "Lynched for Assault," *Vicksburg Herald*, August 17, 1902, 1.

10. Theda Perdue, "The Legacy of Indian Removal," *Journal of Southern History* 78, no. 1 (February 2012): 27–28.

11. Charles Evers and Neil E. Goldschmidt, interview by Robert Penn Warren; Michael W. Fitzgerald, "'We Have Found a Moses': Theodore Bilbo, Black Nationalism, and the Greater Liberia Bill of 1939," *Journal of Southern History* 63, no. 2 (May 1997): 293–320; Charles Evers and Andrew Szanton, *Have No Fear: The Charles Evers Story* (New York: John Wiley & Sons, 1997), 23–24. Many lynchings never received mention in white newspapers. Neither of Newton County's newspapers reported on a "Willie Tingle," but the *Newton Record* reported that "unknown parties" killed an "Albert Tingle" at the old fairgrounds in November 1934. The incident occurred just a few months after two Bilbo stump speeches in the area. According to Evers, the man's crime had been insulting a white woman. The paper listed few specifics. "Negro Found Dead at Decatur Fairground," *Newton Record*, November 8, 1934, 1.

12. Medgar Evers, "Why I Live in Mississippi," *Ebony*, November 1958, 66; Evers and Szanton, *Have No Fear*, 60–64.

13. Frederick Cooper, *Africa since 1940: The Past of the Present* (New York: Cambridge University Press, 2002), 71–74, and *Decolonization and African Society*, 348–360; Caroline Elkins, *Imperial Reckoning: The Untold Story of Britain's Gulag in Kenya* (New York: Owl, 2005), 1–30; John Lonsdale, "Britain's Mau Mau," in *Penultimate Adventures with Britannia: Personalities, Politics and Culture in Britain*, ed. Wm. Roger Louis (London: I. B. Tauris, 2008), 275–277. Not all workers were expelled from settler estates in the Highlands. Some ex-squatters were hired as wage workers, although many were not. Bruce Berman sums up a very tough situation: "While the Central Province administration was seeking ways of forcing the 'excess' population out of the reserves, settlers in the Highlands were forcing squatters off their estates, and the Secretariat in Nairobi responded to the growing number of unemployed Africans in the city with the Voluntary Unemployed Persons Ordinance of 1949, the so-called 'spiv' law, under which the unemployed were rounded up and dumped back into the reserves." See Berman, *Control and Crisis in Colonial Kenya: The Dialectic of Domination* (Athens: Ohio State University Press, 1990), 307.

14. Evers, "Why I Live in Mississippi," 65; Charles Evers and Neil E. Goldschmidt, interview by Robert Penn Warren, February 12, 1964; Evers and Szanton, *Have No Fear*, 64, 75–76; Charles Evers, *Evers* (New York: World Publishing Co., 1971), 74–75. After *Ebony* ran a profile of Medgar Evers, whites took special note of his interest in Kenyatta and Mau Mau. The *Jackson Clarion-Ledger* ran an article that referred to Evers as "the Mau Mau admirer." See "Council Official Says JPC Blocked Arrests," *Jackson Clarion-Ledger*, May 19, 1959, 1.

15. Evers and Szanton, *Have No Fear*, 75–76.

16. Mary Dudziak, *Cold War Civil Rights: Race and the Image of American Democracy* (Princeton, NJ: Princeton University Press, 2000), xix, and "Desegregation as a Cold War Imperative," *Stanford Law Review* 41, no. 1 (November 1988): 61–66; John Dittmer, *Local People: The Struggle for Civil Rights in Mississippi* (Urbana: University of Illinois Press, 1994), 24. As Dudziak and others have argued, Black activists seized on the Cold War imperative. In 1951, the Mississippi NAACP adopted the following resolution: "We declare that any proposal to deprive Negro Americans of their rights guaranteed by the Constitution further minimizes the effectiveness of our efforts to win allies for democracy abroad and gives additional propaganda to the communists in their attacks on the American way of life." Resolutions Adopted by the 6th Annual Convention of the Mississippi State Conference of Branches, Jackson, MS, November 3–4, 1951, Folder 2, Box II:C98, National Association for the Advancement of Colored People (hereafter NAACP) Records, Library of Congress, Washington, DC. See also "European Reaction to Discrimination in America as

Expressed in Press Comments Following the Execution of Willie McGee," Crime, Mississippi, 1951–54, General Office File, Box II:A219, NAACP Records. For the ways in which Cold War pressure affected federal Indian policy and civil rights reforms, see Paul C. Rosier, "'They Are Ancestral Homelands': Race, Place, and Politics in Cold War Native America, 1945–1961," *Journal of American History* 92, no. 4 (March 2006): 1300–1326; James L. Roark, "American Black Leaders: The Response to Colonialism and the Cold War, 1943–1953," *African Historical Studies* 4, no. 2 (1971), 253–270; Gerald Horne, *Black and Red: WEB Du Bois and the Afro-American Response to the Cold War* (Albany: State University of New York Press, 1985); Robert Korstad and Nelson Lichtenstein, "Opportunities Found and Lost: Labor, Radicals, and the Early Civil Rights Movement," *Journal of American History* 75, no. 3 (December 1988): 786–811; Thomas Borstelmann, *Apartheid's Reluctant Uncle: The United States and Southern Africa in the Early Cold War* (New York: Oxford University Press, 1993); Gerald Horne, "Who Lost the Cold War? Africans and African Americans," *Diplomatic History* 20, no. 4 (Fall 1996): 613–626; Penny M. Von Eschen, *Race against Empire: Black Americans and Anticolonialism, 1937–1957* (Ithaca, NY: Cornell University Press, 1997); Dudziak, *Cold War Civil Rights*; Thomas Borstelmann, *The Cold War and the Color Line: American Race Relations in the Global Arena* (Cambridge, MA: Harvard University Press, 2001); Carol Anderson, *Eyes off the Prize: The United Nations and the African American Struggle for Human Rights, 1944–1955* (New York: Cambridge University Press, 2003); and Brenda Gayle Plummer, *In Search of Power: African Americans in the Era of Decolonization, 1956–1974* (New York: Cambridge University Press, 2013). John Munro compellingly (if not entirely convincingly) challenges aspects of their basic argument about the effects of McCarthyism in *The Anticolonial Front: The African American Freedom Struggle and Global Decolonisation, 1945–1960* (New York: Cambridge University Press, 2017). To say that acceptable civil rights discourse became narrower in the postwar period is not, however, to argue that anticolonialism and human rights became completely irrelevant to activists. See Carol Anderson, *Bourgeois Radicals: The NAACP and the Struggle for Colonial Liberation, 1941–1960* (New York: Cambridge University Press, 2015).

17. Mary G. Rolinson, *Grassroots Garveyism: The Universal Negro Improvement Association in the Rural South* (Chapel Hill: University of North Carolina Press, 2007), 110–111; Evers and Szanton, *Have No Fear*, 66, 71–75. A Neshoba County man named William McGowan wrote to the NAACP headquarters with a list of locals who had expressed interest in establishing a branch. The prospective members were James Huddleston, W. W. Wilson, Charlie Pickens, A. V. Savage, Albert Miller (Louisville), Melvin Savage, and William McGowan. William McGowan to William Pickens, March 12, 1936, Folder 18, Box I:G106, NAACP Records; William McGowan to William Pickens, March 26, 1936, Folder 18, Box I:G106, NAACP

Records. For figures on the Kemper and Winston branches, see branch lists from 1951 and 1952 in Folder 2, Box II:C98, NAACP Records.

18. Charles Evers and Neil E. Goldschmidt, interview by Robert Penn Warren. There are only a few sources for county-level figures on Black voting in Mississippi in the postwar decade. Both Florence Mars (who spoke to the circuit clerks) and James Barnes (author of a 1955 master's thesis on Black voting in Mississippi) agree that Neshoba County had eight Black registrants in the mid-1950s. The US Commission on Civil Rights produced similar figures. See Mars, *Witness in Philadelphia*, 58–59, 112; Hanes Walton Jr., Sherman C. Puckett, and Donald R. Deskins Jr., *The African American Electorate: A Statistical History* (Los Angeles: CQ Press, 2012), 505–506; and US Commission on Civil Rights, *Report of the United States Commission on Civil Rights, 1959* (Washington: US Commission on Civil Rights, 1959), 578–580. Different figures appear without citation in Sister M. Michele, *The History of the Negro Vote in Mississippi* (master's thesis: Loyola University, 1957), 134. On the difficulties of voter registration among dependent workers before the 1960s, see Dittmer, *Local People*, 29–30.

19. Anthropologist Robert R. Solenberger, who visited Philadelphia in 1950, wrote that the Choctaws he spoke to cited their inability to interpret the Constitution to the satisfaction of the registrar. Nevertheless, in summer 1951, agency superintendent McMullen urged Choctaws to "exercise their legal rights as citizens" by registering, paying poll taxes, and voting in local elections. That fall, BIA tribal relations officer Marie L. Hayes visited east-central Mississippi, where, per her report, Choctaws "indicated as one of their major interests the full right to vote." Tribal Council chairman Emmett York pointed out that "obviously in some communities the Indians do not vote." Council member Tom Ben stated that he had been voting "for six or seven years," but that he was the only member to have done so. According to Hayes, other council members suggested that Choctaws were allowed to vote in Newton, Leake, and Jones Counties, but that "only two or three Indians of the entire Mississippi Choctaw Band exercise the right of the ballot." Tribal Council Minutes, April 13, 1948, and October 23, 1951; Robert R. Solenberger to Lawrence E. Lindley, January 31, 1950, Tribal File, Choctaw (Mississippi), 1947–1958, Records of the NCAI; "Narrative Report of Visit of Tribal Relations Officer, Muskogee Area, to Choctaw Indian Agency, Philadelphia, Mississippi, October 22 to November 2, 1951," 21–22, Tribal File, Choctaw (Mississippi), 1947–1958, Records of the NCAI.

20. Frederick E. Hoxie, *A Final Promise: The Campaign to Assimilate the Indians, 1880–1920* (Lincoln: University of Nebraska Press, 2001), xix, 43–44; Vine Deloria Jr., *Custer Died for Your Sins: An Indian Manifesto*, rev. ed. (Norman: University of Oklahoma Press, 1988), 46; *An Act to Authorize the Secretary of the Interior to Issue Certificates of Citizenship to Indians*, Public Law 68–175, US Statutes at Large 43 (1924): 253.

21. Paul C. Rosier, *Serving Their Country: American Indian Politics and Patriotism in the Twentieth Century* (Cambridge, MA: Harvard University Press, 2009), 64–70; John Collier, "The American Congo," *Survey* 50, no. 9 (August 1923): 467–476; Laurence M. Hauptman, "Africa View: John Collier, the British Colonial Service and American Indian Policy, 1933–1945," *Historian* 48, no. 3 (May 1986): 368. For an overview of the Indian New Deal, see Graham D. Taylor, *The New Deal and American Indian Tribalism: The Administration of the Indian Reorganization Act, 1934–45* (Lincoln: University of Nebraska Press, 1980); Lawrence C. Kelly, *The Assault on Assimilation: John Collier and the Origins of Indian Policy Reform* (Albuquerque: University of New Mexico Press, 1983).

22. Katherine M. B. Osburn, "'In a Name of Justice and Fairness': The Mississippi Choctaw Indian Federation versus the BIA, 1934," in *Beyond Red Power: American Indian Politics and Activism since 1900*, ed. Daniel M. Cobb and Loretta Fowler (Santa Fe, NM: School for Advanced Research, 2007), 109–125. Malinda Maynor Lowery points out how such confusion exposed fundamental weaknesses in the structure of the IRA. See Lowery, *Lumbee Indians in the Jim Crow South: Race, Identity, and the Making of a Nation* (Chapel Hill: University of North Carolina Press, 2010), 129–131.

23. *Constitution and By-Laws of the Mississippi Band of Choctaw Indians* (Washington, DC: Office of Indian Affairs, 1946) in Box 4, Constitutions and By-Laws, General Records Concerning Indian Organization, Records of the Bureau of Indian Affairs, RG 75, NARA. There is a wide literature on blood and race in settler contexts. Most pertinent for our purposes are Mikaëla M. Adams, *Who Belongs? Race, Resources, and Tribal Citizenship in the Native South* (New York: Oxford University Press, 2016), 129–131; and Katherine M. B. Osburn, *Choctaw Resurgence in Mississippi: Race, Class, and Nation Building in the Jim Crow South, 1830–1977* (Lincoln: University of Nebraska Press, 2014), 37–56, and "'Any Sane Person': Race, Rights, and Tribal Sovereignty in the Construction of the Dawes Rolls for the Choctaw Nation," *Journal of the Gilded Age and Progressive Era* 9, no. 4 (October 2010): 451–471. For a discussion of the IRA's (mis)definition of Indianness in another Southern context, see Lowery, *Lumbee Indians in the Jim Crow South*, 121–148. One of the shibboleths of the budding field of settler-colonial studies is the notion that settlers used blood and race alternately to define Indians out of existence and to construct as inclusive as possible a category of "blackness." See Patrick Wolfe, "Settler Colonialism and the Elimination of the Native," *Journal of Genocide Research* 8, no. 4 (December 2006): 387–409, and "Land, Labor, and Difference: Elementary Structures of Race," *American Historical Review* 106, no. 3 (June 2001): 866–905.

24. *Constitution and By-Laws of the Mississippi Band of Choctaw Indians*, 1–4; A. H. McMullen to the voters of the Mississippi Choctaw Indians, May 25, 1945, Folder 2, Box 23, Series 9, John E. Rankin Collection, University of Mississippi.

25. Donald L. Fixico, *Termination and Relocation: Federal Indian Policy, 1945–1960* (Albuquerque: University of New Mexico Press, 1990), 21–44; Statement by the President upon Signing Bill Creating the Indian Claims Commission, *Legislative Insight*, https://congressional-proquest-com.proxy.lib.fsu.edu/legisinsight?id=PL79-726PS&type=PRES_SIGN_STMT (accessed September 24, 2019); Harry S. Truman to Harold D. Smith, February 25, 1946, Harry S. Truman Library and Museum, available online at https://www.trumanlibrary.gov/library/research-files/correspondence-between-president-harry-s-truman-and-harold-d-smith (accessed September 24, 2019).

26. Tribal Council Minutes, April 8, 1947, July 17, 1947, January 13, 1948, and April 13, 1948. The July minutes indicate that the tribe was occasionally allotted money for land purchases even as they sought broader resolution of the Article 14 issue. In this meeting, the superintendent announced an allotment of $10,000, bringing the total available to the tribe for land purchases to $16,600. The Tribal Council decided use $2,000 to purchase a farm in Conehatta from a man named Paul Bush. Committeemen were urged to "make a further survey for farms that might be purchased and especially farms that had necessary improvements including residences, barns, and carry a good soil type with sufficient farm lands open in order for a family to make immediate use."

27. Tribal Council Minutes, July 20, 1948, and January 12, 1949; "Indians Prepare to Push Claims against 'Great White Father,'" *Jackson Clarion-Ledger*, August 8, 1949, 1; Gordon Brown, "Choctaws Suing U.S. for $200,000,000," *Hattiesburg American*, November 17, 1949, 14; Osburn, *Choctaw Resurgence in Mississippi*, 151–153; "Hearing for Indian Claims Set Oct. 6," *Jackson Clarion-Ledger*, July 17, 1953; "Indians Were Paid, Government Argues," *Jackson Clarion-Ledger*, October 8, 1953, 4; "Opinion of the Commission," Indian Claims Commission Decisions, https://cdm17279.contentdm.oclc.org/digital/collection/p17279coll10/id/570/rec/2; "US Court Refuses Claims of Choctaws," *Jackson Clarion-Ledger*, February 4, 1956, 1.

28. These discussions centered on Choctaws living on tribal lands, not sharecroppers. By all accounts, Choctaw sharecroppers lived in deplorable conditions—generally shacks—on land that they did not own. Tribal Council Minutes, July 10, 1946, October 12, 1948, October 12, 1954, October 9, 1956, and April 12, 1960; Robert R. Solenberger to Lawrence E. Lindley, January 31, 1950, Tribal File, Choctaw (Mississippi), 1947–1958, Records of the NCAI; *Constitution and By-Laws of the Mississippi Band of Choctaw Indians*, 1.

29. Tribal Council Minutes, October 12, 1948; "Indian Agency Asks Cooperation of Those Who Employ Children under 16 Farm Work, Help Keep Them in School," *Neshoba Democrat*, November 17, 1950, 1, 5.

30. Osburn, *Choctaw Resurgence in Mississippi*, 133, 140–143; Tribal Council Min-

utes, October 14, 1947. On indirect rule in comparative perspective, see Mahmood Mamdani, *Neither Settler nor Native: The Making and Unmaking of Permanent Minorities* (Cambridge, MA: Belknap Press of Harvard University Press, 2020), 37–100.

31. My understanding of notions of tradition and modernity in the twentieth-century South owes to Andrew K. Frank, "Modern by Tradition: Seminole Innovation in the Contemporary South," *Native South* 10 (2017): 76–95.

32. Charles F. Wilkinson et al., "The Trust Obligation," in *Indian Self-Rule: First-Hand Accounts of Indian-White Relations from Roosevelt to Reagan*, ed. Kenneth R. Philp (Logan: Utah State University Press, 1995), 302–310; US Congress, House of Representatives, Subcommittee of the Committee on Appropriations, *Interior Department Appropriation Bill for 1949*, 80th Cong., 2nd Sess., 1948, 898; Richard Kluger, *Simple Justice: The History of Brown v. Board of Education and Black America's Struggle for Equality* (New York: Vintage, 2004), 793; Lee D. Baker, *From Savage to Negro: Anthropology and the Construction of Race, 1896–1954* (Berkeley: University of California Press, 1998), 168–187, 208–228; Thomas Clarkin, *Federal Indian Policy in the Kennedy and Johnson Administrations, 1961–1969* (Albuquerque: University of New Mexico Press, 2001), 7–12.

33. Paul C. Rosier, "They Are Ancestral Homelands: Race, Place, and Politics in Cold War Native America, 1945–1961," *Journal of American History* 92, no. 4 (March 2006): 1301.

34. Rosier, *Serving Their Country*, 145–146.

35. Fixico, *Termination and Relocation*; Donald L. Fixico, *The Urban Indian Experience in America* (Albuquerque: University of New Mexico Press, 2000), 207–209; Tribal Council Minutes, July 14, 1953, and October 13, 1953.

36. US Congress, House of Representatives, Committee of the Whole House on the State of the Union, *Report with Respect to the House Resolution Authorizing the Committee on Interior and Insular Affairs to Conduct an Investigation of the Bureau of Indian Affairs (Pursuant to House Resolution 89)*, 83rd Cong., 2nd Sess., 1954, H. Rep. 2680, 3, 18, 31–32.

37. Cleddie Bell to W. O. Roberts, January 4, 1954, in Tribal Council Minutes, October 13, 1953; Tribal Council Minutes, January 12, 1954. As the BIA considered the fate of the Choctaw hospital, the board of trustees at the Neshoba County Hospital lobbied BIA personnel in Washington, DC, to let them lease the Choctaw hospital for obstetric and pediatric services. The board told the BIA that it would serve "the eligible indigent Indian . . . without segregation or discrimination." Glenn L. Emmons to John C. Stennis, February 26, 1954, Folder 3, Box 2, Department of the Interior, John C. Stennis Papers.

38. Tribal Council Minutes, April 13, 1954, July 13, 1954, and October 12, 1954; Fixico, *Termination and Relocation*, 92; Osburn, *Choctaw Resurgence in Mississippi*,

161–162. The law contained a provision that "hospitals now in operation for a specific tribe or tribes of Indians shall not be closed prior to July 1, 1956, without the consent of the governing body of the tribe or its organized council." See *An Act to Transfer the Maintenance and Operation of Hospital and Health Facilities for Indians to the Public Health Service, and for Other Purposes*, Public Law 568, U.S. Statutes at Large 68 (1954): 674.

39. Douglas K. Miller, *Indians on the Move: Native American Mobility and Urbanization in the Twentieth Century* (Chapel Hill: University of North Carolina Press, 2019), 7, 68–70. See also La Verne Madigan, *The American Indian Relocation Program* (New York: Association on American Indian Affairs, 1956); Fixico, *Termination and Relocation* and *The Urban Indian Experience in America*; James B. LaGrand, *Indian Metropolis: Native Americans in Chicago, 1945–75* (Urbana: University of Illinois Press, 2002); Nicolas G. Rosenthal, *Reimagining Indian Country: Native American Migration and Identity in Twentieth-Century Los Angeles* (Chapel Hill: University of North Carolina Press, 2012).

40. The literature on this sort of contradiction is rich. See especially Osburn, *Choctaw Resurgence in Mississippi*, 159–179; Frank, "Modern by Tradition"; Eric Hobsbawm and Terence Ranger, eds., *The Invention of Tradition* (New York: Cambridge University Press, 1983); William Beinart, *Twentieth-Century South Africa* (New York: Oxford University Press, 2001), 162–165; Cooper, *Africa since 1940*, 38–65; and Jocelyn Alexander, *The Unsettled Land: State-Making and the Politics of Land in Zimbabwe, 1893–2003* (Athens: Ohio University Press, 2006), 5–10, 46–48. Victor M. Kaneubbe to the National Congress of American Indians, October 11, 1957, Tribal File, Choctaw (Mississippi), 1947–1958, Records of the NCAI.

41. Jason Sokol, *There Goes My Everything: White Southerners in the Age of Civil Rights, 1945–1975* (New York: Vintage, 2007), 47–53; "United States Supreme Court Rules Out Segregation by Unanimous Vote of the Nine Court Justices," *Neshoba Democrat*, May 20, 1954, 1; Mars, *Witness in Philadelphia*, 53–56; Evers and Szanton, *Have No Fear*, 80. A 1959 Gallup poll revealed that *Brown* made many white Southerners suspicious of communist influence on the Supreme Court. See Michael J. Klarman, "Race and Rights," in *The Cambridge History of Law in America*, Vol. 3, ed. Michael Grossberg and Christopher Tomlins (New York: Cambridge University Press, 2008), 426.

42. Charles C. Bolton, "Mississippi's School Equalization Program, 1945–1954: 'A Last Gasp to Try to Maintain a Segregated Educational System,'" *Journal of Southern History* 66, no. 4 (November 2000): 781–814; Jason Morgan Ward, *Defending White Democracy: The Making of a Segregationist Movement and the Remaking of Racial Politics, 1936–1965* (Chapel Hill: University of North Carolina Press, 2011), 121–140; Meeting of the Delta Council Board of Directors, June 25, 1946, Folder 18, Box 22,

Agricultural Extension L. I. Jones Collection; "White Says State Fighting to Survive in School Vote," *Jackson Clarion-Ledger*, December 17, 1954, 1, 11; "OK School Amendment by 2 ½ to 1 Margin," *Jackson Clarion-Ledger*, December 22, 1954, 1.

43. Study: Philadelphia Separate School District, 1955, Folder 0–110, Box 5, Records of the Mississippi Cooperative Extension Service—Community Development Department, University Archives, Mississippi State University, Starkville, MS. Black schools in Mississippi lagged behind white schools in consolidation (a trend that dated to the Progressive Era whereby smaller, community-based schools combined into larger, graded schools), largely due to neglect on the part of all-white school boards. For instance, the Longdale School, of which Black residents of that community were immensely proud, survived until 1963. See Johnson, *History of Longdale High School, 1949–1963*; and Bolton, "Mississippi's School Equalization Program, 1945–1954," 787–793. The county school district faced the added pressure of public scandal, as Superintendent I. M. Latimer spent the late 1950s under investigation for embezzlement of tens of thousands of dollars in school funds. "Neshoba Schools Get $10,224.31 in Auditor Suit," *Jackson Clarion-Ledger*, December 30, 1960, 8.

44. L. O. Hopkins to John C. Stennis, March 2, 1953, Folder 31, Box 1, Civil Rights, John C. Stennis Papers; J. T. McCully to John C. Stennis, December 21, 1955, Folder 41, Box 1, Civil Rights, John C. Stennis Papers; Natalie G. Adams and James H. Adams, *Just Trying to Have School: The Struggle for Desegregation in Mississippi* (Jackson: University Press of Mississippi, 2018), 32, 192–193.

45. Mars, *Witness in Philadelphia*, 59; Pete Daniel, *Lost Revolutions: The South in the 1950s* (Chapel Hill: University of North Carolina Press, 2000), 60.

46. Tom Ethridge, "Mississippi Notebook," *Jackson Clarion-Ledger*, December 4, 1956, 3; "Council Says JPC Blocked Arrests," *Jackson Clarion-Ledger*, May 19, 1959, 1. For a discussion of the theme of settler anxiety in the late-colonial period, see Will Jackson, "The Settler's Demise: Decolonization and Mental Breakdown in 1950s Kenya," in *Anxieties, Fear and Panic in Colonial Settings: Empires on the Verge of a Nervous Breakdown*, ed. Harald Fischer-Tiné (London: Palgrave Macmillan, 2016), 73–96.

47. "Tighter Voting Law Apparently Approved," *Hattiesburg American*, November 3, 1954, 1; Dennis J. Mitchell, *A New History of Mississippi* (Jackson: University Press of Mississippi, 2014), 403–404; "12 More Charters Issued by State," *Jackson Clarion-Ledger*, December 4, 1956, 19; "Citizens' Council Leaders Meet Here with Governor," *Jackson Clarion-Ledger*, May 23, 1957, 10; Charles M. Hills, "Affairs of State," *Jackson Clarion-Ledger*, October 23, 1957, 7.

48. "Kemper County Ag Agent Honored for Finding New Sources of Income," *Columbian-Progress*, October 27, 1955, 1; Bob Hobson to John C. Stennis, May 22,

1956, Folder 10, Box 7, Civil Rights, John C. Stennis Papers; John C. Stennis to Bob Hobson, May 28, 1956, Folder 10, Box 7, Civil Rights, John C. Stennis Papers.

49. "Fairchilds Is New President of the Lions," *Scott County Times*, July 16, 1958, 1; Forest Citizens Council ad, *Scott County Times*, October 16, 1957, 9; Mr. and Mrs. Richard Ware, interview by Howard Langfitt, transcript, Jackson, MS, February 10, 1956, WLBT "Farm Family of the Week" Collection; "Measells Elected Chairman Forest Citizens Council," *Scott County Times*, December 22, 1955, 9; "Officers of Newton County Citizens' Council Elected," *Newton Record*, April 11, 1957.

50. Evers and Szanton, *Have No Fear*, 94–96; Howard Cole, interview by Chester M. Morgan, transcript, Philadelphia, MS, September 13, 1973, Center for Oral History and Cultural Heritage, University of Southern Mississippi. Charles Evers, interviewer unknown, transcript, Fayette, MS, December 3, 1971, Center for Oral History and Cultural Heritage, University of Southern Mississippi.

51. Yasuhiro Katagiri, *The Mississippi State Sovereignty Commission: Civil Rights and States' Rights* (Jackson: University Press of Mississippi, 2001), 5–6; L. C. Hicks to Ney M. Gore, Jr., July 11, 1957, SCR 2-112-1-1-1-1-1, Mississippi State Sovereignty Commission Files (hereafter MSSC), Mississippi Department of Archives and History, available online at https://www.mdah.ms.gov/arrec/digital_archives/sovcom/result.php?image=images/png/cd05/038124.png&otherstuff=2|112|1|1|1|1|1|37531|#; Zack J. Van Landingham to Director, State Sovereignty Commission, April 7, 1959, SCR 2-112-1-3-1-1-1, MSSC, https://www.mdah.ms.gov/arrec/digital_archives/sovcom/result.php?image=images/png/cd05/038129.png&otherstuff=2|112|1|3|1|1|1|37536|. Whether L. W. Payne was ever an informant for the Sovereignty Commission is not clear.

52. Charles M. Payne, *I've Got the Light of Freedom: The Organizing Tradition and the Mississippi Freedom Struggle* (Berkeley: University of California Press, 1995), 36–42; "Policeman Kills Man, Is Cleared," *McComb Enterprise-Journal*, October 27, 1959, 1; "Negro Killed by Police Officer," *Neshoba Democrat*, October 29, 1959, 1; "G-Men in Neshoba Slaying," *Jackson Clarion-Ledger*, November 10, 1959, 1.

53. NAACP News and Views, March 25, 1959, Branch Files, Box III:C75, NAACP Records. The NAACP had largely avoided issues around mechanization since the late 1940s. See Bradford Jordan to Walter White, January 15, 1947, Labor, Agriculture, Wage Ceiling, Box II:B85, NAACP Records; Madison Jones to Walter White, March 25, 1947, Labor, Agriculture, Wage Ceiling, Box II:B85, NAACP Records.

54. Tribal Council Minutes, January 13, 1959.

55. Elkins, "Race, Citizenship, and Governance," 212–219; Wendy Webster, "'There'll Always Be an England': Representations of Colonial Wars and Immigration, 1948–1968," *Journal of British Studies* 40, no. 4 (October 2001): 557; Martin Thomas, "A Path Not Taken? British Perspectives on French Colonial Violence

after 1945," in *Wind of Change: Harold Macmillan and British Decolonization*, ed. L. J. Butler and Sarah Stockwell (New York: Palgrave Macmillan, 2013), 165. Andrew Cohen provides an up-to-date discussion of the historiography of the Central African Federation in the introduction to *The Politics and Economics of Decolonization in Africa: The Failed Experiment of the Central African Federation* (New York: I. B. Tauris, 2017), 1–19. See also Caroline Elkins, "The Re-assertion of the British Empire in Southeast Asia," *Journal of Interdisciplinary History* 39, no. 3 (Winter 2009): 361–385.

56. Borstelmann, *The Cold War and the Color Line*, 102, 104; William I. Hitchcock, *The Age of Eisenhower: America and the World in the 1950s* (New York: Simon & Schuster, 2018), 296–301; "The Quarter Loaf," *Nation*, September 7, 1957, 101; *Report of the United States Commission on Civil Rights, 1959*, 548.

CHAPTER 4: ENCLOSURE: SETTLER AGRICULTURE IN THE 1950S

1. Pete Daniel's is the best account of this process. See Daniel, *Dispossession: Discrimination against African American Farmers in the Age of Civil Rights* (Chapel Hill: University of North Carolina Press, 2013). For farm statistics on east-central Mississippi, see US Department of Commerce, Bureau of the Census, *Census of Agriculture*, 1945, 1969. For outmigration in the 1950s, see Gladys K. Bowles and James D. Tarver, *Net Migration of the Population, 1950–60: By Age, Sex, and Color* (Washington, DC: Economic Research Service, USDA, 1965), 725, 736–737, 742–743, 746, 752. Both Daniel and Jack Temple Kirby compared land consolidation in the South to the English enclosure movement. See Pete Daniel, *Breaking the Land: The Transformation of Cotton, Tobacco, and Rice Cultures since 1880* (Urbana: University of Illinois Press, 1985), and Kirby, *Rural Worlds Lost: The American South, 1920–1960* (Baton Rouge: Louisiana State University Press, 1987). For a more recent take, see Wendell Berry, "Our Deserted Country," in *Our Only World: Ten Essays* (Berkeley, CA: Counterpoint, 2015), 105–158. Attala County's agents were frank in their depictions of these changes. See J. F. Buchanan, Annual Narrative Report, Attala County, MS, 1956, 1, Box 196, Records of the Extension Service, RG 33, NARA.

2. Of the numerous studies of the Choctaws' economic health, the most complete for our purposes is Economic Development Planning Office of the Mississippi Band of Choctaw Indians, *Mississippi Band of Choctaw Indians Overall Economic Development Program, 1978–1982*, n.p., 1977, Neshoba County Public Library, Philadelphia, MS.

3. Ellen Meiksins Wood, *The Origin of Capitalism: A Longer View* (Brooklyn, NY: Verso, 2017), 177–181; Wendell Berry, *The Unsettling of America: Culture and Agriculture* (San Francisco: Sierra Club Books, 1977), 39–48.

4. Gregory S. Wilson, "Deindustrialization, Poverty, and Federal Area Redevel-

opment in the United States, 1945–1965," in *Beyond the Ruins: The Meanings of Deindustrialization*, ed. Jefferson Cowie and Joseph Heathcott (Ithaca, NY: ILR Press of Cornell University Press, 2003), 181; Numan V. Bartley, "The Southern Enclosure Movement," *Georgia Historical Quarterly* 71, no. 3 (Fall 1987): 440; Jocelyn Alexander, *The Unsettled Land: State-making and the Politics of Land in Zimbabwe, 1893–2003*. Athens: Ohio University Press, 2006, 51. For a longer-term study, see Michael de Klerk, "Seasons That Will Never Return: The Impact of Farm Mechanization on Employment, Incomes and Population Distribution in the Western Transvaal," *Journal of Southern African Studies* 11, no. 1 (October 1984): 84–105. The most complete accounts of the massive migration of Black Southerners to the North during the twentieth century are Nicholas Lemann, *The Promised Land: The Great Black Migration and How It Changed America* (New York: Knopf, 1991); and Isabel Wilkerson, *The Warmth of Other Suns: The Epic Story of America's Great Migration* (New York: Random House, 2010).

5. M. S. Shaw et al., County Agent Leader Annual Report, Mississippi, 1954, Box 225, Records of the Extension Service, RG 33, NARA; C. S. Norton et al., Combined Annual Report of County Extension Workers, Neshoba County, MS, 1950, Box 199, Records of the Extension Service, RG 33, NARA. Neshoba County had had about a dozen county agents since 1918. For a list of the agents between 1918 and 1937, see "Assignment 17: Agriculture," 1937, Box 10773, WPA Files, MDAH.

6. M. M. Hubert and W. E. Ammons, County Agent Leader Annual Report (Negro), Mississippi, 1950, Box 192, Records of the Extension Service, RG 33, NARA; W. E. Ammons, County Agent Leader Annual Report (Negro), Mississippi, 1960, Box 168, Records of the Extension Service, RG 33, NARA; "Supplement to Assignment 10: Negroes," January 29, 1937, Box 10772, WPA Files, MDAH; "Associate Agent Is Retiring," *Jackson Clarion-Ledger*, August 12, 1969, 5.

7. UC Commission on Civil Rights, *Equal Opportunity in Farm Families: An Appraisal of Services Rendered by Agencies of the United States Department of Agriculture* (Washington, DC: Government Printing Office, 1965), 22–38.

8. Mississippi Extension Service, 60–61, 67–68, Alabama-Mississippi Field Trip and Interviews, Box 8, Records of the US Commission on Civil Rights, RG 453, NARA.

9. Clay Lyle, Director's Report, Mississippi, 1952, Box 196, Records of the Extension Service, RG 33, NARA; Clay Lyle, Director's Report, Mississippi, 1958, Box 185, Records of the Extension Service, RG 33, NARA; Clay Lyle, Director's Report, Mississippi, 1959, Box 159, Records of the Extension Service, RG 33, NARA.

10. C. S. Norton and Joe C. Fulton, Annual Narrative Report, Neshoba County, MS, 1950, 22, Box 199, Records of the Extension Service, RG 33, NARA; Esther L.

Kerr and Mary I. Barnett, Annual Narrative Report, Neshoba County, MS, 1952, 26, Box 201, Records of the Extension Service, RG 33, NARA; Margaret Threadgill, Christine Brand, and Nell D. Herrin, Annual Narrative Report, Neshoba County, MS, 1959, Box 165, Records of the Extension Service, RG 33, NARA.

11. US Commission on Civil Rights, *Equal Opportunity in Farm Programs*, 41.

12. M. S. Shaw, associate director of extension work in Mississippi, reported in 1954 that the "4-H Club approach is recognized as one of the most effective methods of Extension teaching. Demonstrations carried on by club members are watched closely by parents and neighbors. It is often true that parents of 4-H Club members base their farming practice on the teaching obtained from Club demonstrations." See Shaw et al., County Agent Leader Annual Report, Mississippi, 1954, 36–37, Box 225, Records of the Extension Service, RG 33, NARA.

13. Berry, *Unsettling of America*, 41; Pete Daniel, "Not Predestination: The Rural South and Twentieth-Century Transformation," in *The American South in the Twentieth Century*, ed. Craig S. Pascoe, Karen Trahan Leathem, and Andy Ambrose (Athens: University of Georgia Press, 2005), 97; US Commission on Civil Rights, *Equal Opportunity in Farm Programs*, 57, 97.

14. US Department of Agriculture, Economic Research Service, *The Cotton Industry in the United States* (Washington DC: Government Printing Office, 1996), 68–69; C. S. Norton and Joe C. Fulton, Annual Narrative Report, Neshoba County, MS, 1950, 22, Box 199, Records of the Extension Service, RG 33, NARA; "County Agent Again Urges Poison Cotton," *Neshoba Democrat*, June 16, 1950, 1, 7; C. S. Norton and Joe C. Fulton, Annual Narrative Report, Neshoba County, MS, 1951, 7–8, Box 189, Records of the Extension Service, RG 33, NARA; C. S. Norton and Joe C. Fulton, Annual Narrative Report, Neshoba County, MS, 1952, 14–15, Box 201, Records of the Extension Service, RG 33, NARA; C.S. Norton and Joe C. Fulton, Annual Narrative Report, Neshoba County, MS, 1953, Box 312, Records of the Extension Service, RG 33, NARA. For the toxicity of BHC and toxaphene, see US Department of Health and Human Services, Agency for Toxic Substances and Disease Registry, Division of Toxicology and Human Health Science, *Public Health Statement: Hexachlorocyclohexane* (Atlanta, 2005), https://www.atsdr.cdc.gov/ToxProfiles/tp43-c1-b.pdf; and US Department of Health and Human Services, Agency for Toxic Substances and Disease Registry, Division of Toxicology and Human Health Science, *Public Health Statement: Toxaphene* (Atlanta, 2014), https://www.atsdr.cdc.gov/ToxProfiles/tp94-c1-b.pdf. The squeeze of 1950 was not altogether a surprise. See, for instance, C. S. Norton's 1949 report: "The mechanization on the large cotton farms is coming into its own. Too, it appears now that cotton marketing quotas will be enforced in 1950. Therefore, the small cotton farmers, which constitute a large percentage of the farmers in Neshoba County, will be forced to turn

to other enterprises for their major cash crop." Norton, Annual Narrative Report, Neshoba County, MS, 1949, Box 231, Records of the Extension Service, RG 33, NARA

15. C. S. Norton et al., Annual Narrative Report, Neshoba County, MS, 1954, Box 233, Records of the Extension Service, RG 33, NARA; "Farm Pattern Changing Fast," *Neshoba Democrat*, November 20, 1958, n.p.; *Census of Agriculture*, 1950, 1959; B. H. Dixon to John C. Stennis, September 4, 1951, Folder 3, Box 6, Agriculture, John C. Stennis Papers, MSU.

16. Clay Lyle, Director's Report, Mississippi, 1952, Box 196, Records of the Extension Service, RG 33, NARA; C. S. Norton et al., Annual Narrative Report, Neshoba County, MS, 1956, Box 201, Records of the Extension Service, RG 33, NARA; *Census of Agriculture*, 1950, 1959; Joe C. Taylor and W. T. Cornelius, Annual Narrative Report, Newton County, MS, 1951, Box 189, Records of the Extension Service, RG 33, NARA.

17. Dorothy Dickins, *Levels of Living of Young White Farm-Operator Families in Mississippi* (State College: Mississippi State College, Agricultural Experiment Station, 1959), 13–14; Dorothy Dickins, *Levels of Living of Young Negro Farm-Operator Families in Mississippi* (State College: Mississippi State College, Agricultural Experiment Station, 1959), 13; L. J. Henry, interview by Gary Chickaway, Jimmy Benn, and Elvis Benn, transcript, April 29, 1977, University of Florida Digital Collections, https://ufdc.ufl.edu/UF00007865/00001 (accessed November 12, 2019); Clay Lyle, Director's Report, Mississippi, 1958, Box 185, Records of the Extension Service, RG 33, NARA.

18. B. H. Dixon to John C. Stennis, September 4, 1951, Folder 3, Box 6, Agriculture, John C. Stennis Papers, MSU; C. I. Smith to John C. Stennis, October 4, 1951, Folder 3, Box 6, Agriculture, John C. Stennis Papers, MSU.

19. T. J. Scott to James O. Eastland, May 27, 1955, Folder 20, Box 30, State/Local Files, Constituent Files, James O. Eastland Collection; Glenn Emmons to James O. Eastland, October 11, 1955, Folder 20, Box 30, State/Local Files, Constituent Files, James O. Eastland Collection; Douglas K. Miller, *Indians on the Move: Native American Mobility and Urbanization in the Twentieth Century* (Chapel Hill: University of North Carolina Press, 2019), 4.

20. *Census of Agriculture*, 1950, 1959. Interestingly, area forester James E. Allen even had the *Neshoba Democrat* run an article suggesting that farmers should plant more seedlings because "we may be cutting too many trees to supply fresh oxygen." "We May Be Cutting Too Many Trees to Supply Fresh Oxygen," *Neshoba Democrat*, June 25, 1959, 1.

21. H. J. Putnam, "The Influence of Size of Farms on Family Labor Earnings, Land Use, Etc.," November 5, 1946, unpublished report in C. M. Chaffee, Missis-

sippi Narrative Progress Report on Agricultural Development through Test Demonstration, 1946, 15–16, Box 196, Records of the Extension Service, RG 33, NARA; Clay Lyle, Director's Report, Mississippi, 1958, Box 185, Records of the Extension Service, RG 33, NARA. Quite predictably, the Extension Service's attitude echoed that of the South African Industrial and Agricultural Requirements Commission, which in 1941 had declared its aim "to reduce the total number of farmers . . . by facilitating the migration from rural to urban areas." See Stefan Schirmer, "Motives for Mechanisation in South African Agriculture, c1940–1980," *African Studies* 63, no. 1 (July 2004): 12.

22. US Commission on Civil Rights, *Equal Opportunity in Farm Programs*, 57–82; *Census of Agriculture*, 1945, 1959.

23. Inez Gunn to John C. Stennis, February 22, 1957, Folder 53, Box 1, Agriculture, John C. Stennis Papers, MSU.

24. John C. Stennis to T. B. Fatherree, March 1, 1957, Folder 53, Box 1, Agriculture, John C. Stennis Papers, MSU; T. B. Fatherree to John C. Stennis, March 5, 1957, Folder 53, Box 1, Agriculture, John C. Stennis Papers, MSU; John C. Stennis to T. B. Fatherree, March 7, 1957, Folder 53, Box 1, Agriculture, John C. Stennis Papers, MSU; T. B. Fatherree to John C. Stennis, March 12, 1957, Folder 53, Box 1, Agriculture, John C. Stennis Papers, MSU.

25. T. B. Fatherree to John C. Stennis, April 9, 1957, Folder 53, Box 1, Agriculture, John C. Stennis Papers, MSU; Audrey S. Mosley, U.S., *Find a Grave Index, 1600s-Current* [database online] (Provo, UT: Ancestry.com Operations, 2012).

26. Michael Thompson and Ted Ownby, "Howard Langfitt," in *The Mississippi Encyclopedia*, ed. Ted Ownby et al. (Jackson: University Press of Mississippi, 2017), 709.

27. Mr. and Mrs. J. A. Howle, interview by Howard Langfitt, transcript, Jackson, MS, July 1, 1955, WLBT "Farm Family of the Week" Collection.

28. Howle, interview.

29. Mr. and Mrs. R. B. Moore, interview by Howard Langfitt, transcript, Jackson, MS, May 10, 1957, WLBT "Farm Family of the Week" Collection.

30. Mr. and Mrs. J. U. Fulcher, interview by Howard Langfitt, transcript, Jackson, MS, June 7, 1956, WLBT "Farm Family of the Week" Collection; Mr. and Mrs. W. K. Boutwell, interview by Howard Langfitt, transcript, Jackson, MS, January 18, 1957, WLBT "Farm Family of the Week" Collection.

31. For the history of WLBT and the civil rights movement, see Steven D. Classen, *Watching Jim Crow: The Struggles over Mississippi TV, 1955–1969* (Durham, NC: Duke University Press, 2004). For some connections between the Farm Bureau's segregationist leadership and the White Citizens' Councils, see Pete Daniel, *Lost Revolutions*, 195–196. As late as November 2018, the webpage of the Mississippi

Farm Bureau contained the following paragraph on the organization's role after 1954: "Nationally, Farm Bureau entered the role of the major organization serving as a watchdog to preserve individual freedom and initiative. Issue after issue was defeated by Farm Bureau at the grassroots which would have led agriculture down the road toward more socialism." The bureau's history page is now under construction. Screen shot in possession of author.

32. Neshoba Rural Area Development Association, *Comprehensive Overall Economic Program (OEDP) for Neshoba County, Mississippi* (Philadelphia, 1962), Folder 0–111, Box 6, Records of the Mississippi Cooperative Extension Service—Community Development Department, University Archives, Mississippi State University; Newton County Rural Areas Development Committee, *Newton County, Mississippi, Overall Economic Development Plan*, 1962, 46–50.

33. The estimate for the decline in lumber jobs is conservative. The 1949 figure could have been as high as 27,300, meaning a 55 percent drop. See James E. Moak, *Economic Opportunities in Mississippi's Pine Lumber Industry* (State College: Mississippi Agricultural Experiment Station, 1961), 17; C. S. Norton, Annual Narrative Report, Neshoba County, MS, 1950, 5–6, Box 199, Records of the Extension Service, RG 33, NARA; C. S. Norton et al., Annual Narrative Report, Neshoba County, MS, 1959, Box 165, Records of the Extension Service, RG 33, NARA.

34. "80 Machines Have Arrived Here for Training Workers," *Neshoba Democrat*, January 12, 1945, 1; Charles Madden Tolbert, "A Sociological Study of the Choctaw Indians in Mississippi," (PhD diss., Louisiana State University, 1958), 126; Economic Development Planning Office of the Mississippi Band of Choctaw Indians, *Mississippi Band of Choctaw Indians Overall Economic Development Program, 1978–1982*, 21; Florence Mars, *Witness in Philadelphia* (Baton Rouge: Louisiana State University Press, 1977), 273–274. In 1959 L. W. Payne reported that "diversification, mechanization and the soil bank program have drastically altered the agricultural picture in the county and provided people with more spare time than ever before. This has cause a need for male industrial employment in this area." L. W. Payne, Annual Narrative Report, Neshoba County, MS, 1959, Box 165, Records of the Extension Service, RG 33, NARA.

35. "Interview Labor for New Factory," *Kemper County Messenger*, August 8, 1946, 1; "Lions Fete Teachers," *Kemper County Messenger*, September 12, 1946, 1; "Prospects for Furniture Factory in Dekalb Soon," *Kemper County Messenger*, September 18, 1947, 1; "McLean Tells Lions That No Industry Coming Here," *Kemper County Messenger*, January 27, 1949, 1; "Factory with $30,000 Month Payroll Considering Dekalb," *Kemper County Messenger*, February 3, 1955, 1.

36. Angela Stuesse and Laura E. Helton, "Low-Wage Legacies, Race, and the Golden Chicken in Mississippi: Where Contemporary Immigration Meets Afri-

can American Labor History," *Southern Spaces*, December 31, 2013, available online at https://southernspaces.org/2013/low-wage-legacies-race-and-golden-chicken-mississippi-where-contemporary-immigration-meets-african-american-labor-history/.

37. Esther L. Kerr, Christine Brand, and Bettie S. Mosley, Annual Narrative Report, Neshoba County, MS, 1957, Box 205, Records of the Extension Service, RG 33, NARA; Julia H. Barnes, Annual Narrative Report, Leake County, MS, 1960, Box 174, Records of the Extension Service, RG 33, NARA; C. S. Norton et al., Annual Narrative Report, Neshoba County, MS, 1959, Box 165, Records of the Extension Service, RG 33, NARA.

38. Mississippi Legislature, Senate, *Report of the Temporary Fact-Finding Committee on the Development of Mississippi Resources pursuant to Senate Concurrent Resolution No. 137, Mississippi Legislature Regular Session 1956* (Jackson, 1957)

39. James N. Gregory, Mapping the Southern Diaspora, http://depts.washington.edu/moving1/map_diaspora.shtml (accessed November 12, 2019).

40. Miller, *Indians on the Move*, 69; Tribal Council Minutes, April 8, 1952; April 13, 1954, and January 11, 1955. Some Choctaws would later be relocated to Cincinnati, as well. Louise Willis's father, for instance, found work at S&H Green Stamps, a Cincinnati-based maker of trading stamps, before moving his family back to Bogue Chitto. Louise Willis, interview by John K. Mahon, transcript, Philadelphia, MS, December 4, 1973, Southern Indian Oral History Project, University of Florida.

41. "Relocation Service Set for Indians," *Neshoba Democrat*, September 13, 1956, 1; Tribal Council Minutes, October 23, 1956; Charlie Denson, interview by Samuel Proctor, transcript, Standing Pine, MS, December 3, 1973, Southern Indian Oral History Project, University of Florida.

42. Records indicate that most who moved to Tennessee were from the Bogue Chitto community. Exhibit G: Forestry Activity in Pearl River Community, Philleo Nash to Stewart L. Udall, April 21, 1965, Box 27, Office Files of James E. Officer, 1959–67, Office of the Associate Commissioner, Records of the Bureau of Indian Affairs, RG 75, NARA; George Baker, "Golddust: New Home of the Braves," *Nashville Tennessean*, September 24, 1961, 9, 23; Sue Ann Tanzer Roberts, "Golddust: Choctaws Scatter When Dreamland Disappoints Tribe," *Jackson Sun*, July 11, 1976, 1-B–2-B.

43. Claudia Goldin and Robert A. Margo, "The Great Compression: The Wage Structure in the United States at Mid-Century," *Quarterly Journal of Economics* 107, no. 1 (February 1992): 3; Jefferson Cowie, *The Great Exception: The New Deal and the Limits of American Politics* (Princeton, NJ: Princeton University Press, 2016), 9; Charles C. Killingsworth, *Structural Unemployment in the United States* (Washington,

DC: Department of Labor, 1964), 9–12; Thomas J. Sugrue, *Origins of the Urban Crisis: Race and Inequality in Postwar Detroit* (Princeton, NJ: Princeton University Press, 1996), 151. See also Thomas Piketty and Emmanuel Saez, "Income Inequality in the United States, 1913–1998," *Quarterly Journal of Economics* 118, no. 1 (February 2003): 1–39.

44. Sugrue, *Origins of the Urban Crisis*, 15; "Recession in Detroit," *Time*, April 14, 1958, 18. Lee E. Ohanian, of the conservative Hoover Institution, argues that the deindustrialization of what is now called the "Rust Belt" between 1950 and 1980 was the result of a lack of competitive pressure on manufacturers in the region. I cite him not to endorse this view but to demonstrate the broad acceptability of the view that deindustrialization began in the 1950s rather than the 1970s. See Ohanian, "Competition and the Decline of the Rust Belt," Economic Policy Paper 14–6, Federal Reserve Bank of Minneapolis (December 2014).

45. Testimony of Walter P. Reuther, Hearings before the United States Commission on Civil Rights, Detroit, MI, 1960, 44–45, 50–51, 59.

46. "The Automation Depression," *Nation*, November 29, 1958, 399; Killingsworth, *Structural Unemployment in the United States*, 7–9; US Congress, House of Representatives, Subcommittee on Unemployment and the Impact of Automation of the Committee on Education and Labor, *Impact of Automation on Employment*, 87th Cong., 1st Sess., 1961, 13; Michigan State Advisory Committee to the United States Commission on Civil Rights, *Employment Problems of Nonwhite Youth*, 3–4. See also Robert L. Allen, *Black Awakening in Capitalist America: An Analytic History* (Garden City, NJ: Anchor, 1970), 115–117, 211–238, 282–283.

47. Testimony of Walter P. Reuther, Hearings before the United States Commission on Civil Rights, Detroit, MI, 1960, 50. See also the statement and remarks of Walter P. Reuther in US Congress, Subcommittee on Economic Stabilization of the Joint Committee on the Economic Report, *Automation and Technological Change: Hearings before the Subcommittee on Economic Stabilization of the Joint Committee on the Economic Report*, 84th Cong., 1st Sess., 1955, 97–149.

48. US Department of Commerce. Bureau of the Census, *United States Census*, 1910, 1920, and 1940; Clinton Collier, interview by Orley B. Caudill, transcript, Morton, MS, July 28, 1981, Center for Oral History and Cultural Heritage, University of Southern Mississippi; Sugrue, *Origins of the Urban Crisis*, 126, 145–146.

49. Arraner Stephens Spivey, interview by Preston Hughes, digital audio, unknown location, February 26–27, 2002, USM.

50. Terence McArdle, "Obituary: Otis Rush," *Baltimore Sun*, October 4, 2018, A10; Edward Komara, "Ike 'Big Ike' Darby," in *The Blues Encyclopedia*, ed. Edward Komara (New York: Routledge, 2006), 249; Karen Freeman, "Musselwhite Finds 'Sanctuary,'" *McComb Enterprise-Journal*, October 29, 2004, 13.

51. Eric Hobsbawm, *The Age of Extremes, 1914–1991* (London: Abacus, 1995), 289, 293; Paul Hofmann, "Bunche Says '60 Is Year of Africa," *New York Times*, February 17, 1960, 15.

CHAPTER 5: MISSISSIPPI'S 1960

1. For Mississippi's Balance Agriculture with Industry (BAWI) program, see James C. Cobb, *Selling of the South: The Southern Crusade for Industrial Development, 1936–1990*, 2nd ed. (Urbana: University of Illinois Press, 1993), 5–34.

2. Bessie L. McCoy, Annual Narrative Report, Kemper County, MS, 1960, Box 173, Records of the Extension Service, RG 33, NARA; Mary F. Perry and Mamie H. Shields, Annual Narrative Report, Winston County, MS, 1960, Records of the Extension Service, RG 33, NARA; Charles S. Kerg, "Cotton States Baseball Loop Folds," *Delta Democrat-Times*, November 30, 1955, 11.

3. Paul K. Conkin, *A Revolution Down on the Farm: The Transformation of American Agriculture since 1929* (Lexington: University Press of Kentucky, 2008), 80–91; Christopher Isett and Stephen Miller, *The Social History of Agriculture: From the Origins to the Current Crisis* (New York: Rowman & Littlefield, 2017), 323–335. The most recent report on the environmental impact of commercial farming is P. R. Shukla et al., ed., "Technical Summary, 2019," in *Climate Change and Land: An IPCC Special Report on Climate Change, Desertification, Land Degradation, Sustainable Land Management, Food Security, and Greenhouse Gas Fluxes in Terrestrial Ecosystems* (available online at https://www.ipcc.ch/site/assets/uploads/sites/4/2019/11/03_Technical-Summary-TS.pdf).

4. C. S. Norton et al., Annual Narrative Report, Neshoba County, MS, 1960, Records of the Extension Service, RG 33, NARA.

5. L. W. Payne, Annual Narrative Report, Neshoba County, MS, 1960, Records of the Extension Service, RG 33, NARA.

6. "Protect Cotton Allotments Urged by Senator John Stennis," *Neshoba Democrat*, February 25, 1960, 12; "Everyone Loses When Cotton Acres Are Idle," *Neshoba Democrat*, March 24, 1960.

7. "Neshoba Leads State in Releasing Acreage," *Neshoba Democrat*, April 14, 1960, 1; C. S. Norton et al., Annual Narrative Report, Neshoba County, MS, 1959, Box 165, Records of the Extension Service, RG 33, NARA; C. S. Norton et al., Annual Narrative Report, Neshoba County, MS, 1960, Records of the Extension Service, RG 33, NARA.

8. "Less Work in Cotton," *Newton Register*, n.d. 1960, in C. P. Miller, Lex C. Mason, and Henry D. Morgan, Annual Narrative Report, Newton County, MS, 1960, Records of the Extension Service, RG 33, NARA; "Dairying is Big Business," *New-*

ton *Register*, n.d. 1960, in C. P. Miller, Lex C. Mason, and Henry D. Morgan, Annual Narrative Report, Newton County, MS, 1960, Records of the Extension Service, RG 33, NARA. Newton County's 1962 application for federal redevelopment aid stated that "the greatest problem in Newton County is underemployment for a large percentage of the work force. One of the greatest causes of this is the decreasing need for labor on the farm. With the modern equipment being used on the farms, one man can do the job that in previous years required ten. The difference between the total investment on the farm and the net returns is widening tremendously. This is putting the small farmer out of business. They cannot compete with the larger farmer with the high cost of machinery." *Newton County, Mississippi, Overall Economic Development Plan* (Newton, 1962), 46–47, 56–62. Newton County's net migration between 1950 and 1960 was –6,566. See Gladys K. Bowles and James D. Tarver, *Net Migration of the Population, 1950–60: By Age, Sex, and Color* (Washington, DC: Economic Research Service, USDA, 1965), 743.

9. J. F. Buchanan et al., Annual Narrative Report, Attala County, MS, 1960, Box 196, Records of the Extension Service, RG 33, NARA; James E. Williams, Annual Narrative Report, Attala County, MS, 1960, Box 196, Records of the Extension Service, RG 33, NARA.

10. *Agricultural Situation* 44, no. 11, November 1960, 15.

11. Tribal Council Minutes, July 12, 1960.

12. "Wells-Lamont to Close for Two-Weeks Period," *Neshoba Democrat*, February 4, 1960, 1.

13. "Questions . . . Answers," *Neshoba Democrat*, February 11, 1960, 1; "Bond Issue Election Date Set March 8," *Jackson Clarion-Ledger*, February 8, 1960, 16; Karen Kruse Thomas, "The Hill-Burton Act and Civil Rights: Expanding Hospital Care for Black Southerners, 1939–1960," *Journal of Southern History* 72, no. 4 (November 2006): 824.

14. "2400 miles Travelled to Make Personal Contacts for Industry," *Neshoba Democrat*, June 18, 1959, 1; "Industrial Committee of C of C Encouraging Manufacturers to Locate Business in Philadelphia," *Neshoba Democrat*, June 4, 1959, 1. In 1960 east-central Mississippi unions were as follows: Bricklayers, AFL-CIO Local Union 9 (Union); Clothing Workers, AFL-CIO Locals 701 (Macon) and 720 (Louisville); Machinists, AFL-CIO Lodge 577; Maintenance of Way Employees, AFL-CIO Sub-lodge 1073 (Union) and Sub-lodge 2312 (Macon); Railway Carmen, AFL-CIO Local Union 1166 (Macon); Railway Conductors, Ind. L Division 667 (Louisville); Woodworkers, AFL-CIO Local Union 5–208 (Louisville). See US Department of Labor, Bureau of Labor-Management Reports, *Register of Reporting Labor Organizations, June 30, 1960, Part IV, Southeastern States* (Washington, DC: Government Printing Office, 1960).

15. "Indian Affairs Official to Meet with CC Group," *Neshoba Democrat*, October 30, 1958, 1; "Industry May Locate in This Area to Use Indian Labor," *Neshoba Democrat*, November 6, 1958, 1; Tribal Council Minutes, April 12, 1960, and October 11, 1960.

16. Tribal Council Minutes, October 13, 1960.

17. US Department of Labor, Bureau of Labor Statistics, *The Structure of Unemployment in Areas of Substantial Labor Surplus*, by Joseph S. Zeisel and Robert L. Stein (Washington, DC: Government Printing Office, 1960), 1–2; "The Depressed-Area Problem," *Time*, November 28, 1960, 90; *US News & World Report*, June 20, 1960, 104.

18. US Department of Labor, Bureau of Employment Security, *Area Labor Market Trends, January 1960* (Washington, DC: Government Printing Office, 1960), 4; US Department of Labor, Bureau of Employment Security, "Manpower—the Challenge of the 1960s," *The Labor Market and Employment Security*, March 1960 (Washington, DC: Government Printing Office, 1960), 9–11; US Department of Labor, Bureau of Labor Statistics, *Technological Change and Productivity in the Bituminous Coal Industry, 1920–60* (Washington, DC: Government Printing Office, 1961), 1–4, 46–55; Timothy J. Minchin, *Empty Mills: The Fight against Imports and the Decline of the U.S. Textile* (Lanham, MD: Rowman & Littlefield, 2013), 8; Thomas J. Sugrue, *Origins of the Urban Crisis: Race and Inequality in Postwar Detroit* (Princeton, NJ: Princeton University Press, 1996), 125–152.

19. "It May Be the Little Things," *Neshoba Democrat*, December 1, 1960, 2; "Coleman Urges Care in Racial Problems," *Jackson Clarion-Ledger*, January 7, 1960, 1, 7. The "practical segregationist" designation for Coleman comes from Joseph Crespino. See Crespino, *In Search of Another Country: Mississippi and the Conservative Counterrevolution* (Princeton, NJ: Princeton University Press, 2007), 11, 33–35, 55, 57, 211. For a look at growth statistics from the period that assesses the impact of racial turmoil on industrial expansion, see James C. Cobb, *The Selling of the South: The Southern Crusade for Industrial Development, 1936–1990*, 2nd ed. (Urbana: University of Illinois Press, 1993), 122–150.

20. James H. Meriwether, *Proudly We Can Be Africans: Black Americans and Africa, 1935–1961* (Chapel Hill: University of North Carolina Press, 2002), 181; Jean Allman, "Between the Present and History: African Nationalism and Decolonization," in *The Oxford Handbook of Modern African History*, ed. John Parker and Richard Reid (New York: Oxford University Press, 2013), 224; Tom Ethridge, "Mississippi Notebook," *Jackson Clarion-Ledger*, February 5, 1960, 5. Ethridge viewed the fates of white South Africans and white Southerners as linked: "The global forces of integration are pressuring South Africa today but [if] her white government falls, it seems inevitable that the same ruthless forces will turn against Mississippi and other Soutern [sic] states, on an all-out

basis." See Ethridge, "Mississippi Notebook," *Jackson Clarion-Ledger*, October 21, 1960, 5.

21. William Beinart, *Twentieth-Century South Africa* (New York: Oxford University Press, 2001), 165–169; Thomas Borstelmann, *The Cold War and the Color Line: American Race Relations in the Global Arena* (Cambridge, MA: Harvard University Press, 2001), 126–128; "'Masses Led Astray' Says Verwoerd," *London Observer*, March 27, 1960, 1.

22. "House Praises Government of South Africa," *Delta Democrat-Times*, April 13, 1960, 1; Gerald Horne, "The White Atlantic," in *From the Barrel of a Gun: The United States and the War against Zimbabwe, 1965–1980* (Chapel Hill: University of North Carolina Press, 2001); Zoe L. Hyman, "American Segregationist Ideology and White Southern Africa, 1948–1975" (PhD diss., University of Sussex, 2011), 122–127.

23. "Kenya's Dirty Word: Tolerance," *Windsor Star*, June 20, 1960, 30; "Kenya Settlers Plan to Leave White Highlands," *Guardian*, June 27, 1960, 13; Thomas Jenkins, "Kenya Settlers Get Ready to Move: Unwanted in the Land They Love," *Detroit Free Press*, March 12, 1960, 6; Alexandra Fuller, *Don't Let's Go to the Dogs Tonight: An African Childhood* (New York: Random House, 2003), 21.

24. Ezekiel C. Smith to A. H. Rosenfeld, June 29, 1960, in "Black Belt Survey," Box 6, Records of the Commission on Civil Rights, RG 453. For a description of the difficulties the Commission on Civil Rights experienced in getting a foothold in the state, see Murray Cox, "Civil Rights in Mississippi," n.d., Folder 14, Box 1, Allen Eugene Cox Papers, MSU.

25. Ezekiel C. Smith to A. H. Rosenfeld, June 29, 1960, in "Black Belt Survey," Box 6, Records of the Commission on Civil Rights.

26. Smith to Rosenfeld. Mississippi State Sovereignty Commission files confirm that local teachers Ethel Smith, Henry Smith, Jack Smith, Willy Howard Roeby, Orietta Stewart, and Eva Sherwood were considered "would-be agitators." Report by Tom Scarbrough, Noxubee County, MS, September 6, 1960, SCR 2-113-0-7-2-1-1, MSSC, available online at https://da.mdah.ms.gov/sovcom/result.php?image=images/png/cd05/038580.png&otherstuff=2|113|0|7|2|1|1|37986|.

27. Smith to Rosenfeld.

28. Albert Jones, memo, July 12, 1960, SCR 2-112-1-11-1-1-1, MSSC, MDAH, available online at https://www.mdah.ms.gov/arrec/digital_archives/sovcom/result.php?image=images/png/cd05/038145.png&otherstuff=2|112|1|11|1|1|1|37552|# ; excerpt from January Report of Mississippi Field Survey made by Messrs. Bonnell and Amidon, "Black Belt Survey," Box 6, Records of the Commission on Civil Rights, RG 453, NARA.

29. Excerpt from January Report of Mississippi Field Survey made by Messrs.

Bonnell and Amidon, "Black Belt Survey," Box 6, Records of the Commission on Civil Rights .

30. Albert Jones, memo, July 12, 1960, SCR 2–112–1-11–1-1–1, MSSC, MDAH, available online at https://www.mdah.ms.gov/arrec/digital_archives/sovcom/result .php?image=images/png/cd05/038145.png&otherstuff=2|112|1|11|1|1|1 |37552|#; "Official Says College Won't Be Integrated," Jackson Clarion-Ledger, August 17, 1960, 10; "Attacked by Drunks, White Minister Says," Jackson Clarion-Ledger, August 20, 1960, 1; "White Citizens Charge Negro School Is for Financial Gain," Jackson Clarion-Ledger, August 21, 1960, 1, 11.

31. "Controversial Negro School Issue Ends in Abandonment of Plans," Newton Record, August 31, 1960, 1; "Germany Giving Up School, Aide Says," clipping, August 28, 1960, Folder 28, Box 1, Allen Eugene Cox Papers, MSU.

32. *Constitution and By-Laws of the Mississippi Band of Choctaw Indians* (Washington, DC: Office of Indian Affairs, 1946), 2, in Box 4, Constitutions and By-Laws, General Records Concerning Indian Organization, Records of the Bureau of Indian Affairs, RG 75, NARA; Phillip Martin to Fred E. Seaton, November 8, 1960, Folder 11, Box 249, AAIA Records; Tribal Council Minutes, January 13, 1959, February 23, 1960, July 12, 1960, October 11, 1960, and December 29, 1960.

33. US Congress, House of Representatives, Fact Sheet No. 38D (Supp. 1), 86th Congress, 2nd Sess., *Congressional Record* 106 (January 25, 1960), Appendix, 633.

CONCLUSION

1. Estelle Fine, "Campaigns Fail in Miss.," *Southern Courier*, September 30–October 1, 1967, 1. On ASC (also called ASCS) elections, see Pete Daniel, *Dispossession: Discrimination against African American Farmers in the Age of Civil Rights* (Chapel Hill: University of North Carolina Press, 2013), 61–64.

2. Robert Sherrill, "It Isn't True that Nobody Starves in America," *New York Times Magazine*, June 4, 1967, 103. The most complete treatment of white Southerners' abandonment of farm laborers is de Jong, *You Can't Eat*. See also Frances Fox Piven and Richard A. Cloward, *Regulating the Poor: The Functions of Public Welfare*, updated ed. (New York: Vintage, 1993), 200–221; and Linda Flowers, *Throwed Away: Failures of Progress in Eastern North Carolina* (Knoxville: University of Tennessee Press, 1992).

3. Gregory S. Wilson, *Communities Left Behind: The Area Redevelopment Administration, 1945–1965* (Knoxville: University of Tennessee Press, 2009), 32–33; Tami J. Friedman, "'Free Enterprise' or Federal Aid? The Business Response to Economic Restructuring in the Long 1950s," in *Capital Gains: Business and Politics in Twentieth-Century America*, ed. Richard R. John and Kim Phillips-Fein (Philadelphia: University of Pennsylvania Press, 2017), 119–138.

4. Neshoba Rural Area Development Association, *Comprehensive Overall Economic Program (OEDP) for Neshoba County, Mississippi*, 1962, 70, Folder 0–111, Box 5, Records of the Mississippi Cooperative Extension Service—Community Development Department, University Archives, Mississippi State University, Starkville, MS; Newton County Rural Areas Development Committee, *Newton County, Mississippi, Overall Economic Development Plan*, 1962, 61–62; Kemper County Rural Area Development Committee, *Over-all Economic Development Program (OEDP)*, 1963 14; Leake County Rural Area Development Committee, *Comprehensive Overall Economic Development Plan (OEDP) for Leake County, Mississippi*, 1962, 18.

5. "Area Redevelopment Act Offering Aid in Employment Opportunities," *Newton Record*, June 7, 1961, 8; Report from SNCC Field Secretary, The Freedom Ballot for Governor, Joan Bowman, October 23, 1963, available online at https://www.crmvet.org/lets/lball63.htm (emphasis mine); William L. Taylor to Ronald Friedenberg, May 14, 1963, Mississippi, Records Relating to Equal Protection and the Administration of Justice, 1961–1965, Federal Programs Division, Box 1, Records of the US Commission on Civil Rights, RG 453, NARA; Vivian W. Henderson, *The Economic Status of Negroes: In the Nation and in the South* (Atlanta: Southern Regional Council, 1963), 5.

6. One of the perpetrators of the murder was Primitive Baptist preacher Edgar Ray Killen, who had earlier opposed the Bay Ridge Christian College (Chapter 5). Gene Roberts and Hank Klibanoff, *The Race Beat: The Press, the Civil Rights Struggle, and the Awakening of a Nation* (New York: Vintage, 2006), 356; Joseph Lelyveld, "A Stranger in Philadelphia, Mississippi," *New York Times Magazine*, December 27, 1964, 5; "Lawmen Search Pearl in Philadelphia Area," *Jackson Clarion-Ledger*, June 28, 1964, 1, 16; Douglas Martin, "Olen Burrage Dies at 82; Linked to Killings in 1964," *New York Times*, March 18, 2013.

7. US Department of Labor, Bureau of Labor Statistics, *The Negroes in the United States: Their Economic and Social Situation* (Washington, DC: Government Printing Office, 1966), 47. Mary Lou Farmer, a Choctaw woman who had farmed for her entire life, was on welfare by the time Samuel Proctor interviewed her in 1973. Mary Lou Farmer, interview by Samuel Proctor, transcript, Conehatta, MS, December 3, 1973, Southern Indian Oral History Project, University of Florida; Gail Falk, "Negroes Move Ahead after 1964 Killings," *Southern Courier*, November 11–12, 1967, 4, 6; "Farmers Home Administration Area and County Committeemen—Mississippi," Folder 11, Box 34, State/Local Files, Constituent Files, James O. Eastland Collection, University of Mississippi, Oxford, MS; Joseph Brenner et al., *Hungry Children* (Atlanta: Southern Regional Council, 1967), 4, 9. Daniel M. Cobb's is the fullest treatment of the Choctaws' experience with redevelopment. See Cobb, "The War on Poverty in Mississippi and Oklahoma: Beyond Black and White," in

The War on Poverty: A New Grassroots History, 1964–1980, ed. Annelise Orleck and Lisa Gayle Hazirjian (Athens: University of Georgia Press, 2011), 387–395.

8. US Commission on Civil Rights, *The Unfinished Business: Twenty Years Later* (Washington, DC: Government Printing Office, 1977), 104–107.

9. US Commission on Civil Rights, *The Decline of Black Farming in America* (Washington, DC: Government Printing Office, 1982), 2, 177; See also Tommy W. Rogers, *A Demographic Analysis of Poverty in Mississippi* (Jackson: Governor's Office of Human Resources and Community Services, 1979), iii, 198–225.

10. Cobb, "The War on Poverty in Mississippi and Oklahoma," 392–395; Katherine M. B. Osburn, *Choctaw Resurgence in Mississippi: Race, Class, and Nation Building in the Jim Crow South, 1830–1977* (Lincoln: University of Nebraska Press, 2014), 203–214.

11. A. S. Mlambo, *A History of Zimbabwe* (New York: Cambridge University Press, 2014), 220–225; Ariel Levy, "Who Owns South Africa?" *New Yorker*, May 13, 2019; Mahmood Mamdani, "Why South Africa Can't Avoid Land Reforms," *New York Times*, June 17, 2019; Brenna Bhandar, *Colonial Lives of Property: Law, Land, and Racial Regimes of Ownership* (Durham, NC: Duke University Press, 2018), 32 (emphasis mine).

BIBLIOGRAPHY

PRIMARY

Manuscript Collections

Agricultural Extension L. I. Jones Collection, Special Collections, Mitchell Memorial Library, Mississippi State University, Starkville, MS
Eugene Butler Papers, Special Collections, Mitchell Memorial Library, Mississippi State University, Starkville, MS
Allen Eugene Cox Papers, Special Collections, Mitchell Memorial Library, Mississippi State University, Starkville, MS
James O. Eastland Collection, Department of Archives and Collections, J. D. Williams Library, University of Mississippi, Oxford, MS
Genealogy Collection, Philadelphia–Neshoba County Public Library, Philadelphia, MS
General Records Concerning Indian Organization, Records of the Bureau of Indian Affairs, Record Group 75, National Archives and Records Administration (NARA), Washington, DC
Mississippi Band of Choctaw Indians Tribal Council Meeting Minutes, Mississippi Band of Choctaw Indians Tribal Archive, Choctaw, MS
National Association for the Advancement of Colored People Records, Library of Congress, Washington, DC
John E. Rankin Collection, Department of Archives and Collections, J. D. Williams Library, University of Mississippi, Oxford, MS
Records of the Extension Service, Record Group 33, National Archives and Records Administration (NARA), Kansas City, MO
Records of the Mississippi Cooperative Extension Service—Community Development Department, Special Collections, Mitchell Memorial Library, Mississippi State University, Starkville, MS
Records of the Mississippi Forestry Association, Special Collections, Mitchell Memorial Library, Mississippi State University, Starkville, MS
Records of the National Congress of American Indians, National Museum of the American Indian Archive Center, Suitland, MD
Records of the US Commission on Civil Rights, Record Group 453 National Archives and Records Administration (NARA), College Park, MD
John C. Stennis Papers, Special Collections, Mitchell Memorial Library, Mississippi State University, Starkville, MS

Work Projects Administration (WPA) Files—Source Material on Mississippi History, Mississippi Department of Archives and History, Jackson, MS

Microfilm Collections

Association on American Indian Affairs Records
Papers of the National Association for the Advancement of Colored People
Peonage Files of the US Department of Justice, 1901–1945

Online Collections

Central Classified Files—Choctaw, National Archives and Records Administration (NARA)
CRMvet.org
Indian Claims Commission Decisions, Oklahoma State University Digital Collections
King Papers, Martin Luther King, Jr. Research and Education Institute, Stanford University
Lynching in America, Equal Justice Initiative
Mapping the Southern Diaspora, James N. Gregory
Mississippi State Sovereignty Commission Files, Sovereignty Commission Online, Mississippi Department of Archives and History (MDAH)
Monroe Work Today
Harry S. Truman Library and Museum
WLBT "Farm Family of the Week" Collection, Special Collections, Mississippi State University (MSU)
WPA Federal Writers' Project County Files, Mississippi Library Commission

Newspapers and Periodicals

Agricultural Situation
Atlanta Constitution
Atlantic
Baltimore Sun
Biloxi Daily Herald
Choctaw Plaindealer
Citizens' Council
Columbian-Progress
Daily Oklahoman

Delta Democrat-Times
Detroit Free Press
Ebony
Fortune
Greenwood Commonwealth
Guardian
Harper's
Hattiesburg American
Jackson Clarion-Ledger
Jackson Daily News
Jackson Sun
Jackson Weekly Clarion-Ledger
Kansas City Plaindealer
Kemper County Messenger
Kosciusko Star-Herald
London Observer
Macon Beacon
McComb Enterprise-Journal
Meridian Daily Clarion
Mississippi Union Advocate
Nashville Tennessean
Natchez Weekly Democrat
Nation
Neshoba Democrat
New Republic
Newton Record
New Yorker
New York Times
New York Times Magazine
Playboy
Richland Beacon-News
Saturday Evening Post
Scott County Times
Southern Courier
Time
Union Appeal
US News & World Report
Vicksburg Herald
Wall Street Journal

Weekly Standard
Westville News
Windsor Star
Winston County Journal

Interviews

Claude Allen, Southern Indian Oral History Project, University of Florida Digital Collections, 1973

Dick Allen, Mississippi Forestry Association Records, Special Collections, Mitchell Memorial Library, Mississippi State University, 1988

Turner Catledge, Center for Oral History and Cultural Heritage, University of Southern Mississippi, 1971

Obie Clark, Center for Oral History and Cultural Heritage, University of Southern Mississippi, 1997

Howard Cole, Center for Oral History and Cultural Heritage, University of Southern Mississippi, 1973

Clinton Collier, Center for Oral History and Cultural Heritage, University of Southern Mississippi, 1981

James McBride Dabbs, Harry Ransom Center, University of Texas at Austin, 1958

Charlie Denson, Southern Indian Oral History Project, University of Florida, 1973

Thomas A. DeWeese, Mississippi Forestry Association Records, Special Collections, Mitchell Memorial Library, Mississippi State University, 1979

Charles Evers, Center for Oral History and Cultural Heritage, University of Southern Mississippi, 1971

Charles Evers and Neil E. Goldschmidt, Who Speaks for the Negro? Collection, Vanderbilt University, 1964

Mary Lou Farmer, Southern Indian Oral History Project, University of Florida Digital Collections, 1973

L. J. Henry, Southern Indian Oral History Project, University of Florida Digital Collections, 1977

Lillie Jones, Center for Oral History and Cultural Heritage, University of Southern Mississippi, 1974

Joe Moore, Center for Oral History and Cultural Heritage, University of Southern Mississippi, 2003

Arraner Stephens Spivey, Center for Oral History and Cultural Heritage, University of Southern Mississippi, 2002

Mary Lillian Peters (Ogden) Whitten, Center for Oral History and Cultural Heritage, University of Southern Mississippi, 1973

Louise Willis, Southern Indian Oral History Project, University of Florida Digital Collections, 1973

Baxter York, Southern Indian Oral History Project, University of Florida Digital Collections, 1974

Government Documents and Publications

Congressional Record

CQ Almanac

Legislative Insight

64th Cong., 2nd Sess., House Document 1464: Additional Land and Indian Schools in Mississippi.

Bowles, Gladys K., and James D. Tarver. *Net Migration of the Population, 1950–60: By Age, Sex, and Color.* Washington, DC: Economic Research Service, USDA, 1965.

Dickins, Dorothy. *The Labor Supply and Mechanized Cotton Production.* State College: Mississippi State College, Agricultural Experiment Station, 1949.

———. *Levels of Living of Young Negro Farm-Operator Families in Mississippi.* State College, Mississippi State College, Agricultural Experiment Station, 1959.

———. *Levels of Living of Young White Farm-Operator Families in Mississippi.* State College, Mississippi State College, Agricultural Experiment Station, 1959.

Federal Writers' Project. *Mississippi: The WPA Guide to the Magnolia State.* Jackson: University Press of Mississippi, 2009.

James, Lee M. *Mississippi's Forest Resources and Industries.* Forest Resource Report No. 4. Washington, DC: Government Printing Office, 1951.

Kemper County Rural Area Development Committee. *Over-all Economic Development Program (OEDP).* 1963.

Killingsworth, Charles C. *Structural Unemployment in the United States.* Washington, DC: Government Printing Office, 1964.

Kimbrough, E. A. *Case Studies of Small Tractors on Hill Farms of Mississippi.* State College: Mississippi State College, Agricultural Experiment Station, 1951.

Kneeland, Hildegarde, and Hazel K. Stiebeling. "The Farm Business and Farm Home." In United States Department of Agriculture, *Yearbook of Agriculture, 1933,* edited by Milton S. Eisenhower. Washington, DC: GPO, 1933.

Lord Hailey. *Native Administration in the British African Territories: Part I. East Africa: Uganda, Kenya, Tanganyika.* London: His Majesty's Stationary Office, 1950.

Leake County Rural Area Development Committee. *Comprehensive Overall Economic Development Plan (OEDP) for Leake County, Mississippi.* 1962.

Mississippi Forestry Commission. *Mississippi's Assessment of Forest Resources and Forest Resource Strategy.* Jackson: Mississippi Forestry Commission, 2010.

Mississippi Legislature. Senate. *Report of the Temporary Fact-Finding Committee on the Development of Mississippi Resources pursuant to Senate Concurrent Resolution No. 137, Mississippi Legislature Regular Session 1956.* Jackson, 1957.

Moak, James E., and Lawrence J. Kerr. *Economic Opportunities in Mississippi's Pine Lumber Industry.* State College: Mississippi Agricultural Experiment Station, 1961.

National Emergency Council. *Report on Economic Conditions of the South.* Washington, DC: Government Printing Office, 1938.

Newton County Rural Areas Development Committee. *Newton County, Mississippi, Overall Economic Development Plan.* 1962.

Parvin, D. W. *Development of the Dairy Industry in Mississippi.* State College: Mississippi State College, Agricultural Experiment Station, 1945.

Rogers, Tommy W. *A Demographic Analysis of Poverty in Mississippi.* Jackson: Governor's Office of Human Resources and Community Services, 1979.

Shukla, P. R., et al., eds. "Technical Summary, 2019." In *Climate Change and Land: An IPCC Special Report on Climate Change, Desertification, Land Degradation, Sustainable Land Management, Food Security, and Greenhouse Gas Fluxes in Terrestrial Ecosystems.* https://www.ipcc.ch/site/assets/uploads/sites/4/2019/11/03_Technical-Summary-TS.pdf.

Special Committee on Farm Tenancy. *Report of the Special Committee on Farm Tenancy.* Washington, DC: Government Printing Office, 1937.

US Commission on Civil Rights. *The Decline of Black Farming in America.* Washington, DC: Government Printing Office, 1982.

———. *Equal Opportunity in Farm Families: An Appraisal of Services Rendered by Agencies of the United States Department of Agriculture.* Washington, DC: Government Printing Office, 1965.

———. *Hearings before the United States Commission on Civil Rights: Hearings Held in Detroit, Michigan, December 14–15, 1960.* Washington, DC: Government Printing Office, 1961.

———. *Report of the United States Commission on Civil Rights, 1959.* Washington, DC: Government Printing Office, 1959.

———. *The Unfinished Business: Twenty Years Later.* Washington, DC: Government Printing Office, 1977.

US Congress. House of Representatives. Committee of the Whole House on the State of the Union. *Report with Respect to the House Resolution Authorizing the Committee on Interior and Insular Affairs to Conduct an Investigation of the Bureau of Indian Affairs (Pursuant to House Resolution 89).* 83rd Cong., 2nd Sess., 1954. H. Rep. 2680.

———. Committee on Agriculture. *Cotton: Hearings before the Subcommittee of the Committee on Agriculture.* 78th Cong., 2nd Sess., 1944.

———. Committee on Agriculture. *Study of Agricultural and Economic Problems of the Cotton Belt*. 80th Cong., 1st Sess., 1947.

———. Committee on Education and Labor. *Labor-Management Relations Act: Report (to Accompany HR 3020)*. 80th Cong., 1st Sess., 1947, HR Rep. 245.

———. Committee on Indian Affairs. "Land Claims, &c. Under 14th Article Choctaw Treaty." May 11, 1836. 24th Cong., 1st Sess.

———. Committee on Investigation of the Indian Service. *Condition of the Mississippi Choctaws: Hearing before the Committee on Investigation of the Indian Service*. 64th Cong., Union, MS, March 16, 1917.

———. Subcommittee of the Committee on Appropriations. *Interior Department Appropriation Bill for 1949*. 80th Cong., 2nd Sess., 1948.

———. Subcommittee on Unemployment and the Impact of Automation of the Committee on Education and Labor. *Impact of Automation on Employment*. 87th Cong., 1st Sess., 1961.

US Congress. Senate. Committee on Labor and Public Welfare. *Antidiscrimination in Employment*. 80th Cong., 1st Sess., 1947.

———. Subcommittee of the Committee on Indian Affairs. *Choctaw Indians of Mississippi: Hearing before the Subcommittee of the Committee on Indian Affairs*, 76th Cong., 3rd Sess., 1940.

———. Subcommittee of the Committee on Indian Affairs. *Survey of the Conditions of the Indians in the United States: Hearings before a Subcommittee of the Committee on Indian Affairs*. 71st Cong., 3rd Sess., 1930.

US Department of Agriculture. *Agricultural Statistics, 1936*. Washington, DC: Government Printing Office, 1936.

———. Bureau of Agricultural Economics. *Farmers View the Postwar World: A Survey of the Cornbelt, the Cotton Region of the Southeast, and the Central Valley of California*. Washington, DC: Government Printing Office, 1944.

———. Economic Research Service. *The Cotton Industry in the United States*. Washington, DC: Government Printing Office, 1996.

———. Foreign Agricultural Service. *Notes on the Agricultural Economies of the Countries in Africa, III. Eastern and Southern Africa*. Washington, DC: Government Printing Office, 1959.

———. *Soil Survey of Neshoba County, Mississippi*. Washington, DC: Government Printing Office, 1981.

———. *What Peace Can Mean to American Farmers: Post-War Agriculture and Employment*. Washington, DC: Government Printing Office, 1945.

US Department of Agriculture and State Agricultural Extension Services. *Facts about Cotton and Southern Farming: Background Information for Farm Leaders*. Washington, DC: Government Printing Office, 1946.

186 | BIBLIOGRAPHY

US Department of Commerce. Bureau of the Census. *United States Census*. 1910.
———. Bureau of the Census. *United States Census*. 1920.
———. Bureau of the Census. *United States Census*. 1940.
———. Bureau of the Census. *United States Census of Agriculture*. 1920.
———. Bureau of the Census. *United States Census of Agriculture*. 1925.
———. Bureau of the Census. *United States Census of Agriculture*. 1930.
———. Bureau of the Census. *United States Census of Agriculture*. 1935.
———. Bureau of the Census. *United States Census of Agriculture*. 1940.
———. Bureau of the Census. *United States Census of Agriculture*. 1945.
———. Bureau of the Census. *United States Census of Agriculture*. 1950.
———. Bureau of the Census. *United States Census of Agriculture*. 1954.
———. Bureau of the Census. *United States Census of Agriculture*. 1959.
———. Bureau of the Census. *United States Census of Agriculture*. 1964.
———. Bureau of the Census. *United States Census of Agriculture*. 1969.
———. Bureau of the Census. *United States Census of Agriculture*. 1982.
———. Bureau of Foreign Commerce. Near Eastern and African Division. *Investment in Rhodesia and Nyasaland*. Washington, DC: Government Printing Office, 1956.
———. Business and Defense Services Administration. *World Survey of Agricultural Machinery and Equipment: Africa and Australia-Oceania*. Washington, DC: Government Printing Office, 1960.
US Department of Health and Human Services. Agency for Toxic Substances and Disease Registry, Division of Toxicology and Human Health Science. *Public Health Statement: Hexachlorocyclohexane* (Atlanta, 2005), https://www.atsdr.cdc.gov/ToxProfiles/tp43-c1-b.pdf.
———. Agency for Toxic Substances and Disease Registry, Division of Toxicology and Human Health Science. *Public Health Statement: Toxaphene* (Atlanta, 2014), https://www.atsdr.cdc.gov/ToxProfiles/tp94-c1-b.pdf.
US Department of Labor. Bureau of Employment Security. *Area Labor Market Trends, January 1960*. Washington, DC: Government Printing Office, 1960.
———. Bureau of Employment Security. "Manpower—the Challenge of the 1960s." *The Labor Market and Employment Security, March 1960*. Washington, DC: Government Printing Office, 1960.
———. Bureau of Labor-Management Reports. *Register of Reporting Labor Organizations, June 30, 1960, Part IV, Southeastern States*. Washington, DC: Government Printing Office, 1960.
———. Bureau of Labor Statistics. *The Negroes in the United States: Their Economic and Social Situation*. Washington, DC: Government Printing Office, 1966.
———. Bureau of Labor Statistics. *The Structure of Unemployment in Areas of Sub-*

stantial Labor Surplus, by Joseph S. Zeisel and Robert L. Stein. Washington, DC: Government Printing Office, 1960.

———. Bureau of Labor Statistics. *Technological Change and Productivity in the Bituminous Coal Industry, 1920–60.* Washington, DC: Government Printing Office, 1961.

US Department of State. *Foreign Relations of the United States, 1955–1957, Volume XVIII, Africa.* Washington, DC: Government Printing Office, 1989.

Wallace, Henry A. "The Year in Agriculture." In United States Department of Agriculture, *Yearbook of Agriculture, 1934,* edited by Milton S. Eisenhower. Washington, DC: Government Printing Office, 1934.

SECONDARY

Books, Articles, and Theses

Adams, Mikaëla M. *Who Belongs? Race, Resources, and Tribal Citizenship in the Native South.* New York: Oxford University Press, 2016.

Adams, Natalie G., and James H. Adams. *Just Trying to Have School: The Struggle for Desegregation in Mississippi.* Jackson: University Press of Mississippi, 2018.

Aiken, Charles S. *The Cotton Plantation South since the Civil War.* Baltimore: Johns Hopkins University Press, 1998.

Alexander, Jocelyn. *The Unsettled Land: State-making and the Politics of Land in Zimbabwe, 1893–2003.* Athens: Ohio University Press, 2006.

Allen, Robert L. *Black Awakening in Capitalist America: An Analytic History.* Garden City, NJ: Anchor, 1970.

Allman, Jean. "Between the Present and History: African Nationalism and Decolonization." In *The Oxford Handbook of Modern African History,* edited by John Parker and Richard Reid. New York: Oxford University Press, 2013.

———. "The Fate of All of US: African Counterrevolutions and the Ends of 1968." *American Historical Review* 123, no. 3 (June 2018): 728–732.

Anderson, Carol. *Bourgeois Radicals: The NAACP and the Struggle for Colonial Liberation, 1941–1960.* New York: Cambridge University Press, 2015.

———. *Eyes off the Prize: The United Nations and the African American Struggle for Human Rights, 1944–1955.* New York: Cambridge University Press, 2003.

Anthony, Constance G. *Mechanization and Maize: Agriculture and the Politics of Technology Transfer in East Africa.* New York: Columbia University Press, 1988.

Arrighi, Giovanni. *The Political Economy of Rhodesia.* The Hague: Mouton, 1967.

Arsenault, Raymond. "White on Chrome: Southern Congressmen and Rhodesia, 1962–1971." *Issue* 2, no. 4 (Winter 1972): 46–57.

Asch, Chris Myers. *The Senator and the Sharecropper: The Freedom Struggles of James*

O. Eastland and Fannie Lou Hamer. Chapel Hill: University of North Carolina Press.

Atanasoski, Neda, and Kalindi Vora. *Surrogate Humanity: Race, Robots, and the Politics of Technological Futures*. Durham, NC: Duke University Press, 2019.

Baldwin, James. *I Am Not Your Negro*. Compiled and edited by Raoul Peck. New York: Vintage International, 2017.

Baker, Lee D. *From Savage to Negro: Anthropology and the Construction of Race, 1896–1954*. Berkeley: University of California Press, 1998.

Baptist, Edward E. *The Half Has Never Been Told: Slavery and the Making of American Capitalism*. New York: Basic Books, 2014.

Bartley, Numan V. *The New South, 1945–1980*. Baton Rouge: Louisiana State University Press, 1995.

———. "The Southern Enclosure Movement." *Georgia Historical Quarterly* 71, no. 3 (Fall 1987): 438–450.

Bayly, C. A. *The Birth of the Modern World, 1780–1914*. Oxford: Blackwell, 2004.

———. *Remaking the Modern World, 1900–2015: Global Connections and Comparisons*. Hoboken, NJ: Wiley Blackwell, 2018.

Beck, E. M., and Stewart E. Tolnay. "A Season for Violence: The Lynching of Blacks and Labor Demand in the Agricultural Production Cycle in the American South." *International Review of Social History* 37, no. 1 (1992): 1–24.

Beinart, William. "Soil Erosion, Conservationism and Ideas about Development: A Southern African Exploration, 1900–1960." *Journal of Southern African Studies* 11, no. 1 (October 1984): 52–83.

———. *Twentieth-Century South Africa*. New York: Oxford University Press, 2001.

Belich, James. *Replenishing the Earth: The Settler Revolution and the Rise of the Anglo-world*. New York: Oxford University Press, 2009.

Benjamin, Walter. "Critique of Violence." In *Reflections: Essays, Aphorisms, Autobiographical Writings*. Translated by Edmund Jeffcott. New York: Schocken, 1986.

Bennett, Evan P. *When Tobacco Was King: Families, Farm Labor, and Federal Policy in the Piedmont*. Gainesville: University Press of Florida, 2014.

Berlin, Ira. *The Making of African America: The Four Great Migrations*. New York: Viking, 2010.

Berman, Bruce. *Control and Crisis in Colonial Kenya: The Dialectic of Domination*. Athens: Ohio State University Press, 1990.

Berman, Bruce, and John Lonsdale. *Unhappy Valley: Conflict in Kenya and Africa*. Athens: Ohio University Press, 1992.

Berry, Wendell. *Our Only World: Ten Essays*. Berkeley, CA: Counterpoint, 2015.

———. *The Unsettling of America: Culture and Agriculture*. San Francisco: Sierra Club Books, 1977.

———. *The World-Ending Fire: The Essential Wendell Berry*. Berkeley, CA: Counterpoint, 2017.

Bhandar, Brenna. *Colonial Lives of Property: Law, Land, and Racial Regimes of Ownership*. Durham, NC: Duke University Press, 2018.

Blackmon, Douglas A. *Slavery by Another Name: The Re-Enslavement of Black Americans from the Civil War to World War II*. New York: Anchor, 2009.

Blevins, Brooks. *Cattle in the Cotton Fields: A History of Cattle Raising in Alabama*. Tuscaloosa: University of Alabama Press, 1998.

Bolton, Charles C. "Mississippi's School Equalization Program, 1945–1954: 'A Last Gasp to Try to Maintain a Segregated Educational System.'" *Journal of Southern History* 66, no. 4 (November 2000): 781–814.

Boris, Eileen. "Fair Employment and the Origins of Affirmative Action in the 1940s." *NWSA Journal* 10, no. 3 (Autumn 1998): 142–151.

Borstelmann, Thomas. *Apartheid's Reluctant Uncle: The United States and Southern Africa in the Early Cold War*. New York: Oxford University Press, 1993.

———. *The Cold War and the Color Line: American Race Relations in the Global Arena*. Cambridge, MA: Harvard University Press, 2001.

Brenner, Joseph, Robert Coles, Alan Mermann, Milton J.E. Senn, Cyril Walwyn, and Raymond Wheeler. *Hungry Children*. Atlanta: Southern Regional Council, 1967.

Brown, Alfred John. *History of Newton County, Mississippi, from 1834 to 1894*. Jackson, MS: Clarion-Ledger Company, 1894.

Brown, D. Clayton. *King Cotton in Modern America: A Cultural, Political, and Economic History since 1945*. Jackson: University Press of Mississippi, 2011.

Brownell, Josiah. *The Collapse of Rhodesia: Population Demographics and the Politics of Race*. New York: I. B. Tauris, 2011.

Bruton, Paul W. "Cotton Acreage Reduction and the Tenant Farmer." *Law and Contemporary Problems* 1, no. 3 (June 1934): 275–291.

Bruyneel, Kevin. *Settler Memory: The Disavowal of Indigeneity and the Politics of Race in the United States*. Chapel Hill: University of North Carolina Press, 2021.

Burbank, Jane, and Frederick Cooper. *Empires in World History: Power and the Politics of Difference*. Princeton, NJ: Princeton University Press, 2010.

Burns, James. "The Western in Colonial Southern Africa." In *The Western in the Global South*, edited by MaryEllen Higgins, Rita Keresztesi, and Dayna Oscherwitz, 11–23. New York: Routledge, 2015.

Byrd, Jodi A. *The Transit of Empire: Indigenous Critiques of Colonialism*. Minneapolis: University of Minnesota Press, 2011.

———. "'Variations under Domestication': Indigeneity and the Subject of Dispossession." *Social Text* 135, vol. 36, no. 2 (June 2018): 123–141.

Caison, Gina. *Red States: Indigeneity, Settler Colonialism, and Southern Studies*. Athens: University of Georgia Press, 2018.

Carson, James Taylor. "'The Obituary of Nations': Ethnic Cleansing, Memory, and the Origins of the Old South." *Southern Cultures* 14, no. 4 (Winter 2008): 6–31.

Cell, John W. *The Highest Stage of White Supremacy: The Origins of Segregation in South African and the American South*. New York: Cambridge University Press, 1982.

Clarkin, Thomas. *Federal Indian Policy in the Kennedy and Johnson Administrations, 1961–1969*. Albuquerque: University of New Mexico Press, 2001.

Classen, Steven D. *Watching Jim Crow: The Struggles over Mississippi TV, 1955–1969*. Durham, NC: Duke University Press, 2004.

Cobb, Daniel M. "The War on Poverty in Mississippi and Oklahoma: Beyond Black and White." In *The War on Poverty: A New Grassroots History, 1964–1980*, edited by Annelise Orleck and Lisa Gayle Hazirjian, 387–410. Athens: University of Georgia Press, 2011.

Cobb, James C. *The Most Southern Place on Earth: The Mississippi Delta and the Roots of Regional Identity*. New York: Oxford University Press, 1992.

———. *Redefining Southern Culture: Mind and Identity in the Modern South*. Athens: University of Georgia Press, 1999.

———. *The Selling of the South: The Southern Crusade for Industrial Development, 1936–1990*, 2nd ed. Urbana: University of Illinois Press, 1993.

Cohen, Andrew. *The Politics and Economics of Decolonization in Africa: The Failed Experiment of the Central African Federation*. New York: I. B. Tauris, 2017.

Cohen, Lizabeth. *A Consumers' Republic: The Politics of Mass Consumption in Postwar America*. New York: Alfred A. Knopf, 2003.

Cohen, William. *At Freedom's Edge: Black Mobility and the Southern White Quest for Racial Control, 1861–1915*. Baton Rouge: Louisiana State University Press, 1991.

Collier, John. "The American Congo." *Survey* 50, no. 9 (August 1923): 467–476.

Cone, L. Winston, and J. F. Lipscomb. *The History of Kenya Agriculture*. Nairobi: University Press of Africa, 1972.

Conkin, Paul K. *A Revolution Down on the Farm: The Transformation of American Agriculture since 1929*. Lexington: University Press of Kentucky, 2008.

Cooper, Frederick. *Africa since 1940: The Past of the Present*. New York: Cambridge University Press, 2002.

———. *Decolonization and African Society: The Labor Question in French and British Africa*. Cambridge: Cambridge University Press, 1996.

Cowie, Jefferson. *The Great Exception: The New Deal and the Limits of American Politics*. Princeton, NJ: Princeton University Press, 2016.

Crespino, Joseph. *In Search of Another Country: Mississippi and the Conservative Counterrevolution*. Princeton, NJ: Princeton University Press, 2007.

Dailey, Jane. *White Fright: The Sexual Panic at the Heart of America's Racist History*. New York: Basic Books, 2020.
Daniel, Pete. *Breaking the Land: The Transformation of Cotton, Tobacco, and Rice Cultures since 1880*. Urbana: University of Illinois Press, 1985.
———. *Dispossession: Discrimination against African American Farmers in the Age of Civil Rights*. Chapel Hill: University of North Carolina Press, 2013.
———. "The Legal Basis of Agrarian Capitalism: The South since 1933." In *Race and Class in the American South since 1890*, edited by Melvyn Stokes and Rick Halpern. Providence, RI: Berg, 1994.
———. *Lost Revolutions: The South in the 1950s*. Chapel Hill: University of North Carolina Press, 2000.
———. "Not Predestination: The Rural South and Twentieth-Century Transformation." In *The American South in the Twentieth Century*, edited by Craig S. Pascoe, Karen Trahan Leathem, and Andy Ambrose, 91–105. Athens: University of Georgia Press, 2005.
———. *The Shadow of Slavery: Peonage in the South, 1901–1969*. Urbana: University of Illinois Press, 1972.
Deininger, Klaus, and Hans P. Binswanger. "Rent Seeking and the Development of Large-Scale Agriculture in Kenya, South Africa, and Zimbabwe." *Economic Development and Cultural Change* 43, no. 3 (April 1995): 493–522.
de Jong, Greta. *You Can't Eat Freedom: Southerners and Social Justice after the Civil Rights Movement*. Chapel Hill: University of North Carolina Press, 2016.
Deloria, Vine, Jr. *Custer Died for Your Sins: An Indian Manifesto*, rev. ed. Norman: University of Oklahoma Press, 1988.
Derrida, Jacques. "Force of Law: The 'Mystical Foundation of Authority.'" In *Acts of Religion*. New York: Routledge, 2002.
Dittmer, John. *Local People: The Struggle for Civil Rights in Mississippi*. Urbana: University of Illinois Press, 1994C.
Du Bois, W. E. B. *Black Reconstruction in America, 1860–1880*. New York: Free Press, 1998.
Dudziak, Mary. *Cold War Civil Rights: Race and the Image of American Democracy*. Princeton, NJ: Princeton University Press, 2000.
———. "Desegregation as a Cold War Imperative." *Stanford Law Review* 41, no. 1 (November 1988): 61–120.
Elkins, Caroline. *Imperial Reckoning: The Untold Story of Britain's Gulag in Kenya*. New York: Owl, 2005.
———. "The Re-assertion of the British Empire in Southeast Asia." *Journal of Interdisciplinary History* 39, no. 3 (Winter 2009): 361–385.
Elkins, Caroline, and Susan Pederson, eds. *Settler Colonialism in the Twentieth Century*. New York: Routledge, 2005.

Engstrom, David Freeman. "The Lost Origins of American Fair Employment Law: Regulatory Choice and the Making of Modern Civil Rights, 1943–1972." *Stanford Law Review* 63, no. 5 (May 2011): 1071–1143.

Eschen, Penny M. Von. *Race against Empire: Black Americans and Anticolonialism, 1937–1957*. Ithaca, NY: Cornell University Press, 1997.

Evans, Ivan. *Cultures of Violence: Lynching and Racial Killing in South Africa and the American South*. New York: Manchester University Press, 2009.

Evers, Charles. *Evers*. New York: World Publishing Co., 1971.

Evers, Charles, and Andrew Szanton. *Have No Fear: The Charles Evers Story*. New York: John Wiley & Sons, 1997.

First, Ruth. *Black Gold: The Mozambican Miner, Proletarian and Peasant*. New York: St. Martin's Press, 1983.

Fite, Gilbert C. *Cotton Fields No More: Southern Agriculture, 1865–1980*. Lexington: University Press of Kentucky, 1984.

Fitzgerald, Michael W. "'We Have Found a Moses': Theodore Bilbo, Black Nationalism, and the Greater Liberia Bill of 1939." *Journal of Southern History* 63, no. 2 (May 1997): 293–320.

Fixico, Donald L. *Termination and Relocation: Federal Indian Policy, 1945–1960*. Albuquerque: University of New Mexico Press, 1990.

———. *The Urban Indian Experience in America*. Albuquerque: University of New Mexico Press, 2000.

Flowers, Linda. *Throwed Away: Failures of Progress in Eastern North Carolina*. Knoxville: University of Tennessee Press, 1992.

Foner, Eric. *Nothing but Freedom: Emancipation and Its Legacy*. Baton Rouge: Louisiana State University Press, 2007.

Forner, Karlyn. *Why the Vote Wasn't Enough for Selma*. Durham, NC: Duke University Press, 2017.

Frank, Andrew K. "Modern by Tradition: Seminole Innovation in the Contemporary South." *Native South* 10 (2017): 76–95.

Frank, Andrew K., and Kristofer Ray. "Indians as Southerners; Southerners as Indians: Rethinking the History of a Region." *Native South* 10 (2017): vii–xiv.

Frederickson, George M. *White Supremacy: A Comparative Study in American and South African History*. New York: Oxford University Press, 1981.

Freund, Bill. "Forced Resettlement and the Political Economy of South Africa." *Review of African Political Economy* 29 (July 1984): 49–63.

Friedman, Tami J. "'Free Enterprise' or Federal Aid? The Business Response to Economic Restructuring in the Long 1950s." In *Capital Gains: Business and Politics in Twentieth-Century America*, edited by Richard R. John and Kim Phillips-Fein, 119–138. Philadelphia: University of Pennsylvania Press, 2017.

Fuller, Alexandra. *Don't Let's Go to the Dogs Tonight: An African Childhood*. New York: Random House, 2003.

Geary, Daniel, and Jennifer Sutton. "Resisting the Wind of Change: The Citizens' Councils and European Decolonization." In *The U.S. South and Europe: Transatlantic Relations in the Nineteenth and Twentieth Centuries*, ed. Cornelis A. van Minnen and Manfred Berg, 265–282. Lexington: University Press of Kentucky, 2013.

George, Carol V. R. *One Mississippi, Two Mississippi: Methodists, Murder, and the Struggle for Racial Justice in Neshoba County*. New York: Oxford University Press, 2015.

Goldin, Claudia, and Robert A. Margo. "The Great Compression: The Wage Structure in the United States at Mid-Century." *Quarterly Journal of Economics* 107, no. 1 (February 1992): 1–34.

Goldstein, Alyosha. "The Ground Not Given: Colonial Dispositions of Land, Race, and Hunger." *Social Text* 135, 36, no. 2 (June 2018): 83–106.

Goluboff, Risa L. "The Thirteenth Amendment in Historical Perspective." *Journal of Constitutional Law* 11, no. 5 (July 2009): 1451–1473.

Gondola, Ch. Didier. *Tropical Cowboys: Westerns, Violence, and Masculinity in Kinshasa*. Bloomington: Indiana University Press, 2016.

Grant, Nicholas. *Winning Our Freedoms Together: African Americans and Apartheid, 1945–1960*. Chapel Hill: University of North Carolina Press, 2017.

Grossberg, Michael, and Christopher Tomlins. *The Cambridge History of Law in America, Vol. 3*. New York: Cambridge University Press, 2008.

Grove, Wayne A., and Craig Heinicke. "Better Opportunities or Worse? The Demise of Cotton Harvest Labor, 1949–1964." *Journal of Economic History* 63, no. 3 (September 2003): 736–767.

Hagood, Margaret Jarman. "Discussion." *Rural Sociology* 4, no. 3 (September 1939): 313–314.

Hahn, Steven. "Hunting, Fishing, and Foraging: Common Rights and Class Relations in the Postbellum South." *Radical History Review* 26 (1982): 37–64.

———. *A Nation under Our Feet: Black Political Struggles in the Rural South from Slavery to the Great Migration*. Cambridge, MA: Belknap Press of Harvard University Press, 2003.

———. *The Roots of Southern Populism: Yeoman Farmers and the Transformation of the Georgia Upcountry, 1850–1890*. New York: Oxford University Press, 1983.

Hamilton, C. Horace. "The Social Effects of Recent Trends in the Mechanization of Agriculture." *Rural Sociology* 4, no. 1 (March 1939): 3–19.

Hauptman, Laurence M. "Africa View: John Collier, the British Colonial Service and American Indian Policy, 1933–1945." *Historian* 48, no. 3 (May 1986): 359–374.

Henderson, Vivian W. *The Economic Status of Negroes: In the Nation and in the South*. Atlanta: Southern Regional Council, 1963.

Herbin-Triant, Elizabeth A. *Threatening Property: Race, Class, and Campaigns to Legislate Jim Crow Neighborhoods.* New York: Columbia University Press, 2019.

Hitchcock, William I. *The Age of Eisenhower: America and the World in the 1950s.* New York: Simon & Schuster, 2018.

Hobsbawm, Eric. *The Age of Extremes, 1914–1991.* London: Abacus, 1995.

Hobsbawm, Eric, and Terence Ranger, eds. *The Invention of Tradition.* New York: Cambridge University Press, 1983.

Hochschild, Arlie. *The Second Shift: Working Families and the Revolution at Home.* New York: Viking, 1989.

Holley, Donald. *The Second Great Emancipation: The Mechanical Cotton Picker, Black Migration, and How They Shaped the Modern South.* Fayetteville: University of Arkansas Press, 2000.

Honey, Michael. "Operation Dixie: Labor and Civil Rights in the Postwar South." *Mississippi Quarterly* 45, no. 4 (Fall 1992): 439–452.

Horne, Gerald. *Black and Red: WEB Du Bois and the Afro-American Response to the Cold War.* Albany: State University of New York Press, 1985.

———. *From the Barrel of a Gun: The United States and the War against Zimbabwe, 1965–1980.* Chapel Hill: University of North Carolina Press, 2001.

———. "Who Lost the Cold War? Africans and African Americans." *Diplomatic History* 20, no. 4 (Fall 1996): 613–626.

Hoxie, Frederick E. *A Final Promise: The Campaign to Assimilate the Indians, 1880–1920.* Lincoln: University of Nebraska Press, 2001.

Hudson, Angela Pulley, and Hatty Ruth Miller. "Unsettling Histories of the South." *Southern Cultures* 25, no. 3 (Fall 2019): 30–45.

Hudson, Winson, and Constance Curry. *Mississippi Harmony: Memoirs of a Freedom Fighter.* New York: Palgrave Macmillan, 2002.

Hyman, Zoe L. "American Segregationist Ideology and White Southern Africa, 1948–1975." PhD diss., University of Sussex, 2011.

Isett, Christopher, and Stephen Miller. *The Social History of Agriculture: From the Origins to the Current Crisis.* New York: Rowman & Littlefield, 2017.

Jackson, Will. "The Settler's Demise: Decolonization and Mental Breakdown in 1950s Kenya." In *Anxieties, Fear and Panic in Colonial Settings: Empires on the Verge of a Nervous Breakdown,* edited by Harald Fischer-Tiné. London: Palgrave Macmillan, 2016.

Jacobs, Margaret D. "Seeing Like a Settler Colonial State." *Modern American History* 1, no. 2 (July 2018): 257–270.

James, C. L. R. *A History of Pan-African Revolution.* Oakland, CA: PM Press, 2012.

Jenkins, Jeffrey A., and Justin Peck. "Building toward Major Policy Change: Congressional Action on Civil Rights." *Law and History Review* 31, no. 1 (February 2013): 139–198.

Johnson, Charles S., Edwin R. Embree, and W. W. Alexander. *The Collapse of Cotton Tenancy: Summary of Field Studies and Statistical Surveys, 1933–35*. Chapel Hill: University of North Carolina Press, 1935.

Johnson, David. "Settler Farmers and Coerced African Labour in Southern Rhodesia, 1936–46." *Journal of African History* 33, no. 1 (1992), 111–128.

Johnson, Inez Calloway. *History of Longdale High School, 1949–1963*. Jackson, MS: I. C. Johnson, 1999.

Johnson, Walter. *The Broken Heart of America: St. Louis and the Violent History of the United States*. New York: Basic Books, 2020.

———. *River of Dark Dreams: Slavery and Empire in the Cotton Kingdom*. Cambridge, MA: Belknap Press of Harvard University Press, 2013.

Kanogo, Tabitha. *Squatters and the Roots of Mau Mau, 1905–63*. Athens: Ohio University Press, 1987.

Katagiri, Yasuhiro. *The Mississippi State Sovereignty Commission: Civil Rights and States' Rights*. Jackson: University Press of Mississippi, 2001.

Katznelson, Ira. *Fear Itself: The New Deal and the Origins of Our Time*. New York: Liveright, 2013.

Kelley, Robin D. G. "The Rest of Us: Rethinking Settler and Native." *American Quarterly* 69, no. 2 (June 2017): 267–276.

Kelly, Lawrence C. *The Assault on Assimilation: John Collier and the Origins of Indian Policy Reform*. Albuquerque: University of New Mexico Press, 1983.

Kennedy, Dane. *Islands of White: Settler Society and Culture in Kenya and Southern Rhodesia, 1890–1939*. Durham, NC: Duke University Press, 1987.

Kidwell, Clara Sue. "The Choctaw Struggle for Land and Identity in Mississippi, 1830–1918." In *After Removal: The Choctaw in Mississippi*, edited by Samuel J. Wells and Roseanna Tubby, 64–93. Jackson: University Press of Mississippi, 1986.

King, J. Crawford, Jr. "The Closing of the Southern Range: An Exploratory Study." *Journal of Southern History* 48, no. 1 (February 1982): 53–70.

Kirby, Jack Temple. *Rural Worlds Lost: The American South, 1920–1960*. Baton Rouge: Louisiana State University Press, 1987.

Klarman, Michael J. *From Jim Crow to Civil Rights: The Supreme Court and the Struggle for Racial Equality*. New York: Oxford University Press, 2004.

———. "The White Primary Rulings: A Case Study in the Consequences of Supreme Court Decisionmaking." *Florida State University Law Review* 29, no. 1 (Fall 2001): 55–107.

Klerk, Michael de. "Seasons That Will Never Return: The Impact of Farm Mechanization on Employment, Incomes and Population Distribution in the Western Transvaal." *Journal of Southern African Studies* 11, no. 1 (October 1984): 84–105.

Kluger, Richard. *Simple Justice: The History of Brown v. Board of Education and Black America's Struggle for Equality*. New York: Vintage, 2004.

Komara, Edward, ed. *The Blues Encyclopedia*. New York: Routledge, 2006.

Kotef, Hagar. *The Colonizing Self: Or, Home and Homelessness in Israel/Palestine*. Durham, NC: Duke University Press, 2020.

Korstad, Robert, and Nelson Lichtenstein. "Opportunities Found and Lost: Labor, Radicals, and the Early Civil Rights Movement." *Journal of American History* 75, no. 3 (December 1988): 786–811.

Kruse, Kevin M., and Stephen Tuck, eds. *Fog of War: The Second World War and the Civil Rights Movement*. New York: Oxford University Press, 2012.

LaGrand, James B. *Indian Metropolis: Native Americans in Chicago, 1945–75*. Urbana: University of Illinois Press, 2002.

Lemann, Nicholas. *The Promised Land: The Great Black Migration and How It Changed America*. New York: Knopf, 1991.

Le Sueur, James D., ed. *The Decolonization Reader*. New York: Routledge, 2003.

Lipscomb, J. F. *We Built a Country*. London: Faber & Faber, 1956.

Lonsdale, John. "Britain's Mau Mau." In *Penultimate Adventures with Britannia: Personalities, Politics and Culture in Britain*, edited by Wm. Roger Louis, 259–273. London: I. B. Tauris, 2008.

———. "The Depression and the Second World War in the Transformation of Kenya." In *Africa and the Second World War*, edited by David Killingray and Richard Rathbone, 97–142. London: MacMillan, 1986.

Low, D. A., and J. M. Lonsdale. "Towards the New Order, 1945–1963." In *History of East Africa*, vol. 3, edited by D. A. Low and Alison Smith, 1–63. Oxford: Clarendon Press, 1976.

Lowery, Malinda Maynor. *Lumbee Indians in the Jim Crow South: Race, Identity, and the Making of a Nation*. Chapel Hill: University of North Carolina Press, 2010.

———. "The Original Southerners: American Indians, the Civil War, and Confederate Memory," *Southern Cultures* 25, no. 4 (Winter 2019): 19.

Madigan, La Verne. *The American Indian Relocation Program*. New York: Association on American Indian Affairs, 1956.

Mamdani, Mahmood. *Neither Settler nor Native: The Making and Unmaking of Permanent Minorities*. Cambridge, MA: Belknap Press of Harvard University Press, 2020.

Mars, Florence. *Witness in Philadelphia*. Baton Rouge: Louisiana State University Press, 1977.

Martin, Philip. *Chief*. Brandon, MS: Quail Ridge Press, 2009.

Mauldin, Erin Stewart. "Freedom, Economic Autonomy, and Ecological Change in the Cotton South, 1865–1880." *Journal of the Civil War Era* 7, no. 3 (September 2017): 401–424.

———. *Unredeemed Land: An Environmental History of Civil War and Emancipation in the Cotton South*. New York: Oxford University Press, 2018.

Mbembe, Achille. *On the Postcolony*. Berkeley: University of California Press, 2001.

McRae, Elizabeth Gillespie. *Mothers of Massive Resistance: White Women and the Politics of White Supremacy*. New York: Oxford University Press, 2018.

Meriwether, James H. *Proudly We Can Be Africans: Black Americans and Africa, 1935–1961*. Chapel Hill: University of North Carolina Press, 2002.

Michele, Sister M. *The History of the Negro Vote in Mississippi*. MA thesis, Loyola University, 1957.

Miller, Douglas K. *Indians on the Move: Native American Mobility and Urbanization in the Twentieth Century*. Chapel Hill: University of North Carolina Press, 2019.

Minchin, Timothy J. *Empty Mills: The Fight Against Imports and the Decline of the U.S. Textile*. Lanham, MD: Rowman & Littlefield, 2013.

Mitchell, Dennis J. *A New History of Mississippi*. Jackson: University Press of Mississippi, 2014.

Mlambo, A. S. *A History of Zimbabwe*. New York: Cambridge University Press, 2014.

Mosley, Paul. *The Settler Economies: Studies in the Economic History of Kenya and Southern Rhodesia, 1900–1963*. New York: Cambridge University Press, 1983.

Munro, John. *The Anticolonial Front: The African American Freedom Struggle and Global Decolonisation, 1945–1960*. New York: Cambridge University Press, 2017.

Naidu, Suresh. "Labor Mobility and Economic Development in the Post-Bellum U.S. South." Working paper. https://eml.berkeley.edu/ffiwebfac/cromer/e211_spo8/naidu.pdf (accessed June 21, 2021).

Ndlovu-Gatsheni, Sabelo J. "Mapping Cultural and Colonial Encounters, 1880s-1930s." In *Becoming Zimbabwe: A History from the Pre-colonial Period to 2008*, edited by Brian Raftapoulos and A. S. Mlambo, 39–74. Harare, ZI: Weaver Press, 2009.

Nyambara, Pius S. "'That Place Was Wonderful!': African Tenants on Rhodesdale Estate, Colonial Zimbabwe, c. 1900–1952." *International Journal of African Historical Studies* 38, no. 2 (2005): 267–299.

O'Brien, Jean M. "Tracing Settler Colonialism's Eliminatory Logic in *Traces of History*." *American Quarterly* 69, no. 2 (June 2017): 249–255.

Ochiltree, Ian D. "'A Just and Self-Respecting System'?: Black Independence, Sharecropping, and Paternalistic Relations in the American South and South Africa." *Agricultural History* 72, no. 2 (Spring 1998): 352–380.

Ohanian, Lee E. "Competition and the Decline of the Rust Belt," Economic Policy Paper 14–6. Federal Reserve Bank of Minneapolis. December 2014.

Olsson, Tore C. "The South in the World since 1865: A Review Essay." *Journal of Southern History* 87, no. 1 (February 2021): 67–108.

Onselen, Charles van. *Chibaro: African Mine Labour in Southern Rhodesia, 1900–1933.* Johannesburg: Ravan Press, 1980.

———. "Race and Class in the South African Countryside: Cultural Osmosis and Social Relations in the Sharecropping Economy of the South-Western Transvaal, 1900–1950." *American Historical Review* 95, no. 1 (February 1990): 99–123.

———. *The Seed Is Mine: The Life of Kas Maine, a South African Sharecropper, 1894–1985.* New York: Hill & Wang, 1997.

Osburn, Katherine M. B. "'Any Sane Person': Race, Rights, and Tribal Sovereignty in the Construction of the Dawes Rolls for the Choctaw Nation." *Journal of the Gilded Age and Progressive Era* 9, no. 4 (October 2010): 451–471.

———. *Choctaw Resurgence in Mississippi: Race, Class, and Nation Building in the Jim Crow South, 1830–1977.* Lincoln: University of Nebraska Press, 2014.

———. "'In a Name of Justice and Fairness': The Mississippi Choctaw Indian Federation versus the BIA, 1934." In *Beyond Red Power: American Indian Politics and Activism since 1900*, edited by Daniel M. Cobb and Loretta Fowler, 109–125. Santa Fe, NM: School for Advanced Research, 2007.

———. "Mississippi Choctaws and Racial Politics," *Southern Cultures* 14, no. 4 (Winter 2008): 32–54.

Ownby, Ted, Charles Reagan Wilson, Ann J. Abadie, Odie Lindsey, and James G. Thomas, Jr., eds. *The Mississippi Encyclopedia.* Jackson: University Press of Mississippi, 2017.

Padmore, George. *The Life and Struggles of Negro Toilers.* London: Red International of Labor Unions Magazine for the International Trade Union Committee of Negro Workers, 1931.

Palmer, Robin. "The Agricultural History of Rhodesia." In *The Roots of Rural Poverty in Central and Southern Africa*, edited by Robin Palmer and Neil Parsons, 221–254. London: Heinemann, 1977.

———. *Land and Racial Domination in Rhodesia.* Berkeley: University of California Press, 1977.

Payne, Charles M. *I've Got the Light of Freedom: The Organizing Tradition and the Mississippi Freedom Struggle.* Berkeley: University of California Press, 1995.

Perdue, Theda. "The Legacy of Indian Removal." *Journal of Southern History* 78, no. 1 (February 2012): 3–36.

———. "Southern Indians and Jim Crow." In *The Folly of Jim Crow: Rethinking the Segregated South*, edited by Stephanie Cole and Natalie J. Ring, 54–90. College Station: Texas A&M University Press, 2012.

Petty, Adrienne Monteith. *Standing Their Ground: Small Farmers in North Carolina since the Civil War.* New York: Oxford University Press, 2013.

Pierce, Jason E. *Making the White Man's West: Whiteness and the Creation of the American West.* Boulder: University Press of Colorado, 2018.

Piketty, Thomas, and Emmanuel Saez. "Income Inequality in the United States, 1913–1998." *Quarterly Journal of Economics* 118, no. 1 (February 2003): 1–39.

Piven, Frances Fox, and Richard A. Cloward. *Regulating the Poor: The Functions of Public Welfare,* updated ed. New York: Vintage, 1993.

Plummer, Brenda Gayle. *In Search of Power: African Americans in the Era of Decolonization, 1956–1974.* New York: Cambridge University Press, 2013.

Price, Richard N. "The Psychology of Colonial Violence." In *Violence, Colonialism and Empire in the Modern World,* edited by Philip Dwyer and Amanda Nettlebeck, 25–52. London: Palgrave Macmillan, 2018.

Prince, K. Stephen. *Stories of the South: Race and the Reconstruction of Southern Identity, 1865–1915.* Chapel Hill: University of North Carolina Press, 2014.

Rand, Clayton. *Ink on My Hands.* New York: Carrick & Evans, 1940.

Raper, Arthur. "The Role of Agricultural Technology in Southern Social Change." *Social Forces* 25, no. 1 (October 1946): 21–30.

Reidy, Joseph P. *From Slavery to Agrarian Capitalism in the Cotton Plantation South: Central Georgia, 1860–1880.* Chapel Hill: University of North Carolina Press, 1992.

Rifkin, Mark. *Settler Common Sense: Queerness and Everyday Colonialism in the American Renaissance.* Minneapolis: University of Minnesota Press, 2014.

Roark, James L. "American Black Leaders: The Response to Colonialism and the Cold War, 1943–1953." *African Historical Studies* 4, no. 2 (1971), 253–270.

Roberts, Gene, and Hank Klibanoff. *The Race Beat: The Press, the Civil Rights Struggle, and the Awakening of a Nation.* New York: Vintage, 2006.

Rolinson, Mary G. *Grassroots Garveyism: The Universal Negro Improvement Association in the Rural South.* Chapel Hill: University of North Carolina Press, 2007.

Rosenthal, Nicolas G. *Reimagining Indian Country: Native American Migration and Identity in Twentieth-Century Los Angeles.* Chapel Hill: University of North Carolina Press, 2012.

Rosenthal, Robert J. "Exclusions of Employees under the Taft-Hartley Act." *ILR Review* 4, no. 4 (July 1951): 556–570.

Rosier, Paul C. *Serving Their Country: American Indian Politics and Patriotism in the Twentieth Century.* Cambridge, MA: Harvard University Press, 2009.

———. "'They Are Ancestral Homelands': Race, Place, and Politics in Cold War Native America, 1945–1961." *Journal of American History* 92, no. 4 (March 2006): 1300–1326.

Rothman, Adam. *Slave Country: American Expansion and the Origins of the Deep South*. Cambridge, MA: Harvard University Press, 2005.

Ruminski, Jarret. *The Limits of Loyalty: Ordinary People in Civil War Mississippi*. Jackson: University Press of Mississippi, 2017.

Said, Edward W. *Culture and Imperialism*. New York: Alfred A. Knopf, 1993.

Saunt, Claudio. *Unworthy Republic: The Dispossession of Native Americans and the Road to Indian Territory*. New York: Norton, 2020.

Saville, Julie. *The Work of Reconstruction: From Slave to Wage Laborer in South Carolina, 1860–1870*. New York: Cambridge University Press, 1994.

Schirmer, Stefan. "Motives for Mechanisation in South African Agriculture, c1940–1980." *African Studies* 63, no. 1 (July 2004): 3–28.

Shepard, Todd. *The Invention of Decolonization: The Algerian War and the Remaking of France*. Ithaca, NY: Cornell University Press, 2006.

Shepherd, A. W. "Capitalist Agriculture in Africa." *Africa Development* 6, no. 3 (July-September 1981): 5–21.

Slotkin, Richard. *Gunfighter Nation: The Myth of the Frontier in Twentieth-Century America*. New York: HarperPerennial, 1993.

Smallwood, Stephanie E. "Reflections on Settler Colonialism, the Hemispheric Americas, and Chattel Slavery." *William and Mary Quarterly* 76, no. 3 (July 2019): 407–416.

Sokol, Jason. *There Goes My Everything: White Southerners in the Age of Civil Rights, 1945–1975*. New York: Vintage, 2007.

Stanley, Amy Dru. *From Bondage to Contract: Wage Labor, Marriage, and the Market in the Age of Slave Emancipation*. New York: Cambridge University Press, 1998.

Stein, Judith. *Pivotal Decade: How the United States Traded Factories for Finance in the Seventies*. New Haven, CT: Yale University Press, 2010.

Street, James H. *The New Revolution in the Cotton Economy: Mechanization and Its Consequences*. Chapel Hill: University of North Carolina Press, 1957.

Stuesse, Angela, and Laura E. Helton. "Low-Wage Legacies, Race, and the Golden Chicken in Mississippi: Where Contemporary Immigration Meets African American Labor History." *Southern Spaces*, December 31, 2013. https://southernspaces.org/2013/low-wage-legacies-race-and-golden-chicken-mississippi-where-contemporary-immigration-meets-african-american-labor-history/.

Sugrue, Thomas J. *The Origins of the Urban Crisis: Race and Inequality in Postwar Detroit*. Princeton, NJ: Princeton University Press, 1996.

Surplus People Project. *Forced Removals in South Africa: Volume 1: General Overview*. Cape Town: Surplus People Project, 1983.

———. *Forced Removals in South Africa: Volume 2: Eastern Cape*. Cape Town: Surplus People Project, 1983.

Taylor, Graham D. *The New Deal and American Indian Tribalism: The Administration of the Indian Reorganization Act, 1934–45.* Lincoln: University of Nebraska Press, 1980.

Thomas, Karen Kruse. "The Hill-Burton Act and Civil Rights: Expanding Hospital Care for Black Southerners, 1939–1960." *Journal of Southern History* 72, no. 4 (November 2006): 823–870.

Thomas, Martin. "A Path Not Taken? British Perspectives on French Colonial Violence after 1945." In *Wind of Change: Harold Macmillan and British Decolonization,* edited by L. J. Butler and Sarah Stockwell, 159–179. New York: Palgrave Macmillan, 2013.

Tolbert, Charles Madden. "A Sociological Study of the Choctaw Indians in Mississippi." PhD diss., Louisiana State University, 1958.

Veracini, Lorenzo. "Settler Collective, Founding Violence, and Disavowal: The Settler Colonial Situation." *Journal of Intercultural Studies* 29, no. 4 (November 2008): 363–379.

Wallerstein, Immanuel. "What Hope Africa? What Hope the World?" In *After Liberalism.* New York: New Press, 1995.

Walton, Hanes, Jr., Sherman C. Puckett, and Donald R. Deskins Jr. *The African American Electorate: A Statistical History.* Los Angeles: CQ Press, 2012.

Ward, Jason Morgan. *Defending White Democracy: The Making of a Segregationist Movement and the Remaking of Racial Politics, 1936–1965.* Chapel Hill: University of North Carolina Press, 2011.

wa Thiong'o, Ngugi. *Decolonising the Mind: The Politics of Language in African Literature.* London: James Currey, 1988.

Webster, Wendy. "'There'll Always Be an England': Representations of Colonial Wars and Immigration, 1948–1968." *Journal of British Studies* 40, no. 4 (October 2001): 557–584.

White, Richard. *The Republic for Which It Stands: The United States during Reconstruction and the Gilded Age, 1865–1896.* New York: Oxford University Press, 2017.

Wilkerson, Isabel. *The Warmth of Other Suns: The Epic Story of America's Great Migration.* New York: Random House, 2010.

Wilkinson, Charles F., LaDonna Harris, Steven Unger, Helen Peterson, and Benjamin Reifel. "The Trust Obligation," in *Indian Self-Rule: First-hand Accounts of Indian-White Relations from Roosevelt to Reagan,* edited by Kenneth R. Philp, 302–310. Logan: Utah State University Press, 1995.

Williams, B. O. "The Impact of Mechanization of Agriculture on the Farm Population of the South." *Rural Sociology* 4, no. 3 (September 1939): 300–311.

Wilson, Gregory S. *Communities Left Behind: The Area Redevelopment Administration, 1945–1960.* Knoxville: University of Tennessee Press, 2009.

———. "Deindustrialization, Poverty, and Federal Area Redevelopment in the

United States, 1945–1965." In *Beyond the Ruins: The Meanings of Deindustrialization*, edited by Jefferson Cowie and Joseph Heathcott, 181–198. Ithaca, NY: ILR Press of Cornell University Press, 2003.

Wolfe, Patrick. "Land, Labor, and Difference: Elementary Structures of Race." *American Historical Review* 106, no. 3 (June 2001): 866–905.

———. "Settler Colonialism and the Elimination of the Native." *Journal of Genocide Research* 8, no. 4 (December 2006): 387–409.

———. *Traces of History: Elementary Structures of Race*. Brooklyn, NY: Verso, 2016.

Wood, Ellen Meiksins. *The Origin of Capitalism: A Longer View*. Brooklyn, NY: Verso, 2017.

Woodman, Harold D. *New South—New Law: The Legal Foundations of Credit and Labor Relations in the Postbellum Agricultural South*. Baton Rouge: Louisiana State University Press, 1995.

———. "Post–Civil War Southern Agriculture and the Law." *Agricultural History* 53, no.1 (January 1979): 319–337.

Woodruff, Nan Elizabeth. *American Congo: The African American Freedom Struggle in the Delta*. Cambridge, MA: Harvard University Press, 2003.

———. "Mississippi Delta Planters and Debates over Mechanization, Labor, and Civil Rights in the 1940s." *Journal of Southern History* 60, no. 2 (May 1994): 263–284.

———. "Pick or Fight: The Emergency Farm Labor Program in the Arkansas and Mississippi Deltas during World War II." *Agricultural History* 64, no. 2 (Spring 1990): 74–85.

Woods, Clyde. *Development Arrested: The Blues and Plantation Power in the Mississippi Delta*. Brooklyn, NY: Verso 1998.

Yellow Bird, Michael. "Cowboys and Indians: Toys of Genocide, Icons of American Colonialism." *Wicazo Sa Review* 19, no. 2 (Autumn 2004): 33–48.

Youé, Christopher. "Black Squatters on White Farms: Segregation and Agrarian Change in Kenya, South Africa, and Rhodesia, 1902–1963." *International History Review* 24, no. 3 (September 2002): 558–602.

Zeichner, Oscar. "The Legal Status of the Agricultural Laborer in the South." *Political Science Quarterly* 55, no. 3 (September 1940): 412–428.

Zimmerman, Andrew. *Alabama in Africa: Booker T. Washington, the German Empire, and the Globalization of the New South*. Princeton, NJ: Princeton University Press, 2010.

Films

Sissako, Abderrahmane, dir. *Bamako*. 2006. New York: New Yorker Films, 2007. DVD.

INDEX

African National Congress, 119
Agricultural Adjustment Act, 23–25
Agricultural Adjustment Administration (AAA), 36, 39, 89, 96
Agricultural Stabilization and Conservation Service (ASC; ASCS), 88–89, 96–97, 111, 125–126, 128, 136n11, 175n1
Alexander, L. S., 120
Algeria, 31, 118
Allen, Dick, 37–38
Amis, Lampkin, 22
Angola, 79, 118
anti-enticement laws, 14, 18, 140n17
Area Redevelopment Act, 126–127
Area Redevelopment Administration, 126
Attala County, MS, 4, 14, 18, 45, 59, 81, 91, 106, 112, 140n16, 153n8, 163n1
automation, 98, 103–105, 117

Balanced Farm and Home (BFH) Program, 110, 114
Baldwin, James, 53, 125
baseball, 109
Bates, G. N., 120
Bay Ridge Christian College, 121–123
Bell, Cleddie, 53, 70
Bell, Cubert, 102
Bell, Willie, 102
Benson, Ezra Taft, 88
Biddle, Francis, 42–43
Bilbo, Theodore, 55–56, 153n11
blues musicians, 106–107

Bowman, Joan, 127
Brown v. Board of Education, 67, 71–79, 160n41
Bryant, John, 120–121
Bulman, Milton Lee, 42
Bunche, Ralph, 107
Bureau of Indian Affairs (BIA), 26–27, 54, 61–62, 66, 68–71, 101–102, 156n19, 159n37
Burrage, Olen, 128

Central African Federation (Northern Rhodesia), 79, 118
Chaney, James, 128
chibalo, 14
chibaro, 14
Choctaws. *See* Mississippi Band of Choctaw Indians
Citizens' Council (White Citizens' Council), 7–8, 75–77, 95, 97, 119, 122–124
Civil Rights Act of 1957, 80
Civil Rights Act of 1964, 125, 128
Civil Rights Commission, 8, 80, 85–88, 104, 108, 120–122, 127, 129
Civil War (United States), 12–13, 16, 134n6
Clark, Tom C., 42
Cobb, Cully, 24
Cold War, 50, 58, 67–68, 71, 79, 83, 102
Coleman, J. P., 75, 118
Collier, Clinton, 20, 25–26, 105–106, 129
Collier, John, 60–61

communism, 19, 51, 58, 68, 72, 79, 129, 154n16, 160n41
Community Action Program, 130
Congress of Industrial Organizations (CIO), 43–45, 172n14
cotton
    allotments, 88–89, 111–112
    and Choctaws, 22, 26–27, 65–66, 102–103, 113–114
    cultivation of, 1, 5, 10, 23, 25–26, 86–87
    diversification from, 35–38, 89–90, 92, 95–97, 165–66n14
    and the economy, 23–24, 29, 32–33, 41–42, 135n8
    and the labor question, 10–12
    and mechanization, 2, 30–31, 33–35, 38–41, 44, 46–49, 97, 103, 112–113, 165n14
    and neoslavery, 14, 18–19
cotton picker, 2, 30–31, 33–34, 39–40, 44, 46–47, 113
Cotton States League, 109
cowboys, 53–54, 57
Crossett Experimental Forest, 37
Crump, Ed, 39

dairy farming, 35–38, 46, 87, 90, 96–97, 112
Dancing Rabbit Creek, Treaty of, 1, 2, 11, 16, 27, 32, 63–64, 130
Darby, "Big Ike," 106–107
deindustrialization, 103–106, 117–118, 170n44
Delta Council, 31, 44, 72
Delta region, 2, 5, 18, 20, 26, 30, 31, 35, 39, 44, 56, 59, 65–66, 72, 107
Detroit, MI, 101, 103, 105

DeWeese Lumber Company, 22, 37–38
diversification, 8, 31, 35–38, 95, 168n34
Dixiecrats (States' Rights Democratic Party), 46
Dixon, B. H., 38, 89, 91
Dixon, MS, 105
Dockery, Joe, 44
Dorman, Clarence, 33

Eastland, James O., 2, 8, 45, 91, 114
Economic Opportunity Act of 1964, 130
Eisenhower, Dwight D., 70, 79–80
Emmons, Glenn, 91
environmental degradation, 25, 82, 109, 171n3
Equal Opportunity in Farm Programs (United States Commission on Civil Rights), 85, 129
Ethridge, Tom, 51, 74–75, 118, 173n20
Evers, Charles, 20–21, 46, 54–59, 72, 76–77, 153n11
Evers, Medgar, 20–21, 46, 54–58, 74, 120, 153n11
Extension Service, 8, 33–38, 40–41, 54, 75, 83–92, 96, 100, 110–112, 127, 146n10, 147n12, 152–53n8, 165n12, 167n21. *See also specific employees*

Fair Employment Practices Committee (FEPC), 44–45
Farm Bureau, 44, 75–76, 95–97, 124, 167–68n31
Farmers Home Administration (FHA), 88, 92–94, 128
Farm Family of the Week, 94–97

INDEX | 205

Fatherree, T. B., 93–94
Federal Bureau of Investigation (FBI), 17–18, 42
fence laws (stock laws), 14, 139n8
Florida, 65, 102
4-H clubs, 38, 84–90, 165n12
Freedom Summer, 123, 128

George, T. B., 22
Germany, Horace, 121–123
Golddust, TN, 102–103
Goodman, Andrew, 128
Griffin, Shep, 15–16

Hall, Toxey, 42
Harpole, H. H. "Boots," 75
Harrison, Pat, 45
Henry, L. J., 90
Hill-Burton Act, 115
Hollis, J. O., 46
Home Demonstration Clubs, 54, 84, 86–87, 96, 100, 109, 153n8
Hopson, Richard, 30–31
Howard, Theodore Roosevelt Mason (T. R. M.), 58, 78
Hoyt, A. J., 16
Huxley, Julian, 61

Indian removal, 1–3, 5, 17
Indian Reorganization Act (IRA), 61–62, 66, 68, 157nn22–23
Isaac, Calvin, 129

Jackson, Luther, 78
Johnson, Andrew, 12
Johnson, E. J., 85
Johnson, Lyndon B., 125
Johnston, Oscar, 39–40, 46–47
Jones, Lillie, 20, 74

Kemper County, MS, 1, 4, 14, 15–16, 20–22, 34, 37, 38, 54, 59, 73–74, 75–76, 78, 85–86, 89, 91, 93–94, 99–100, 109, 120–121, 125, 127, 145n7, 153n8
Kennedy, John F., 124, 126
Kenya, 4, 10–11, 20, 28, 31, 47–49, 53, 56–58, 71, 74, 79, 118–120, 154n13
Kerr, Esther L., 87
Kikuyu, 28, 56–57, 154n13
Kilgore, Ethyl, 42
Killen, Edgar Ray, 123, 176n6
Korean War, 89
Ku Klux Klan, 17, 21, 75

land bank, 47–48
Langfitt, Howard, 94–97
Lauderdale County, MS, 4, 21, 37, 43, 45, 59, 78, 85
Leake County, MS, 4, 17–18, 21, 26, 34, 37, 46, 54–55, 59, 64, 85–86, 100, 106, 127, 153n8, 156
Lee, George W., 77
Lee, R. C., 15
Lions Club, 99–100
Little Rock crisis, 79–80
Lyle, Clay, 86, 89–90, 92
lynching, 19–23, 55, 56, 141n20, 153n11

Maine, Kas, 28, 48
Malan, D. F., 79
Mars, Charles, 75
Mars, Florence, 52, 72, 74, 156n18
Mashulatubbee, 21
Mau Mau uprising, 28, 57–58, 74, 120, 154n13
McKinley, Frank, 27

McLendon, Robert, 17–18
mechanization
  and Africa, 28, 31, 47–48, 56, 150n34
  and US industry, 117
  and US South, 2, 5, 8–9, 30–41, 44, 46–47, 49, 65, 67, 81, 83, 92, 95–99, 103–104, 109–110, 112–113, 127, 146n9, 162n53, 165–66n14, 168n34
migration, 19, 39–41, 65–66, 81–83, 102–107, 117, 126, 167n21, 172n8
miscegenation, 51, 72
Mississippi Band of Choctaw Indians (MBCI)
  economic advancement of, 78, 99, 116–117, 128–130, 176n7
  and farming, 7–8, 25–27, 41, 47, 65–66, 82, 90, 91, 93, 97, 102–103, 113, 158n28, 176n7
  former towns of, 3, 109
  and Freedom Summer murders, 128
  and Indian Removal, 1–3, 5, 6, 11–13, 47, 125
  and IRA, 52, 60–63, 67, 68
  and lynching, 19–22
  and neoslavery, 15–17, 19, 113
  and political disenfranchisement, 29, 52, 58, 59–60, 78, 156n19
  second removal of, 17
  and settler culture, 6, 52–55, 97, 151–52n5
  and termination/relocation, 4, 68–71, 101–103, 159n37, 169n40
  treaty claims of, 6, 8, 52, 64–65, 108, 123–124
Mississippi Burning case, 123, 128
Mississippi Delta, 2, 5, 18, 20, 26, 30, 31, 35, 39, 44, 56, 59, 65–66, 72, 107
Mississippi State Sovereignty Commission, 8, 77, 121–123, 174n26
Moody, William H., 16
Mosley, J. Y., 93–94
Mosley, Turner, 93–94
Mozambique, 79, 118
musicians, 106–107
Musselwhite, Charlie, 106–107

National Association for the Advancement of Colored People (NAACP), 18, 52, 58–59, 72, 74, 76–78, 154n16, 155–56n17, 162n53
Neshoba County, MS
  Choctaws in, 26–27, 64, 66, 159n37
  and civil rights, 52, 58–59, 72–78, 123, 128, 155n17, 156n18, 161n43
  and economic decline, 98–99, 114–116, 118, 126–127, 168n34
  and farming, 33–38, 41, 84–90, 95–96, 105, 106, 110, 128, 129, 164n5
  and Freedom Summer, 123, 128
  geography of, 4
  neoslavery in, 15–16
  racist violence in, 20–23, 121–123, 128
  and tree farming, 37–38, 88, 92
New Deal, 23–25, 43, 46, 63, 67, 71, 103
Newton County, MS, 4, 17, 20–21, 26, 36, 42, 46, 51, 54, 59, 76, 90, 97–98, 111–112, 121–122, 127,

138n7, 138n8, 153n8, 156n19, 172n8
Northern Rhodesia. *See* Central African Federation
Norton, C. S., 36–38, 41, 84, 89–90, 92, 96, 99, 110–111, 146n9, 165–166n14
Noxapater, MS, 22, 58
Noxubee County, MS, 4–5, 12, 14, 18–19, 21–22, 52, 59, 76, 120–121
Nyasaland, 79

Office of Indian Affairs (OIA). *See* Bureau of Indian Affairs (BIA)
open range, 14
Operation Dixie (CIO), 43–44, 58
outmigration, 19, 39–41, 65–66, 81–83, 102–107, 117, 126, 167n21, 172n8
overall economic development programs (OEDP), 126–128

Padmore, George, 19
Pan-Africanist Congress, 119
Parker, John R., 119
Patterson, Bob "Tut," 75
Patterson, Joe, 122
Payne, L. W., 77, 85–86, 92, 110, 162n51, 168n34
Pearl River, MS, 26, 53, 62, 66, 70
peonage, 14–19, 26, 29, 42–43, 93, 140n16
Perryman, Will E., 85
Philadelphia, MS
  Choctaws in, 3, 26, 34–37, 54, 91, 102, 156n19
  and civil rights, 58–59, 73, 75–78
  and economic decline, 98–99, 114–117

and farming, 91, 96, 98, 102–103, 106
Mars family of, 25, 52, 72, 74, 156n18
population of, 98
Phillip, Riley, 113
Pioneer Society, 119
Plessy v. Ferguson, 67
Posey, Vance, 16
poultry, 86–87, 100
Production and Marketing Administration (PMA). *See* Agricultural Stabilization and Conservation Service
Provinse, John H., 54
Putnam, H. J., 40, 92

race
  and Africa, 4, 119
  and Choctaws, 6, 19, 54–55, 62
  and education, 72–74, 119, 121–123
  and extension work, 85–86, 110
  panic over, 2, 30–31, 51–52, 74–75
  and peonage, 19
  and politics, 43–47
  and settler-colonial theory, 5–6, 49, 157n23
  social construction of, 6, 62, 157n23
  and US South, 2, 4, 12–14
  See also segregation; settler colonialism
Rainey, Lawrence, 78
Reconstruction, 12–14, 23, 25, 29, 105
Reeves, W. T., 123
relocation. *See* Voluntary Relocation Program
Resident Native Labor Ordinance (RNLO), 28, 48

Reuther, Walter, 104–105
Rhodesia. See Zimbabwe
Roosevelt, Franklin D., 23, 44
Rural Electrification Administration, 87
Rush, Otis, 106–107
Rust brothers (John and Mack), 30, 39

Schwerner, Michael, 128
Scott, T. J., 91
Scott County, MS, 4, 17, 59, 76, 100
segregation
    and Africa, 79, 119–120
    breakdown of, 50–51, 58, 71–78, 118
    and Choctaws, 52–55, 67, 69, 72–79, 82, 85, 87–88, 97, 115, 118
    and extension work, 85–88
    and hospitals, 115
    and labor, 82, 99, 108
    and schools, 46, 50, 52, 67, 71–74
    and White Citizens' Councils, 7–8, 75–77
Sells, Cato, 26
settler colonialism
    and Africa, 4, 19–20, 27–28, 47–49, 74–75, 79, 83, 107, 118–120, 152n6
    and decolonization, 4, 7, 50, 58, 71, 74, 82, 84, 108, 118
    defined, 3
    and English enclosure, 82
    growth of, 10–11
    and Native Americans, 52–55, 62, 68
    and race, 5–6, 49, 51, 54, 62
    scholarship on, 3, 137–38n4
    and US South, 1–9, 19–20, 31–32, 48–49, 50–52, 72, 74–75, 79, 83, 107, 109, 126, 130

sharecropping, 1, 3–5, 8–9, 13, 19, 24–28, 30–31, 34, 37–40, 42, 48, 61, 65, 81–82, 91, 103, 120–121, 126, 138n7, 143n34, 158n28
Sharpeville Massacre, 108, 118–119
Shaw, M. S., 100, 111, 165n12
Shelton, Harry, 22
Shuqualak, MS, 120
Simpson, J. David, 51
slavery, 1, 11–12, 14–20, 22, 27, 29, 42–43, 125, 138n5
Smith, C. I., 35–36, 91
Smith, Ezekiel C., 120–121, 123
Smith, Lamar, 77
Smith, Roy, 42
Smith v. Allwright, 43, 56
Society of the Two Souths, 119
South Africa, 4, 7, 10, 20, 28, 48, 51, 71, 74–75, 79, 118–120, 130
South West Africa, 79, 118
Southern Rhodesia. See Zimbabwe
Spivey, Arraner Stephens, 106, 140n16
squatters. See Kikuyu
States' Rights Democratic Party (Dixiecrats), 46
Stennis, John C., 8, 45, 73, 75, 89, 93–94, 111
Stephens, Tom, 16–17
stock laws, 14, 139n8
Student Nonviolent Coordinating Committee (SNCC), 125, 127
Sullens, Fred, 44

Taft-Hartley Act, 45
Taylor, William L., 127
tenancy
    AAA policies regarding, 24–25
    and Choctaws, 25–27
    defined, 13

and eviction, 1, 5, 8–9, 31–40, 46, 48, 81–83, 92–93, 95, 97–99, 101, 113, 125–127
and lynching, 22
and neoslavery, 19, 42
in southern Africa, 28–29, 47–48, 150n34
termination policy, 67–71, 101
Therrell, Jeff, 18
Thiong'o, Ngugi wa, 53
Thomas, Bob and Delma, 42
Thompson, Tommy, 22
Till, Emmett, 77–78
Tillis, Elijah, 120
timber industry, 17, 18, 37–38, 41, 49, 66–67, 92, 95, 96, 112, 116
Tingle, Willie, 20–21, 56
Transvaal, 48, 119
tree farming. *See* timber industry
truancy, 65–66
Truman, Harry S., 46, 64, 68
Tunisia, 31

underemployment, 101, 126–126, 172n8
unemployment, 30, 35, 38, 57, 81, 83, 104, 108, 112, 116–118, 126–130
United States Commission on Civil Rights, 8, 80, 85–88, 104, 108, 120–122, 127, 129
United States Congress, 10, 26, 33, 40, 43–46, 67–70, 123–124
United States Department of Agriculture, 8, 29, 32, 82, 84, 110, 113, 129–130, 153n8. *See also* Agricultural Adjustment Administration; Agricultural Stabilization and Conservation Service; Extension Service; Farmers Home Administration

United States Department of Justice, 15, 42, 80
United States Employment Service (USES), 43
United States v. Leggett, 15–16
United States v. Pickett, 16

vagrancy, 14, 17
Vance, Paul, 70, 114, 116
Verwoerd, Hendrik, 119
Voluntary Relocation Program, 4, 69–71, 91, 101–102
Voting Rights Act, 125, 128

Wagner Act, 45
Waldo, MS, 96, 105
Wallace, Henry A., 24–25
Warren, Earl, 67
Welch, Frank J., 33, 145n5
Wells-Lamont glove factory, 99, 114–115
Wheeler-Howard Act. *See* Indian Reorganization Act
White Citizens' Council, 7–8, 75–77, 95, 97, 119, 122–124
White Highlands. *See* Kenya
Whitten, Mary Lillian Peters (Ogden), 21
Winstead, Arthur, 45–46, 50, 124, 127
Winston County, MS, 1, 4, 21–22, 37, 42, 58–59, 96–97, 153n8, 156n17
WLBT-TV, 94–97
Wolfe, Patrick, 3, 5–6, 49, 137–38n4
Works Progress Administration (WPA), 1, 133n1
World War I, 17, 21, 23, 28
World War II
and African settler states, 47–48, 50, 56–57, 79

World War II, *continued*
  as civil rights watershed, 2, 6, 8, 31, 55–56, 72, 79
  and decolonization, 31, 50
  and the economy, 32–33, 37, 41, 43, 44–45, 104, 108, 117
  and farming, 1, 5, 8, 28–29, 31–41, 48–49, 81, 88, 93, 94, 96, 108–109
  migration during and after, 1, 5, 40, 41, 106
  and Native Americans, 6, 7, 60, 67–68, 93, 130

Wright, Fielding L., 45

York, Baxter, 64
York, Emmett, 6, 78–79, 123–124, 156n19

Zama, 18
Zimbabwe, 4, 7, 11, 20, 28, 51, 71, 79, 83, 118, 130, 152n5